BEYOND AS ABOVE, SO BELOW

UNDERSTANDING HERMETIC TAROT THROUGH THE MUSIC OF MAYNARD JAMES KEENAN

M. KYNDYLL LACKEY

FOREWORD BY
M. M. MELEEN

ILLUSTRATED BY
M. M. MELEEN

ST

ISBN-13: 9798987134788 Paperback

ISBN-13: 9798987134726 eBook

Print edition printed in the United States of America

✾ Created with Vellum

For my Lord Thoth; may it please Him.

As below, so above and beyond I imagine...

— MAYNARD JAMES KEENAN

CONTENTS

Foreword   xiii
Preface   xv
Introduction   xxiii

1. Why Maynard James Keenan?   1
2. General Tarot and Thoth Tarot Basics   8
3. Qabalah Basics   17
4. Sephiroth and Albums   29
5. Pathways on The Tree   35
6. 0. The Fool: "Gravity," A Perfect Circle   44
7. I. The Magus: "Lateralus," Tool   50
8. II. The Priestess: "Parabola," Tool   56
9. III. The Empress: "Orestes," A Perfect Circle   61
10. IV. The Emperor: "Invincible," Tool   66
11. V. The Hierophant: "Sour Grapes," Puscifer   71
12. VI. The Lovers: "Schism," Tool   75
13. VII. The Chariot: "Passenger," Deftones   79
14. VIII. Adjustment: "Green Valley," Puscifer   83
15. IX. The Hermit: "Forty-Six & 2," Tool   87
16. X. Fortune: "Delicious," A Perfect Circle   91
17. XI. Lust: "Queen B," Puscifer   95
18. XII. The Hanged Man: "Reflection," Tool   100
19. XIII. Death: "Horizons," Puscifer   105
20. XIV. Art: "Agostina," Puscifer   109
21. XV. The Devil: "Breathe," Puscifer   114
22. XVI. The Tower: "Ænema," Tool   118
23. XVII. The Star: "Grand Canyon," Puscifer   123
24. XVIII. The Moon: "Culling Voices," Tool   127
25. XIX. The Sun: "Pneuma," Tool   131
26. XX. The Aeon: "Galileo," Puscifer   136
27. XXI. The Universe: "The Grudge," Tool   142
28. Residents in the Sephiroth   149

29. Ace of Wands: "Intension," Tool   153

30. Knight of Wands: "Eulogy," Tool   156

31. Queen of Wands: "Rev. 22:20," Puscifer   160

32. Prince of Wands: "Hooker with a Penis," Tool   165

33. Princess of Wands: "The Outsider," A Perfect Circle   169

34. 2 of Wands: "Thinking of You," A Perfect Circle   173

35. 3 of Wands: "Simultaneous," Puscifer   177

36. 4 of Wands: "Get the Lead Out," A Perfect Circle   181

37. 5 of Wands: "Prison Sex," Tool   185

38. 6 of Wands: "10,000 Days (Wings, Pt. 2)," Tool   189

39. 7 of Wands: "Passive," A Perfect Circle   193

40. 8 of Wands: "Grey Area," Puscifer   197

41. 9 of Wands: "Rose," A Perfect Circle   202

42. 10 of Wands: "Pushit," Tool   206

43. Ace of Cups: "Monsoons," Puscifer   210

44. Knight of Cups: "Oceans," Puscifer   214

45. Queen of Cups: "Jimmy," Tool   218

46. Prince of Cups: "The Hollow," A Perfect Circle   222

47. Princess of Cups: "Breña," A Perfect Circle   226

48. 2 of Cups: "The Humbling River," Puscifer   230

49. 3 of Cups: "Indigo Children," Puscifer   234

50. 4 of Cups: "Stinkfist," Tool   238

51. 5 of Cups: "Momma Sed," Puscifer   242

52. 6 of Cups: "Third Eye," Tool   246

53. 7 of Cups: "Undertow," Tool   251

54. 8 of Cups: "Potions," Puscifer   255

55. 9 of Cups: "Dear Brother," Puscifer   259

56. 10 of Cups: "Sober," Tool   263

57. Ace of Swords: "UPGrade," Puscifer   267

58. Knight of Swords: "Jerk-Off," Tool   272

59. Queen of Swords: "The Weaver," Puscifer   276

60. Prince of Swords: "Vanishing," A Perfect Circle   280

61. Princess of Swords: "Cold and Ugly," Tool   284

62. 2 of Swords: "Fear Inoculum," Tool   288

63. 3 of Swords: "Feathers," A Perfect Circle   292

64. 4 of Swords: "Bread and Circus," Puscifer   296

65. 5 of Swords: "Right in Two," Tool   300

66. 6 of Swords: "Postulous," Puscifer 304

67. 7 of Swords: "7empest," Tool 308

68. 8 of Swords: "Rosetta Stoned," Tool 315

69. 9 of Swords: "Vicarious," Tool 319

70. 10 of Swords: "Descending," Tool 324

71. Ace of Disks: "Lighten Up, Francis," Puscifer 329

72. Knight of Disks: "Sweat," Tool 333

73. Queen of Disks: "Judith," A Perfect Circle 337

74. Prince of Disks: "Eat the Elephant," A Perfect Circle 341

75. Princess of Disks: "Magdalena," A Perfect Circle 345

76. 2 of Disks: "H.," Tool 349

77. 3 of Disks: "TalkTalk," A Perfect Circle 353

78. 4 of Disks: "The Doomed," A Perfect Circle 357

79. 5 of Disks: "Ticks & Leeches," Tool 361

80. 6 of Disks: "Jambi," Tool 365

81. 7 of Disks: "Bottom," Tool 369

82. 8 of Disks: "The Patient," Tool 373

83. 9 of Disks: "Moneyshot," Puscifer 377

84. 10 of Disks: "Autumn," Puscifer 381

85. Fun with Maynard Tarot 385

Afterword 391

Bibliography 395

Notes 397

Acknowledgments 405

FOREWORD

Like tarot itself, Maynard James Keenan's body of musical work is brimming with magick and metaphysical correspondences, describing processes of transformation and transmutation. Since the tarot is actually a symbolic language, it can morph and elastically and endlessly adapt itself, becoming a sort of mnemonic device for sorting and describing any known thing in the Universe. It occupies a niche that is more than just the sorcery of sortilege - like music, it is a form of meditation capable of transporting one to the heights and the depths of the human experience and development.

There are lots of ways to approach learning tarot. But just when you think you have seen every such thing under the sun, along comes *Beyond As Above, So Below:* this unique and inspired work by M. Kyndyll Lackey that utilizes Maynard James Keenan's radiant works to illuminate tarot – or vice versa. One can sense her deep understanding of these two timeless and parallel streams, creating a seamless confluence. Allow her to be your guide and navigator taking you above, and below.

The works of Keenan represent an evolutionary spiral in the musical realm technically, lyrically, and by most any measure, just as

Crowley's magickal work and exploration enriched tarot with Thelemic tenets and took the system to an elevated level. I'm so happy to be able to provide "pictures of the world" from Tabula Mundi's tarot illustrations for this great work to visually kindle your interest, and deeply honored to be on the page with these worthy avatars of their respective crafts.

-- M. M. Meleen, Artist and Author
Tabula Mundi Tarot and *Book M: Liber Mundi*

PREFACE

I should first start out by saying this book is not *about* Maynard James Keenan, but rather, it is **an attempt to teach readers about tarot and the occult systems undergirding it through an exploration of and commentary on Keenan's body of music**—particularly through the analysis of his lyrics from a symbolic and metaphysical perspective. In fact, the exercise described in this book could be completed using most any artist's body of work, as long as it is large enough.

I selected Keenan as the subject here because I have a deep appreciation of and reverence for his collection of works. I find his lyrics to be rich in metaphor and symbolism, as well as emotional connection. Additionally, Keenan's lyrics do not shy away from the shadows. Unafraid of the dark, his words have traversed from brilliance to abyss, and everything in between. These elements combine to produce incredibly sacred and profane songs, repeatedly proving that the sacred and profane are, in every sense, made of the same stuff. The progress of his work reveals the development of artistic expression, from youthful derision to sage compassion, with eternal trickster sprinkled in throughout.

Equal parts rage, sorrow, philosophy, and strength, Keenan seems to work to balance expressions of fire, water, air, and earth in his art, mirroring the wisdom and balance captured within the tarot. Symbolism, intensity, light and dark, the four elements, and the archetypal stages of human growth and development are all classic, fundamental aspects of tarot. Every possible human experience is captured in the akashic records stored inside tarot symbolism, and any life that is long enough will match this diversity of experience. You've lived it, and I have, too, but our journeys will naturally look different from each other at first glance. We may not share a common world view or faith. But, if you're reading this, I'm fairly certain we will share a common set of symbols and language vis-à-vis the collected works of one Maynard James Keenan.

The added benefit of using Keenan as the illustrating example for this system of learning tarot is, of course, his broad knowledge of metaphysics and his own intuition. It is the development of his metaphysical perspective that I believe deeply influenced his song writing, and that is ultimately what led me to engage in this exercise.

So that's what this book is. Here's what this book is not:

- An assertion that my interpretations of the lyrics are the "real" or "true" interpretations. My interpretations are just that. They are not approved or consecrated in any way or by anyone, but they are informed by decades of magickal practice, research, and experience, as well as decades of following Keenan's work.
- A proclamation that Maynard James Keenan is perfect, a prophet, or even a part of this endeavor. It is not a statement of 'Maynard worship,' but rather an attempt to use a clearly defined area of modern culture to help myself and others strengthen our understanding of and relationship to archetypes and occult systems.
- An attempt at a "Top Maynard James Keenan Songs" listicle. This is an analysis I conducted in earnest, using

my decades of occult study and professional tarot practice to inform my interpretations. Correspondences were determined meticulously, with multiple layers of meaning attributed to each match.

- A comprehensive review or anthology of Keenan's work. There were many songs not used here, and Keenan continues to make music, which of course cannot be considered here. There will be multiple times throughout this document when you will intensely disagree with choices I made, forsaking your personal favorite. Why is Lust "Queen B" and not "Rev. 22:20"? Or "Magdalena"? Or "Thinking of You"? Gentle Reader, I assure you I had my reasons—some of them I may even share here...

- A noob fan-girl manifesto. As I mentioned above, I've been studying tarot for a long time, and following Keenan's music even longer.

- "Official" or "approved" in any manner, by Keenan or any organization. This is a labor of love from my own creative Will, undertaken as a spiritual practice of my own accord, with the intention of sharing my love for and knowledge of these subjects with others who may love them, too. Maynard fans and tarot nerds of the world, let us unite in our geekery!

PARAMETERS

Every good experiment begins with boundaries to keep the operations honest. Here are mine:

- Songs assigned to cards have to contain mostly original lyrics by Keenan—no covers of other artists' songs. I know that "Imagine," "No Quarter," "When the Levee Breaks," "The Fiddle and The Drum," "Rocket Man," and many other cover songs Keenan has done are inspiring.

Perhaps they introduced you to the originals. However, those are examples of Keenan paying homage to those artists' creative expressions. In this book, we're considering Keenan's lived experiences and creative expressions, as chronicled in his original music. We'd compromise the integrity of the book and its theory if we included covers. After all, the point is to illustrate how one person's life can be correspondent to all of the 78 cards—no fair mixing in someone else's life experiences!

- Songs can be from any Keenan project (Tool, A Perfect Circle, Puscifer, Tapeworm, etc.).

- Matches are made regardless of musical chronology, project, and album. Matches are made based on lyrical content, meaning, and symbolism—not in the spirit of shoving square pegs into round holes.

- This exercise uses the *Tabula Mundi Tarot* (and the *Crowley-Harris Thoth* tradition upon which it is based) without exception. That is to say, I'm using this deck's order, correspondences, and titles. Mostly, this is because *Tabula Mundi/Thoth* is the tradition that I work with, and it is the system that I believe is most appropriate to apply to Keenan's music. I do include additional interpretations of cards, purely for the sake of sharing what I have learned over the last two-plus decades, in hopes that it will be helpful to those who are learning tarot.

- This is a tool that attempts to bridge two bodies of knowledge: the artistic works of Maynard James Keenan and the occult divination system of the tarot. I have written this specifically to help those with the most basic knowledge about the two systems to increase their knowledge in both. I'm by no means the final authority on either topic, but I have spent enough time studying both to have something to share in the spirit of perpetual learning and exploration.

If you can accept these ideas, this book should hopefully make a lot of sense to you. If you can't... well, you're probably not going to have a good time (wink).

OTHER THEORIES AND PURE SPECULATION

I don't know if Keenan intentionally strived to create songs that musically walk the paths of the tarot and the Qabalistic Tree of Life. If he did, I don't think he did so from the outset. I think it would've been subconscious at first. My guess would be—if it indeed ever was intentional—it became so somewhere around the time of *Ænima* and the subsequent issue of *Salival*, which featured a subtle Qabalistic Tree of Life on the cover. I believe any plan he may have had about reflecting the entire 78-card tarot in his music would've probably come around the time of starting Puscifer.

Keenan also didn't write these songs in any order that I can discern. But if he was intentionally exploring the tarot in this way, I think he may have decided on a "collect them all" strategy in the last approximately fifteen years. This is most evident to me in Puscifer's EPs that contain one or two new original compositions, along with a few re-mixes or covers. In these, the original compositions have consistently been matched songs, as if the album was released expressly to get those particular tracks into the catalog and complete matches. All of this, of course, is pure speculation on my part, but there you have my thoughts on the matter.

You may take issue with how I've done this here. Great! Go make your own. Use the tarot correspondences and song interpretations you like. Hell, change to a different artist. The point is to engage in the study, to think deeply about these archetypes, and to integrate the symbolism further and deeper into your psyche, so that you can draw on these symbols to help navigate this ocean of chaos we call life.

HOW TO USE THIS BOOK

My primary purpose with this book is to teach readers about tarot and related occult systems. Thus, I recommend that you read the first few chapters in order, as I use them to explain some basic concepts that will come up throughout the card sections of the book. Once you arrive at the card entries, feel free to skip around. You might start with your favorite cards, or the cards that you pull in a reading. Another way to use this book is to do a bit of musical divination—set your favorite Keenan playlist to random,[1] and read the entries of the songs that play. Whether you read straight through cover to cover, or bounce around, follow that little tickling inspiration of your curiosity —it will never lead you astray!

As you read about the individual cards, you'll notice each card entry contains four main parts. The first section gives basic correspondences and information about the card, the second analyzes the matched song in relation to the card, the third examines the card in both the *Thoth Tarot* and *Tabula Mundi Tarot,* and the final section provides instructions on how to read the card in a typical tarot spread.

Additionally, there is a spot in each entry to record your "Atu Line" for the card, which is a key line or phrase from the song to help you remember the meaning of the card it's matched with.[2] Because I've found that the most effective mnemonic devices are those we create for ourselves, I'm providing the Atu Lines for the first few cards to give you an idea of what to look for; the rest are left open for you to choose your own. It's been my experience that most songs have multiple lines that could reasonably be used as the Atu Line for its card, which is what makes this exercise fun and engaging. A big part of the learning here is in choosing the Atu Line, because doing so helps you focus on developing a true understanding of the card that can be succinctly expressed in a memorable way.

This book will also be best appreciated if the reader first gathers a few basic items: a *Thoth* or *Thoth*-based tarot deck such as M.M.

Meleen's *Tabula Mundi Tarot*, a journal and pen, Keenan's original music, and the songs' lyrics. It will be most helpful if the reader familiarizes themselves with each track, particularly while reading about its card. All of the music discussed here can be easily—and legally—accessed online, especially now that (nearly) the entire Tool catalog is available to stream. The same is true of the complete lyrics, [3] although I have found errors in online lyric sources, so you may want to listen for yourself and double-check lyrics you find on the web.

I have chosen to use Meleen's beautifully intoxicating *Tabula Mundi* as the imagery for this book for two primary reasons: first, because I feel her deck is a modernized re-telling of the *Thoth Tarot* that gives balanced treatment to both masculine and feminine as well as their integration; and second, because *Tabula Mundi*'s visual imagery is remarkable in its synchronicities with Keenan's lyrical imagery and overall symbolism. Furthermore, *Thoth* has been on the receiving end of endless analysis over the past 60+ years, and it is my firm belief that *Tabula Mundi* is every bit as transformative and deserves to be considered as a preeminent hermetic deck in its own right.

It should go without saying, but stating the obvious has never stopped me before: **the ethical, karmically appropriate, and just plain decent thing to do when enjoying any art is to pay for access to an artist's work whenever there is a fee attached, and it is best to make your purchase directly from the artist whenever possible.**

Remember you are interacting with someone's livelihood, and while you may be tempted to think this is some kind of class warfare thing (*"but that person is wealthy and I'M NOT!"*), know that *there is no cheap way to produce good art.* And the more important a particular piece of art is to you on a personal or spiritual level, the more it deserves your good faith energetic exchange via opening your damn wallet. **In short, don't be a fucking asshole (and yes, I'm talking to YOU).**

As a final note, I am also not attempting to identify MJK with any particular spiritual path. He is in charge of his spiritual life. This is an expression of mine. -MKL

[1] For better results, you can find and follow my complete, book-order playlist "Beyond As Above, So Below" on Spotify @kyndyll.lackey.

[2] The word "Atu" is the Ancient Egyptian word for *key*, see *The Book of Thoth,* p35.

[3] Some music streaming services, such as Spotify and Roon, have a convenient lyrics feature built in.

INTRODUCTION

Though it may seem strange to open a book on the occult and tarot with a discussion of the Bible, I invite you to consider this mythological work as one of the most powerful books of occult knowledge ever written. Biblical passages are known by occultists to be some of the most potent spells on Earth, because over thousands of years, millions upon millions of people have prayed, chanted, recited, and written these precise words in their particular order. Over centuries, repetition has imbued them with meaning and charged them with purpose and belief. Each recitation builds the power of the words, giving them a life of their own and animating them as energetic beings. Whether they practice Christianity or not, every magickian knows the Bible is powerful because so many people believe in the words and have invested themselves in them.

Likewise, songs that gain widespread popularity can reach energetic heights similar to prayers and biblical passages. Over time, millions of people sing these words, rap them, quote them, scream them at shows. They are earworms that get stuck for days, their lyrics swirling around our minds mercilessly, whether we invited them in or not.

Consider, for example, the "one-hit wonders" of the world. Ever 'wonder' why they were successful? It's because those songs struck a chord in our collective unconscious. Esoterically speaking, the writer hit on a perfectly attuned, magically charged set of words, beats, notes, and rhymes—which all correspond to larger universal principles. In short, one-hit wonders are masterfully crafted spells! Popular songs of all genres have hit on effective formulas, making them powerful enough to entrench themselves in our memories, become the soundtracks of our lives, and develop deeply personal meanings to each listener—even beyond what the writer originally intended.

It is for these reasons that I consider musicians—particularly those who develop a large and dedicated following that lasts for years—as some of the most powerful magickians of our time. Their art inspires passion, motivation, love, dance, art, babies, and many other expressions of the Divine here on Earth. And at each live performance, thousands of people dance, sing, jump, mosh, and revel in the sounds these masters make, creating a vortex of energy that intoxicates everyone present.

If you don't believe me, ponder this: how many times have you seen people lose themselves at a concert? I would say we've all seen them: the couple who decides *this* is the moment to declare their love for each other or even conceive a child...the tripper who is seeing the space-time fabric of reality unravel before him...the reveler who just wants to set shit on fire...the provoked and provoking warriors itching for a fight...the worshippers lost in the lyrics and unconcerned that they are screaming right into your ear—all of them are under the influence of the masterful magi on stage. Whether the band knows it or not, they literally are casting a spell upon their audience. Such power should not be taken lightly, and the best musicians don't.

Magick with a 'k'—the practice of changing the environment around us to conform to our will through energetic means—is achieved in a variety of ways, but the oldest and most primal magick is generated through chant and dance. Chant and dance require a rhythm, notes, movement, and an idea—elements that come together to create music. Think of it this way: every concert is a magickal ritual, in which collective energy is intentionally raised and released. Other rituals achieve this through mantras, some through sex, some through meditation—but all magickal rituals have a clear goal to generate as much vital energy as possible, aim it at a desired outcome, and at the moment of the energy's crescendo, 'fire' or release it at the intended target outcome. That is what all acts of magick technically are, and looking at it that way, of course all concerts are 'magical' experiences—they're *magickal* experiences.

When talented musicians and song writers understand the gravity of the energy they are able to move with their art, when they become aware of the archetypes that drive the human mind, and when they invest time in understanding esoteric principles, their impact on others is profoundly intensified. Such is the nature and effect of the music that Maynard James Keenan and his project partners have created over more than thirty years of being in the public eye and ear.

A BRIEF BIOGRAPHY OF MJK

James Herbert Keenan was born in Ravenna, Ohio on April 17, 1964 to Mike and Judith Keenan. His parents divorced when he was four; his father moved to Scottville, Michigan and his mother remained in Ohio, where she remarried. James, or Jimmy as he was called, spent the next ten years living with his mother and step-father in their extremely conservative Southern Baptist household.

It was in this environment that Jimmy developed a distaste for organized religion, especially conservative Christianity, as he witnessed church-sanctioned abuse in a variety of forms during his childhood and beyond. His mother's faith would endure for her lifetime, and this conflict between her religiosity and his cynicism would become a touchstone for some of Jimmy's most important musical and personal works.

When Jimmy was eleven years old, his mother suffered a cerebral aneurysm that would ravage her mobility and health for the rest of her life. Three years after this traumatic event, Judith convinced her son to go live with his father and step-mother for his high school and adolescent years.

In Scottville, Jimmy went to the high school where his father was a teacher and wrestling coach. He picked up both wrestling and cross-country, and excelled academically and athletically while simultaneously nurturing a love of art and music, particularly the music of such popular artists as Joni Mitchell, Led Zeppelin, Pink Floyd, and KISS.

After completing high school in 1982, Jimmy enlisted in the United States Army and completed basic training as well as advanced training at West Point Prep School. Although he was offered the opportunity to continue on at West Point, he declined the appointment and instead used the funds he received through the G.I. Bill to attend Kendall School of Art and Design in Grand Rapids, Michigan.

It was around this time that young Jimmy traded in his childhood name for "Maynard," the name of a fictional character he created during his teen years. This new identity marked a shift in his worldview; he not only adopted an edgier appearance, but he began exploring edgier philosophical and metaphysical ideas via the works of Carl Jung, Joseph Campbell, John Crowley, and (later) Drunvalo Melchizedek, as well as exploring the archetypes found in tarot and astrology.

More than once, Keenan sought and received guidance from tarotists and other mediums who provided important information to help him find and pursue his unique path; these and other extraordinary synchronicities convinced him that there is more to reality than what most people routinely perceive, and the more he broadened his thinking and perceptions, the more he could actively participate in shaping his world. This perspective permanently changed who he was and how he interacted with his life.

Following art school, Keenan spent time living in Boston, honing his artistic style and developing a deep appreciation for punk music as well as a nascent appreciation for wine, an interest that would dramatically reshape his life in middle age. He played in two bands during this time period: TexA.N.S. (Tex and the Anti-Nazi Squad) and Children of the Anachronistic Dynasty (C.A.D.). Neither group was ever signed to a label, but he gained performance experience playing bass and singing. He also found success working in a pet store designing merchandise displays and store layout; it was this skill set that would eventually serve as his bridge to moving across the country to Los Angeles.

In sunny, creative Los Angeles, the pet store job was short-lived, but by that time Keenan realized that his passion lay in music and art, and he found himself surrounded by like-minded people who would soon become friends and bandmates. He found work in set construction for small projects such as music videos, and he continued to develop his musical style by jamming with future Tool bandmates Adam Jones and Danny Carey, as well as friends Tom Morello, Brad Wilk, and Zack de la Rocha of also soon-to-be-famous Rage Against the Machine.

The first of Maynard's wildly successful musical groups, Tool, officially formed in 1990. Along with guitarist Jones, drummer Carey, and bassist Paul D'Amour, Keenan rounded out the group by providing vocals. Their first EP, entitled *Opiate*, was released in 1992, and their first full-length album, the platinum-certified *Undertow*, followed in 1993. Both albums were quite dark in thematic content and sound—*Opiate* was a blistering explosion of young adult angst and anger, railing against religion and hypocrisy, while *Undertow* was a more focused metal album that delved into serious topics such as abuse, addiction, mental illness, and the failures of dogmatic religion.

In 1996, the group released their second studio album, the triple platinum-certified *Ænima*, which was dedicated to the memory of friend and comedian Bill Hicks (who had died in 1994 at the age of 32 of pancreatic cancer). *Ænima* marked a significant thematic and musical turn for the group; named for Carl Jung's concept of the anima/animus, this album's sound was still dark and heavy, but the music had taken on a more complex texture, and the lyrics discussed such concepts as shadow integration, identity crisis, consciousness expansion via the ritual use of entheogens, and the state of American culture at-large. It further incorporated several clips of Hicks' comedy bits, used to reinforce the messages of the songs. The album was an unmitigated massive success, elevating their fanbase to a cult-following status and earning the group a Grammy Award for Best Metal Performance.

Following the release of *Ænima*, the band's work was interrupted by a contract dispute with their record label, and Keenan took this opportunity to explore working with other musicians. In 1999, he began collaborating with a Tool guitar tech named Billy Howerdel on material Howerdel had been writing. Together with drummer Troy Van Leeuwen and bassist Paz Lenchantin, the group formed A Perfect Circle, which released its debut platinum album *Mer de Noms* (French for 'sea of names') in 2000.

The launch of this second musical project gave Keenan the chance to further explore some of the esoteric concepts found in *Ænima*, and he adopted a more feminine presentation during performances of A Perfect Circle songs. *Mer de Noms* was populated with tracks named for various people in Keenan's life, and the songs explored the emotional connections between people, for better and worse. This album included some of Keenan's first songs that were romantic and sexual in nature, an especially surprising twist for his long-time fans. The sound was flowing and melodic, unlike Tool's massive crunching, screaming, battering wall of sound. In this sonic space, Keenan began to flex his clear tenor singing voice.

Tool was also busy in 2000, releasing a limited-edition box set of live performances entitled *Salival*. This collection of mostly live tracks from the *Ænima* tour includes Tool's first cover songs, Led Zeppelin's "No Quarter" and Peach's "You Lied," as well as extended versions of their own "Third Eye" and "Pushit." The album was decidedly metaphysical in nature, confirmed by the Qabalistic Tree of Life diagram that graced its back cover.

Keenan's first child, a son named Devo, was born in August of that year. It was during this time period that he also began exploring the idea of making wine, and soon selected an area near Jerome, Arizona as the future home of his vineyard.

Tool returned to the forefront of Keenan's life the following year, in 2001, when the group released *Lateralus*. Following the smashing success of *Ænima, Lateralus* effortlessly reached No. 1 on the U.S. *Billboard* 200 list the week of its launch, was certified double platinum, and earned the group their second Grammy Award for Best Metal Performance. *Lateralus* marked Tool's formal entry into the world of math rock and progressive metal; these songs showcased dizzying cascades of time signatures, influences of eastern musical instruments, and thematic material that included such occult subjects as the Saturn return and the human subtle energetic body. The band partnered with visionary artist Alex Grey to produce incredible, multilayered packaging and stage sets for their live tour, based on the same metaphysical concepts that the album explored.

After several lengthy tours in support of *Lateralus*, Tool again went into hiatus, continuing to battle with their record label. During this break, Keenan worked on a second album with A Perfect Circle. *Thirteenth Step* was released in 2003, and it too eventually reached platinum status. Named for the twelve-step process frequently used in recovery, *Thirteenth Step* focused heavily on addiction's many faces and impacts, the recovery journey, and the extreme prices addiction's victims often pay.

In the same year, Keenan's mother Judith died from complications of the aneurysm she had suffered twenty-seven years before; this final loss was a watershed moment for her son, and much of his work moving forward would be in service to healing and processing these experiences concerning his mother. Keenan began releasing solo songs under the name Puscifer around this time as well, collaborating with friends from various other bands and projects.

In 2004, A Perfect Circle tackled the American political scene with *eMOTIVe,* a collection of protest and political song covers released just before the 2004 presidential election. At that point, the group announced the conclusion of their work together.

Two years later, Tool released *10,000 Days,* which also was certified platinum, reached No. 1 on the *Billboard* 200 list the week it debuted, and won a third Grammy Award, this time for Best Recording Package. The legal battles with their label persisted, and this time the band members' hiatus from recording would prove to be thirteen years long, leaving Keenan plenty of time to develop other interests.

After touring in support of *10,000* Days, he returned to working with Puscifer, and in 2007 independently released a full-length album entitled *V Is for Vagina.* This album was decidedly different from anything Keenan had ever created with either Tool or A Perfect Circle. For the first time, listeners could clearly point to influences of other musical genres on Keenan's music, including rap, country, gospel, and electronica. The themes were decidedly racier, with several tracks graphically describing sex and sex magick practices. Other songs were parodies, foreshadowing a trend of bringing a comedic element to his work. Still other tracks began to reveal the alchemical nature of Keenan's approach to questions of spirituality and philosophy.

He also expanded the Puscifer brand to include apparel and other merchandise available online, and in 2008 he opened a brick-and-mortar store for the line in his adopted hometown of Jerome, Arizona. The same year, he released his first wines from his winemaking practice, which he had dubbed Merkin Vineyards/Caduceus Cellars.

The years following were filled with a head-spinning mash of wine making; conducting wine tasting events and lectures; touring with all three bands at various intervals; creating several new and remix albums of Puscifer's music; expanding his business ventures in Jerome and throughout Arizona; and falling in love with and marrying his wife, Lei Li.

In 2009, Keenan released a Puscifer EP entitled *C Is for [Insert Sophomoric Genitalia Reference HERE]*. This small collection of new songs doubled down on the radical spirituality of alchemical balance that had first appeared in *V Is for Vagina*. In 2011, Puscifer released its second full-length album, *Conditions of My Parole*, something of a love letter to Keenan's family and his adopted home in the Verde Valley. An EP, *Donkey Punch the Night*, came two years later, show-casing a jaw-droppingly faithful rendition of Queen's "Bohemian Rhapsody," tributes to a fallen friend, and more of his unique blend of sexually empowered spirituality.

Puscifer's third full-length album, *Money Shot*, appeared in 2015. Opening with three sweepingly epic spiritual tracks, *Money Shot* brought Puscifer to a new place, a blend of worldly wisdom and lofty hope. It included a track dedicated to his infant daughter, Agostina, born the year before, as well as critical commentary on America's continuing cultural and political devolution.

In 2016, much to the surprise of fans, Keenan partnered with longtime friend Sarah Jensen to write *A Perfect Union of Contrary Things*, a deeply personal autobiography of this alchemical hermit-trickster-wizard with a magical introduction by Alex Grey. A multi-media book tour followed, in which a different host interviewed Keenan in each city. The book detailed the major events in his familial history and life from childhood, as well as let readers in on his personal philosophy and perspectives on a wide range of issues. The majority of this brief biographical sketch is sourced from this book, and I highly recommend it for developing an in-depth under-standing of Keenan's wide and varied musical works. Though it was a small book by most autobiographical standards, it was nothing short of an enlightenment bomb for Keenan's fans, who had always known him to be quite reclusive, stingy with personal details, and frequently moody toward fans.

Two years later (and fourteen years after officially announcing the group's dissolution), A Perfect Circle surprised the music world in 2018 by releasing *Eat the Elephant*, an album that seemed to pick up where Puscifer's *Money Shot* left off. In this unexpected fourth studio album, A Perfect Circle explored the grief of our times, including the disconnection between people in the United States, warnings against the dangerous political and climate games being played out across the country, and broad appeals for compassion, peace, and brotherhood. The release was accompanied by a brief tour, and upon its completion Keenan resumed work with Tool to finalize their long-awaited fifth album, *Fear Inoculum*.

After a thirteen-year absence from the charts, Tool exploded into the American imagination again on August 30, 2019, when they released *Fear Inoculum* to the elation of fans and critics alike. Just weeks before, Tool finally consented to offering their music on streaming services, and the impact was immediate.[1] All five Tool albums appeared on iTunes' top 10 albums list,[2] and several individual tracks appeared on the top 10 tracks list,[3] where they remained for several weeks. *Fear Inoculum*'s first single, its title track, debuted at #93 on *Billboard*'s top 100 list, the longest song to ever enter the chart. Once again, Tool's new album debuted at the top of the *Billboard* 200 chart and earned them another Grammy Award for Best Metal Performance.

Although the tour was initially cut short by the COVID-19 pandemic, *Fear Inoculum* is widely regarded as both prescient of our times as well as the group's masterpiece. The subject matter of this album is a continuation of the themes found in Puscifer's *Money Shot* and A Perfect Circle's *Eat the Elephant*, drawing them to their natural conclusions about climate change, political unrest, and the contagion of fear. Each song appeals to the better nature of humanity, and compared with early Tool albums, *Fear Inoculum* is almost wholesome in its content. Furthermore, each track conveys strikingly open magickal information, such that the listener wonders what psychic power market the members of Tool have cornered in our information- and logic-driven society.

In 2020, Puscifer released their fourth full-length album, *Existential Reckoning*, which carried and expanded on the ideas broached in Tool's *Fear Inoculum*. Leaning heavily into electronica to mirror the theme of digital and virtual reality, this new album seems to be positioned as a wake-up call to listeners, attempting to rouse them from their electronic and social media spells. Topics include entheogen and psychedelic explorations, electronic and virtual realities, personal power, and sovereignty.

Keenan continues to make wine and music in the Arizona desert today. At the time of this writing, Puscifer has hinted at possible new works, and Tool are about to resume the *Fear Inoculum* tour.

A FOOL FOLLOWS HER WILL

I have been listening to Maynard James Keenan's music for most of my life, and my own occult journey has in some ways chased, and in other ways mirrored, the progression of his musical journey. Sometimes I understood the nature of what I was hearing at the time I first encountered it, and sometimes it took me years of life experience to be able to revisit and understand the ideas contained in the lyrics and melodies. I suspect it's been this way for most of his die-hard fans. We are each on our own journeys, developing our own wisdom, but his music has become a common language of soul progression that we can all speak, if we care to learn it.

My journey took an unexpectedly deep turn one night when I was in a chemically altered state of consciousness, listening to one of my own playlists of music from all of Keenan's projects. I was thinking about how much of a departure A Perfect Circle was from Tool, and how much Tool fans were surprised and, in some ways, blindsided by Keenan's transformation—in his lyrical content, vocal style, and physical appearance—between the two projects. He had become decidedly more feminine in his presentation. As I was musing on this, I thought, perhaps he saw A Perfect Circle as a chance to explore his anima, to understand and experience the Divine Feminine for himself. Maybe *Mer de Noms* was his very conscious attempt to temporarily inhabit Binah, the station on the Qabalistic Tree of Life that represents the Divine—or Supernal—Mother, through performance art.

Interesting... I wondered what other ways his music reflects his explorations of occult systems.

And just like that, I was off to the races. I immediately noticed some definite connections between albums and the sephiroth of the Qabalistic Tree of Life, and songs that seemed to fit the pathways between them (and if this sentence doesn't make sense the first time you read it, keep reading—it will make sense very shortly).

I was having a marvelous time puzzling out which albums and songs belonged where. In the end, I discovered that Keenan's catalogue corresponded not just to the thirty-two paths of the Tree of Life, *but to the entire tarot.* A deck of 78 tarot cards is an incredibly diverse tool that is correspondent to, or in harmony with, the philosophical system of Qabalah and its pictorial representation, the Tree of Life. The tarot represents the totality of human experience and is a working model of the universe as Hermetic magickians understand it. And Keenan's musical life work is an extensive, growing representation of a thinking person's journey in life, which of course can also be told through the symbols of the tarot, Qabalah, and the Tree of Life.

Over the course of many months of tinkering, reading, listening to, and obsessively thinking about Keenan's lyrics, I settled on albums corresponding to sephiroth (spheres on the Tree of Life), because each album is its own little world, a self-contained reality much like a sephira. The pathways between the sephiroth were individual tracks—songs that represented certain archetypes, which corresponded to the major arcana of the tarot. Each song is a time-space capsule of a particular kind of human experience, and there was one in Keenan's catalogue for all twenty-two of the traditional major arcana archetypes. There were also songs that described characters of real and fictitious people, which stunningly matched up with the sixteen court cards from the tarot. A final set of thirty-six songs matched up to the small cards' meanings. All of these correspondences or "matches" were made including works from every Keenan project, and every full-length album Keenan has made through Puscifer's *Existential Reckoning*, without duplicating one song. I was tickled with my little project!

And then the magick truly began. As a professional tarotist and a perpetual student of the occult, I work with tarot and the Qabalistic Tree of Life every day. I'm continuously handling and studying the Crowley-Harris Thoth and other Thoth-based decks (my tarot system of choice), which is based on the teachings of Aleister Crowley. Once I started working on this book in earnest, interesting things started happening. I began to automatically hear songs in my mind when I drew their cards. The associations became effortless mnemonics for remembering which major arcana cards fell on which paths of the Tree. Tarot spells came more easily. I began to experience synchronicities, such as choosing to play a particular album, and then randomly pulling cards that corresponded to that album, which also accurately reflected my day ahead and the even the weather outside at that moment.

On a complete lark, I had grabbed what seemed to me at the time to be a tiny, random thread, and to my utter astonishment as I began to pull, I realized that the thread was indeed connected to something bigger. And not only was I tugging on the sleeve of something bigger, its unraveling was revealing a pattern to me that I had previously never seen, even in decades of earnest fandom and occult studies. To say I was delightfully flabbergasted is an understatement.

I understood cards I had been working with for two decades in an entirely new light. And the songs that have been the soundtrack of my life grew richer, with even more symbolic meaning than ever. It was as if the music that had most enhanced my life for all these years suddenly became... my teachers. Like the flip of a switch, the light was on, and I was on fire.

I soon realized that there was an entire body of occult knowledge contained in Keenan's music. Whether he had intended to do so or not, he had created a rather effective class in Hermetic Qabalah and tarot, and anyone who is familiar with the lyrics of his songs could use them to better understand what the cards meant. With time and study, explorers would begin to see even deeper esoteric concepts in the tarot and in the music, too.

If you are interested in tarot but feel overwhelmed, look, I get it. Seventy-eight cards are a lot to memorize in the beginning. Some of them look and sound so similar! Even after years of practice it's easy to suddenly think, *Oh shit! What's the difference between those two again?* But the beauty of this system is that it meets you where you are, using a body of knowledge you already have ingrained deep within your psyche (via your own personal memories and associations with this music) as a bridge to learning a completely new body of knowledge. In the course of studying these two tools together, your skill in using both will be increased and refined.

For example, do you struggle with telling the 9 and 10 of Swords apart? It's as easy as listening to and feeling the difference between Tool's "Vicarious" and "Descending."

Are the Justice and Judgement cards giving you grief? Their titles are closely related, after all. Well, if you switch to a Thoth-based deck, problem solved! They become Adjustment and The Aeon (wink). But even beyond that, using this system, it is apparent that Puscifer's "Green Valley" and "Galileo" have decidedly different flavors.

And there you go. That mysterious little tarot deck in your hands just got mapped to your own life experiences—your joy, your pain, your hopes, and your fears—because you have already encoded them to your own memories vis-à-vis this particular catalog of music. The hardest part is done, and you felt no pain because you were busy jamming out to the tunes and living your life.

CHAPTER I
WHY MAYNARD JAMES KEENAN?
CELEBRITIES AS AVATARS OF THE DIVINE

Have you ever wondered why people become celebrities? I mean, beyond the obvious explanations like models are beautiful, comics are funny, and musicians are talented. After all, there are millions of people all over the globe who are incredibly beautiful, funny, and talented—why are they not famous? What is it about the celebrity that catapults them to fame? What is the element that captures the attention of the masses, that spellbinds them into adoration, obsession, or even hatred?

I have come to the conclusion that celebrities are avatars—channels of deities. People rise to fame by channeling a particular deity exceptionally well, and their followers who are more than just casual fans are, in effect, worshippers of the deities their favorite celebrities represent.

This is interesting to consider in light of all the many reasons for which people can become famous. Someone can become famous for *what they do*, such as acting, visual arts, music, literature, comedy, or fashion. But people also become famous for *the kinds of characteristics they display*—not only for positive traits such as heroism or generosity, but for negative traits, too, such as pettiness, crassness, selfishness, violence, and cowardice.

After all, famous people include serial killers, politicians, pundits, and heiresses, too, and they all gained notoriety for some reason. I postulate whatever that reason is, it's a clue to the deity they channel. A good example of this is Warren Buffett. Mr. Buffett is not particularly handsome or funny or entertaining. However, he is absolutely famous as a person who is able to generate profound amounts of wealth. People who are drawn to study him could probably also be drawn to deities that represent abundance, such as Lakshmi (Hindu), Mercury (Roman), or Oshun (Yoruba).

Think of it this way: your most beloved celebrities hold keys to understanding your values and thus your own connection to the Divine. The celebrities you love so much that you feel you almost "know" them are placeholders for your own spiritual path and communication with their (and your) patron deities. In this manner, we can break ourselves from the spell of obsession with these mere mortals, and put the wonder where it should be: on the Universe, the Source, the All, God, Goddess, Great Spirit—whatever you call that universal animating force.

I came to this conclusion because my own patron god is the Thrice-Great Mercury-Hermes-Thoth, and I see Keenan as a near perfect avatar of Him. I suspect the reason I have always loved Keenan is that he lines up so perfectly with my own conception of the divine masculine. To be clear, I do not worship Maynard James Keenan—rather, I see in him uniquely human expressions of this particular facet of the Divine, a facet we magickians call Thoth. This perception is what allowed me to make the connection between his music and *Tabula Mundi/Thoth Tarot*, which in turn gave rise to this book.

I make the connection between Keenan and Mercury-Hermes-Thoth for a large variety of reasons, and for the sake of example, here are a few of the Thrice-Great God's teachings and characteristics, and the ways Keenan personifies them.

- **"As above, so below; as within, so without; as the Universe, so my soul."** This is the primary philosophy of Hermeticism as found on the Emerald Tablet (the condensed statement of Thoth's teachings), and this concept has made appearances throughout Keenan's works.
- **Communication** – Thoth is first and foremost a god of communication. This includes verbal, written, and psychic communication, as well as specific forms of communication like poetry and song. Anyone who is a fan of Keenan can attest to his remarkable skills in songwriting and communication, and the vast majority of this book is dedicated to dissecting the works of this master wordsmith.
- **Commerce** – All aspects of commerce are also under the dominion of Mercury-Hermes-Thoth, due to His rulership over communication, consciousness, and perception, as well as over sciences, mathematics, and other systems of knowledge. The words *merchant* and *commerce* are derived from the same Latin root as *Mercury*. Keenan has shown himself to be a consummate master in sales and business, from his early days of pet shop display management, to his phenomenal success in entertainment, to his growing empire of retail and hospitality businesses in Arizona and beyond.
- **Mathematics and musical theory** are both under the purview of Thoth, and Keenan frequently uses mathematics in song writing. "Lateralus" is, of course, the most famous example of this.
- **Magick** – Thoth is the inventor of the practice of magick, and I believe there is more than ample evidence of Keenan's proficiency in this art. From lyrical references to magickal concepts, to the achievement of material success in multiple areas, to the spellbinding effect he

has on fans, Keenan has repeatedly demonstrated his knowledge and ability to effectuate change in his environment in direct accordance with his creative will.

- **Psychopomp** – Mercury-Hermes-Thoth is known to be a psychopomp, or guide in the underworld. Because He is able to travel freely between all the worlds, including those of the living and the dead, He is comfortable with both the light and the dark. Keenan likewise demonstrates this comfort with the light and dark, and his collected works represent a clear journey to integrate the repressed parts of the personality, often referred to as the shadow.

- **Trickster** – Mercury, Hermes, and Thoth are all known to be trickster gods—deities who often toy with human perceptions in an effort to teach them, play with them, and laugh with them. I see this aspect of Thoth in Keenan's comedic and playful works, such as "Cuntry Boner."

- **Lunar Deity** – Despite the fact that lunar deities are traditionally goddesses across most cultures (and unlike Mercury and Hermes, who are of course tied to the planet Mercury), the Egyptian Thoth is tied to the Moon. In addition to the darkness that pervades much of Keenan's works, he also seems to be heavily influenced by the Moon's aspects: cycles, the unknown, psychic connection, and the feminine all play major thematic roles in Keenan's collected works.

- **Male/Female Versatility** – Mercury-Hermes-Thoth is specifically known to be versatile in gender expression. For instance, sometimes Thoth manifests as Seshat, goddess of records, record keeping, magick, and knowledge. The word *hermaphrodite*, an organism with both masculine and feminine qualities, originated from the Greek Hermaphroditos, son of Hermes and Aphrodite, who had both male and female attributes. The alchemical element Mercury and planetary Mercury are also recognized to be both/neither masculine and feminine—able to interact with and alternate between the two. Keenan, too, has performed in both masculine and feminine personas.

- **Caduceus** – The Thrice-Great Mercury-Hermes-Thoth is associated with the caduceus, a magickal staff of entwined, winged serpents that represents knowledge and enlightenment. As most fans know, Keenan named his wine business Caduceus Cellars.

- **Divination** – Thoth is credited as the creator of tarot, which is naturally the inspiration for this project. If Keenan can exhibit so many other aspects of the Thrice-Great God, then why not add one more? In the tarot, Mercury-Hermes-Thoth is represented primarily by The Magus or Magician, and He also rules the astrological signs of Gemini and Virgo, The Lovers and The Hermit respectively. These archetypes have become cornerstones of how I understand Keenan's music and philosophy.

All these connections are wonderous in and of themselves, but there was more. Over the course of this study, it became evident that Keenan explores multiple faces of the Divine beyond the Moon and Mercury. For instance, he frequently writes about the impact of limitations and lessons, which is a direct reflection of Saturn. He also seems to channel the energy of Mars through multiple pieces that focus on conflict, as well as the Sun via plenty of expressions of Sun-worship in his lyrics. In the latter half of his career, he has explored themes closely tied to the goddess Babalon, a modern rejuvenation of the Sumerian goddess of sex and love, Inanna.

In other words, just because I see Thoth in Keenan does not mean I have definitively pinned him down as only an avatar of the Thrice-Great God—quite the contrary. Keenan is not limited by me, you, or even himself. You may see another deity's influence in his works, and you would be right, too. He may consider himself a devoted follower of something else entirely, or nothing at all. And so it is with all humans, because we are all expressions of the Divine, and the Divine manifests in all forms.

BEFORE GOING ANY FURTHER, I hope you'll permit me a small side quest, a brief foray outside the realm of tarot theory and into the realm of broader occult praxis, because there is much that can be done with your love of music and popular culture beyond learning to read tarot.

I invite you to pause for a moment and think about your favorite famous people, and consciously connect them to the aspect of the Divine you're adoring when you admire them. For instance, if Keenan is also one of your favorite celebrities, then you may be a Thoth/Babalon-worshipper like me, or perhaps a Sun, Mars, Moon, or Saturn worshipper. The point is, only you can determine that answer for yourself, and it's a worthwhile exercise for reasons to be made clear imminently.

Who do you love, and why?

I ask you to consider these two questions because, when you know their answers, you can effectively use your personal connections to that area of pop culture to create potent, perspective-shifting spell work for yourself. Personal connections to popular culture—including such things as catch-phrases, lyrics, movie lines, makeup, and clothing—become incredibly effective symbols that you can use in your own magick. It doesn't matter that "it's just a movie (book, song, show, etc.) that someone made up." It doesn't matter that pop culture is created by mere humans—who do you think inspired them?

So, absolutely—write your favorite lyric or movie line that brings the energy you're seeking on your magickal petition, listen to a song that gives voice to your emotions while you perform your magickal workings, don that piece of clothing that reminds you of the superhero whose strengths you need... use the symbols of your fandom—those potent symbols that already speak to you—to help yourself achieve the mindset and results you intend. Use what speaks directly to you in a personal way to attain the objectives you seek, understanding that all the information, ideas, memories, and associations in your consciousness are available expressly for your own use.

CHAPTER 2
GENERAL TAROT AND THOTH TAROT BASICS

Each and every time I sat down to work on this chapter, a wave of imposter syndrome washed over me. Exactly who the fuck do I think I am, really, to write any kind of overview of a topic that has already been explored, explained, and expounded upon by such legends as Aleister Crowley, Carl Jung, Robert Wang, Rachel Pollack, Gerd Ziegler, Lon Milo DuQuette, Robert Place, M.M. Meleen, T. Susan Chang, and Benebell Wen (to name just a tiny fraction)? What could I possibly add to the discourse on this centuries-old esoteric practice?

And yet, if I want to be sure that the rest of this book makes sense and makes for a meaningful reading experience, I must share a few basic concepts first. In absolute honesty, I am by no means attempting to corral the total knowledge of tarot in this short introductory chapter, nor do I wish to recreate the wheel. It simply couldn't be done here, even if I wanted to—there is too much information, historical narrative, philosophy, and theory on tarot to put it all in this small volume. The study and mastery of this tool for spiritual growth could take up lifetimes and libraries, and so many more eloquent masters have already captured much more in their own books than this little nibble I'm providing here.

Instead, what I'm going to attempt to do in this chapter and the following chapter on Qabalah is to give you the running start you need to begin making sense out of tarot vis-a-vis this body of music, assuming you know only a little about either one or both. Just as you don't have to be a trained musician to appreciate and benefit from Keenan's music, you also don't have to be a world-class scholar of tarot to use and benefit from the practice of tarot. In fact, you don't even have to know all the cards' meanings to use and benefit from tarot. As I mentioned earlier, my intention in writing this book is two-fold: to help Keenan fans learn tarot through their existing knowledge of and appreciation for his music, and to help beginning tarot practitioners anchor what they've learned about tarot in something that is a part of their daily lives—the music of a favorite artist. For the purposes of this book, I'm choosing to use Keenan's catalogue of mystically-charged and esoterically-connected music to illustrate each card and to help readers strengthen their understanding of both the songs and the cards.

It is possible to have a lively tarot practice without knowing any of what I'm about to go over, but with these basics under your belt, tarot gets so much better—it becomes more personalized to you and your life, more meaningful, more spiritual. I promise to be efficient, and to only include the bare necessities so we can get on to the good stuff as soon as possible, but my hope is that this will be a spark that inspires readers to follow their curiosity, wherever it may lead. I'll also share my recommendations for additional reading, so that when you're ready to explore further, you'll know where to start.

Ready? Let's go.

WHAT IS TAROT?

Tarot is collection of 78 archetypes illustrated in a deck of as many cards. It is most frequently used as a tool for divination as well as for personal and spiritual development. The archetypes included in any standard tarot deck are common to every culture, civilization, creed, and race on earth, and they embody every basic human concept there is. Birth, death, and rebirth are represented here, as are concepts of the Mother, Father, and Child, as well as human experiences like falling in love, feeling lust, and being betrayed. Thus, the full spectrum of human experience can be expressed with this nifty little pack of cards.

Tarot practitioners use this simple, yet effective tool to access information that is currently outside of their consciousness by allowing the information to come through via symbolism. Rather than getting tangled up in the merry-go-round of the long-standing issues and conundrums of waking life, tarot helps people to "get outside themselves" by recasting their personalities and problems in metaphorical or symbolic terms, so they can be analyzed and "solved" in non-dramatic, non-threatening ways. In other words, tarot provides an avenue for examining yourself under a different light and from a new perspective.

HISTORY OF TAROT

Like most any ancient spiritual tool still in use today, tarot has contested origins. The long and short of it is, tarot began as a mid-15th century Italian card game, which eventually developed occult associations starting in the late 18th century. The Hermetic Order of the Golden Dawn explored the tarot as a deeply cloaked representation of Hermetic truths, and from that study, renowned mystic A.E. Waite and acclaimed artist Pamela Colman Smith created the modern tarot deck as we know it—a deck known as the *Rider-Waite Smith Tarot*.

Published in 1910, many of the images from the Rider-Waite Smith deck have become part of our mainstream consciousness, such as The Hermit, which appears on the *Led Zeppelin IV* album cover. Other examples of well-known Rider-Waite Smith images include The Fool, The Magician, and Death. Today, this deck is widely considered to be the world standard of tarot symbolism.

However, development of the practice of tarot didn't end there. The next major step in the evolution of this esoteric treasure trove came in 1938, when occult genius Aleister Crowley and master artist Lady Frieda Harris began working on a new tarot system, which came to be known as the *Thoth Tarot*. In this project, Crowley and Harris built on the teachings of the Golden Dawn and produced a deck that was much more open in its symbolism. In fact, deeply secret spiritual teachings of the Golden Dawn were laid bare by this upstart *Thoth* deck, and it did not see the light of day until it was published over 25 years after it was completed, well after both its creators were dead and gone.

Lady Harris's hauntingly beautiful images and Crowley's accompanying *Book of Thoth* offer pictorial and written lessons of Thelema, which is widely understood to be the direct philosophical and religious teachings of Crowley. Today, the *Thoth Tarot* remains the premier deck of Hermeticists, magickians, and lefthand-path walkers the world over. I use the *Thoth Tarot* and *Tabula Mundi Tarot* —M.M. Meleen's vibrant, visually arresting deck that is faithful to the *Thoth* tradition—in this exploration of Keenan's music and the tarot for a variety of reasons, but mainly because they are my decks of choice and because this tradition most closely resembles and explains the ideas expressed in Keenan's music.

WHAT MAKES TAROT, TAROT?

There are a few characteristics that make a deck of cards a tarot deck. First of all, the deck has 78 cards—no more, no less.[1] Of the 78 cards, 22 comprise the major arcana, which includes the most well-known cards, such as The Fool, The Magician, The Empress, The Emperor, The Hermit, and Death. The remaining 56 cards are divided into four suits, each consisting of a four-member royal family (commonly called court cards) and numbered cards Ace through 10.

Furthermore, each suit is associated with one of four elements: fire, water, air, and earth. The fire suit is typically called Wands, Rods, or Staffs. The water suit is most often Cups, but can also be called Chalices, Cauldrons, or Bowls. The air suit is commonly called Swords, Blades, or Knives, and the earth suit is usually called Disks, Pentacles, or Coins.

Finally, each and every card in the tarot pack has specific astrological, planetary, Qabalistic, chromatic, and numerological *correspondences* assigned to them. A correspondence is an energetic or magickal relationship or equivalency between two things; in the cards section of the book, we'll discuss correspondences for each card in detail.

Decks of divination cards that do not conform to this structure are called oracle decks, and they are not tarot. Oracle decks do not have a standardized structure or system—they can be whatever their creators design them to be: a deck of 30 goddess cards, for instance, or a set of 50 flower cards, or whatever else the creator desires. Oracle decks are wonderful divination tools, but *they are not tarot*. I say this more than once, because this is often a point of confusion for beginning divination students. Tarot is much more structured than oracles—there are standardized meanings and associations assigned to the cards, and tarot is used in a specific, prescribed manner.

WHAT MAKES THE THOTH TAROT AND OTHER THOTH-BASED DECKS DIFFERENT?

Aleister Crowley trained in the Golden Dawn tradition, and most of the *Thoth* deck conforms to Golden Dawn tenets just as the *Rider-Waite Smith* deck does, albeit with some important tweaks. The tweaks in the *Thoth* deck often represent important ideas in Thelema. For the record, Thelema is a religion, but it can also be practiced as a philosophy. You don't have to be a Thelemite to use the *Thoth* deck.

Thoth, the deity for whom Crowley's tarot deck is named, is the

Egyptian god of writing, communication, magick, and knowledge; He is the creator of the secret teachings of tarot, and is also hailed as the Roman Mercury and the Greek Hermès.

A run-down of the major differences between *Rider-Waite* and *Thoth* decks follows.

Court Cards: In the *Rider-Waite Smith* deck, the royal court is made up of a King, a Queen, a Knight, and a Page (who can represent any young person, male or female). As Lon Mile DuQuette points out, Crowley essentially thought that the Knight was sexier than the King, which conjures images of an old man instead of a virile, dashing hero.[2] So, he decided to call the Kings Knights, and then made the younger members of the court the Prince and Princess to keep a gender balance among the court cards.

Rider-Waite Smith-Based Decks	*Thoth*-Based Decks
King	Knight
Queen	Queen
Knight	Prince
Page	Princess

Major Arcana Titles: Crowley renamed several cards in the major arcana.

Rider-Waite Smith-Based Decks	*Thoth*-Based Decks
The Magician	The Magus
The High Priestess	The Priestess
Justice	Adjustment
The Wheel of Fortune	Fortune
Strength	Lust
Temperance	Art
Judgement	The Aeon
The World	The Universe

Major Arcana Card Interpretations: Crowley's interpretation of several major arcana cards is also different from the standard *Rider-Waite Smith* definitions, which had a more "Christianized" flavor about them. Crowley's interpretations of the three cards listed below, on the other hand, are Thelemic and alchemical in nature.

Rider-Waite Smith-Based Decks	Thoth-Based Decks
Strength – victory of human compassion and enlightenment over beastly tendencies	Lust – joy of life and physical vigor exercised, especially in a sexual sense
Temperance – moderation, balance	Art – alchemical transformation, perfection via integration of opposing forces
Judgement – the last judgement, truth revealed, victory of the faithful over death	The Aeon – the dawning of a new age, a new paradigm of humans as extensions of the Divine

Card Order: Crowley also reversed the order of the Strength (VIII) and Justice (XI) cards; in the *Thoth* deck, Adjustment (Justice) comes before Lust (Strength).

Rider-Waite Smith-Based Decks	Thoth-Based Decks
Strength (Lust) – VIII	Adjustment (Justice) – VIII
Justice (Adjustment) – XI	Lust (Strength) – XI

Attribution: Finally, Crowley also restored the traditional Hebrew letter attributions of the masculine Emperor and feminine Star cards. He made The Emperor Tzaddi (which means fish hook), because the word Tzaddi is related to other masculine words such as Caesar and czar. Likewise, he made The Star Heh (which means window), because Heh is the letter of the divine feminine, as seen in the textual representation of the name of God, YHVH (more about this to come in the Qabalah Basics chapter).

Rider-Waite Smith-Based Decks	Thoth-Based Decks
The Emperor – Heh, the path of Chesed to Tiphareth	The Emperor – Tzaddi, the path of Netzach to Yesod
The Star – Tzaddi, the path of Netzach to Yesod	The Star – Heh, the path of Chesed to Tiphareth

OTHER IMPORTANT DISTINCTIONS

Reversals: The *Thoth* deck does not traditionally use reversals, which is indicated by the backs of the cards; decks that are intended to be read using reversals usually have a back design that is the same right side up or upside down, to disguise the orientation of the cards. A quick glance at the cards confirms the Thoth deck's back design is clearly not reversible.

Instead, the Thoth deck uses the "dignity" of the cards to determine whether an "upright" or "reversed" interpretation is called for. Cards of the same suit reinforce each other, and cards of opposing suits weaken each other. Swords oppose Disks, and Wands oppose Cups. All other combinations are positive.

Symbols and Hebrew Letters on Cards: As mentioned earlier, the *Thoth* deck includes a great deal more information about the cards on the cards themselves. One example of the kinds of "secret" information readily revealed by the *Thoth* deck are the planetary and astrological attributions on the minor arcana cards, and the Hebrew letter correspondences and planetary/elemental attributions on the major arcana cards.

Hermetic Titles Revised and on Cards: As Crowley originally trained in the Golden Dawn, he kept the Hermetic titles of the cards, but in many cases, he shortened or slightly revised them. For example, 2 of Swords, "Lord of Peace Restored," became "Lord of Peace." He also placed title key words on the cards themselves; hence, the 2 of Swords card bears the title "Peace."

Metaphor and Symbolism Throughout the Cards: Crowley also was intent on using Lady Harris' art to further convey Hermetic information about the cards. The colors used in each card, the card back, and the mythological and Qabalistic references throughout the artwork are intentional, and each and every element on each card is there for a reason. This is why the *Thoth* deck retains its enduring allure: students of tarot can go as far down the "rabbit hole" as they want to with this deck—and each deepening layer of symbolism gives way to another beneath it.

As mentioned earlier, there are volumes more that could be said about tarot, but this will suffice for our purposes here. Now that we have a grasp of the tool we're using, and an understanding of its specific tradition, we can examine the major philosophy that animates it: Qabalah.

RECOMMENDED READING

<u>General Tarot</u>
Tarot Deciphered, T. Susan Chang and M.M. Meleen
Tarot Correspondences, T. Susan Chang
Seventy-Eight Degrees of Wisdom, Rachel Pollack

<u>Thoth Tarot</u>
The Book of Thoth (Egyptian Tarot), The Master Therion (Aleister Crowley)
Understanding Aleister Crowley's Thoth Tarot, Lon Milo DuQuette
Book M: Liber Mundi (companion book to the *Tabula Mundi Tarot*), M.M. Meleen
The Qabalistic Tarot, Robert Wang
Tarot: Mirror of the Soul, Gerd Ziegler

CHAPTER 3
QABALAH BASICS

This is indeed the very basics of Qabalah—Qabalistic Kindergarten, if you will. I'm including this section in hopes that it will prevent you from taking the path I initially took: that of mistakenly believing that Qabalah isn't all that important for understanding Hermetic tarot. If you start out with at least a little understanding of Qabalah and some basic astrology[1] as you learn the *Thoth* tarot deck, it will serve you extraordinarily well.

WHAT IS QABALAH?

Qabalah is a spiritual and philosophical system that attempts to explain the universe by organizing and categorizing all energy in existence. It originated within Judaism, and in the intervening centuries, mystics have studied it and applied its principles to metaphysics and the occult, especially tarot. I should note that this has been a controversial undertaking. Those who practice traditional and conservative forms of Judaism do not agree with Kabbalah (this is the traditional spelling) being used in any manner that could be called mystical, and many also disapprove of people outside the

Jewish faith using it at all. Be that as it may, most every tarot deck in existence is based in some part on (mystical) Qabalah, and tarot readers are able to understand their cards much better when they have at least a cursory understanding of this ancient and complex system.

THE TREE OF LIFE

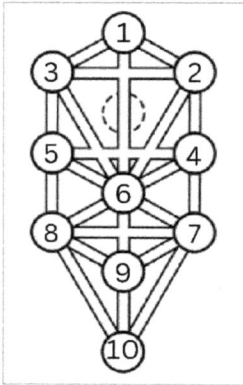

The Tree of Life is the title given to the diagram that illustrates many of Qabalah's main principles. You've probably seen it before—in fact it's included on the back cover of Tool's *Salival* album. The Tree of Life is a geometric design that contains ten spheres with 22 paths connecting them. The main thrust of this model is that the energy of Godhead percolates downward, from the top sphere to the bottom, energizing each sphere along the way. Think of the top sphere as containing pure light, and each of the spheres below it containing some component of the light spectrum, until it reaches the bottom and all the pieces are recollected into visible light.

The top sphere, Kether (1), is the Crown, or Godhead; the bottom sphere, Malkuth (10), is the Kingdom—the physical expression of all that is contained above, which you and I know collectively as "reality." Between Kether and Malkuth are eight spheres which represent major kinds of energetic signatures: 2. Wisdom (Chokmah), 3. Understanding (Binah), 4. Mercy (Chesed), 5. Severity (Geburah), 6. Beauty (Tiphareth), 7. Victory (Netzach), 8. Splendor (Hod), and 9. Foundation (Yesod). Above Kether are three veils that represent the void from which the Tree of Life sprang; they are, from Kether outward, Ain (Nothing), Ain Soph (The Boundless), and Ain Soph Aur (The Boundless Light).

THE SEPHIROTH AND PATHWAYS

The spheres on the Tree are called *sephiroth* (singular *sephira*). Each sephira is something like a world, a "place" where everything of that energy "resides." They each have different themes, associated deities, and correspondences. As you can see in the previous diagram, the spheres are arranged in three columns. On the right side is the Pillar of Mercy or the Pillar of Force; it is the masculine or positive side of the Tree, where all possibility resides. On the left is the Pillar of Severity or the Pillar of Form; this is the feminine or negative side of the Tree, where all is certain. The middle column is known as the Middle Pillar or the Middle Way, which expresses the concepts of unity and balance.

An important side note here: the masculine/mercy/force/positive and the feminine/severity/form/negative dichotomy do not have the traditional good/bad values that we place on those words. They are merely descriptions of the flow of energy from one to the other, like a battery; the Pillar of Mercy is so named because it represents inspiration before it has been solidified into *something*. All things are possible on the Pillar of Mercy. But once energy is solidified in the Pillar of Severity, all other things *the thing* could've been before, are no longer options; a chair, once built, no longer has the potential to be a bed, because it's now locked into the reality of being a chair. In effect, the Pillar of Severity is severe because it destroys other possibilities when it creates.

Kether, as mentioned before, is the top sphere. It represents the Godhead, the Source, the All, the singularity that first issued from the void before anything else. It is the purest, most blinding light in existence—beyond the light of the Sun, beyond what we can even imagine. Kether's standard color is white, and its alternate title is Crown. In Kether, there is no duality, no separation. All is One. Being omniscient, omnipotent, and The All is great, but it gets boring after a while. So, Source breathed out and created a second sphere, Chokmah, with Its exhalation.

Down and to the right from Kether is Chokmah, the second sephira, which is associated with the color gray, and is also known as Wisdom. Chokmah is the Divine Father principle, the energetic force of Kether. This sephira is associated with the zodiac, the heavens. Chokmah is also at the head of the Pillar of Mercy or Force. Now that there was a second sephira, Godhead could experience Itself through interplay with Chokmah; now there was an Other, which meant there could now be duality instead of just singularity. This new experience of "otherness" was also grand, but then Source wondered what this relationship looked like from the outside, so Source spoke aloud and created the third sphere, Binah.

Directly across the Tree from Chokmah and to the lower left of Kether, Binah is the third sephira, known as Understanding. Naturally, if Chokmah is the Divine Father principle, it follows that Binah is the Divine Mother principle. As such, Binah receives the raw energy or force of Chokmah, and uses it to create form—matter. In other words, Chokmah provides the energetic sperm, and Binah receives that insemination and uses it to create form, the child that She will birth. And you can probably guess, Binah is the head of the Pillar of Severity or Form; She corresponds to Saturn, the planet of limitations and lessons. Binah is also often referred to as a black sea, as black is the traditional color of this sephira, and the sea is a metaphor for the womb.

Together, Kether, Chokmah, and Binah are the Supernal Triad, the Holy Trinity. They are so far above our comprehension that we cannot fathom them. They are Duality and Duality combined into the One, and together they create the entire Universe—all we know and Everything Else. They are the great generating engine that spins out all of existence, and below them on the Tree is the Abyss—the vast chasm that separates the material from the ethereal, the mundane from the divine. Relatively few humans ever see beyond the Abyss, and those who do have spent many years and expended much dedicated effort in doing so.

Incidentally, if you examine the Tree of Life diagram again, you'll also notice there is a blank spot in the upper portion of the Tree;[2] it appears that there should be an eleventh sephira, placed just below Kether on the Middle Pillar. That blank space is where the secret or false sephira, Da'ath, is located. Da'ath, also called Knowledge, does not appear on most depictions of the Tree because it represents the Abyss that separates the Supernal Triad from the rest of the sephiroth. Da'ath is the obstacle that humans must overcome to reach enlightenment. People call this obstacle by many names—the shadow, the adversary, the dark night of the soul, the abyss—but ultimately, Da'ath is our own flawed humanity, including our egos, our over-reliance on thought (or Knowledge), our patterns, our identities, and our habits.

So, above the Abyss, the Supernal Triad is busy perpetually permutating, generating, and spitting out all of the matter that makes up the Universe, leading us to the next real sephira, Chesed. Chesed, or Mercy, is the highest sephira on the Pillar of Mercy below the Abyss, and it is the first realm of material existence. Like the four legs of a table, the fourth sephira of Chesed is solid, sturdy, and stable. It grows, achieves, and expands, and is associated (or, to use the concept we discussed earlier, it *corresponds to*) Jupiter, the planet of gifts and expansion. Chesed's color is blue.

To balance Mercy on the Pillar of Force, across the Tree on the Pillar of Form we have Severity. Geburah, or Severity, is the red sephira of war and the realm of Mars. In this sphere are all things conflict, including war, pain, suffering, dominance, and aggression. Things are cut down and destroyed in Geburah, as opposed to growing and expanding in Chesed.

From there, energy passes back onto the Middle Pillar for the first time since Kether, into the sephira of Tiphareth. Tiphareth, or Beauty, is the center of the Tree. Naturally, Tiphareth corresponds to the Sun, the center of our "universe" for the majority of humankind's existence. It traditionally corresponds to the color yellow and the number six. This is as high up the Tree as most mere mortals make it in a lifetime. As such, we associate it with other humans who achieved enlightenment—we call this the center of Christ Consciousness or the Buddha Mind. Thus, this sephira is not only the Sun, it's the Son, as in the son of God the Father and God the Mother. Tiphareth is also the sephira in which we gain Knowledge and Conversation of our Holy Guardian Angels, as per the Thelemic philosophy. From this point on down the Tree, energy continues to slow and solidify—remember, we're headed toward tangible, material reality as we know it in Malkuth. The further down the Tree we descend, energy becomes denser, heavier, murkier, darker.

Our next stop is Netzach, a.k.a. Victory, on the Pillar of Mercy. As the seventh sephira and the realm of the material feminine, Netzach corresponds to Venus, goddess of beauty, fertility, and sensuality. This is a sphere of the body, the emotions, the receptive aspects of existence. Due to Venus' connection with abundance and verdant growth, Netzach is traditionally green.

On the opposite side of the Tree, across from Netzach and on the Pillar of Severity, is Hod. Hod, or Splendor, is the eighth sephira, and it is associated with the mental faculties and the god Mercury. Where Netzach lounges in Her luxurious abundance, Hod is lightning fast, the fleet-footed messenger of thought, rationale, systems, and knowing. Hod is the mind that balances Netzach's body, and it corresponds to the number eight and the color orange.

Beyond Hod, we return to the Middle Pillar and descend into Yesod. Yesod, or Foundation, represents the realm of intuition, psychism, and faith. It corresponds to the Moon, and is usually purple. This sephira is just beyond what we experience in daily reality, and because of that, many (if not most) humans are able to access Yesod through dreams, psychedelic experiences, prayer, and meditation. Yesod is the realm we reach when we have a mystical, supernatural, or religious experience.

From this ninth sephira, we descend, finally, into the mundane reality of Malkuth, the realm of earth and of the Daughter. What is Malkuth? Well, you're sitting in it. You're also breathing it. You are looking at, touching, tasting, hearing, and smelling it. Malkuth is everything we can perceive and interact with in normal consciousness. It's what we all think of as "the real world." At the very bottom of the Tree, everything has been collected and mixed together in this dark, dense, murky mass of matter. It's disgustingly glorious, and it contains a little bit of absolutely everything in the Universe, known and unknown. Malkuth is usually illustrated as a circle divided into four slices—one slice is citrine, one olive, one rust, and the last black —all earthy colors.

It might be tempting to think of Malkuth as the weakest, most primitive and least desirable sephira, and you would be right...and also wrong (I hope you like paradoxes—this book, the tarot, meta-physics, and *reality in general* are full of paradoxical truths). This amazing physical manifestation of Malkuth is the culmination of the efforts of all that God/Source/All desired to create. In a Qabalistic sense, Malkuth is the final result that truly allows God to experience Godself. It's glorious because it's *real*. It's been made *manifest*. Malkuth is the *realm of successful magick*. And because it's the end, there's nowhere to go from there...except back up to the beginning. What began in the Supernal Triad has passed down the Middle Pillar to the Son, and finally at the end, rests in the Daughter. The Daughter (a.k.a. Malkuth, a.k.a. Earth... a.k.a. you and me and everyone else) then gives birth to the next generation, the next itera-tion of The Tree.

And now that we've visited all ten sephiroth, we can (briefly, more on this shortly) consider the pathways between them. There are 22 connecting pathways that join most all of the sephiroth to their neighbors (I'm sure you've noticed that some pathways seem to be missing, and we're going to return to that later). The pathways between the sephiroth represent certain lessons, which makes sense when you consider that traveling from one sephiric "world" to another would necessitate some growth or change. More on this later, but you get the idea for now.

THE FOUR QABALISTIC WORLDS

At this point, you should have in your mind a working model of the Universe in the form of a Tree of Life with 10 sephiroth and pathways between them. There! Neat and tidy, right?

Right...so here's the thing: all of existence is made up of fractals, or patterns that repeat inside themselves, infinitely in either direction. You've seen these before, too, in digital animations and in magnifications of organic material like plants and seashells. Thus, there's not just *one* Tree—there's one Big Tree made up of smaller Trees, which are made up of smaller Trees, and on and on, ad infinitum.

So, take your image of the Qabalistic Tree of Life, and multiply it, connecting each Malkuth to a Kether, and each Kether to a Malkuth, in a never-ending chain. Remember when we talked about how in Malkuth, there's nowhere to go but back up to Kether? Every Malkuth is the Kether of the Tree below it, and every Kether is the Malkuth of the Tree above.

Now, imagine there isn't just one chain of Trees, but infinite chains that are connected side by side—each Pillar of Severity connected to the Pillar of Mercy next to it, and vice versa, on and on. It's three-dimensional. It's living, breathing, moving. *That* is more like the Qabalistic representation of the fabric of the space-time continuum.

"The Big Tree," if you will—the one that represents the totality of All That Is—is made up of four Trees. The first of these four Trees is the Qabalistic world of Atziluth. It's the purest energy emanating directly from Godhead. In this world are the inspirations of all that is, ever was, will come to be. Nothing *exists* here; in Atziluth there are only potentialities. It is a world ruled by the element of fire, the heat at the heart of every process and action, ever. Atziluth is the world of God's ideas, for lack of a better way to put it. In the credo of the Magickian, the Qabalistic world of Atziluth represents the power To Will, the personal, internal force that responds to inspiration.

The second Tree in "The Big Tree" is the Qabalistic world of Briah, which could be best expressed as desire for something to satisfy the inspiration from Atziluth. The fire of Atziluth gives way to the water world of Briah, of psychism and connection and emotion. Again, nothing *exists* yet. Here in Briah, there are only cravings; it's the world of God's hunger, if I might be so bold. In the credo of the Magickian, this is the power To Dare—the willingness to feel, and pursue the object of, attraction.

The third Tree in "The Big Tree" is the Qabalistic world of Yetzirah, the world of ideas. At this point, we start to move a little closer to real *things*, but before we get there, we must envision them. Yetzirah is the world of air, of such insubstantial things as the intellect, knowledge, and identity. Still, nothing *exists* here, but now we have the idea of a thing, that *could* exist. The magickal power here is To Know.

The fourth and final Tree that makes up the "Big" Tree of Life is the Qabalistic world of Assiah. Here, there are finally real things, as energy has slowly descended down through the worlds into the realm of earth—matter. Assiah is the world of solid forms, the material world, existence. The cycle is complete, energy is now at rest in the form of matter, all is quiet. The magickal power of Assiah is To Keep Silent.

The four Qabalistic worlds, now connected into one big Tree, have covered the creation cycle from inspiration to finished product, and all together constitute All That Is, The Tree of Life, and the final magickal power, To Go. To Go represents the combined ability of all the powers: the power to use magick to create the world around you, just as Godhead does, but on a smaller scale.

THE TETRAGRAMMATON AND THE FOUR-FOLD NATURE OF GOD

The Tree of Life is four-fold, and so is the name of God. You've no doubt seen the unpronounceable YHVH as the name of God in scriptures before, or else you've seen the speech-approximated version of that name, Jehovah. Ever wondered about that? Why give anything a name that is not pronounceable?

The name is unpronounceable, because the ancients understood that we could never grasp God with our human minds. We could approximate understanding with symbols that we can wrap our tiny, limited brains around, but we'll never *know God*. Thus, the mystics of old called God by what they could understand, a name composed of letters that represent the four-fold nature of the universe—four-fold as in the elements and the Qabalistic worlds.

In this divine not-name, also known as the Tetragrammaton, the letter Y is the Hebrew letter Yod, representing Atziluth, fire, and the Father. The first H is the Hebrew letter Heh (*Heh primal*), representing Briah, water, and the Mother. The V stands for the Hebrew letter Vau, and it represents Yetzirah, the world of air, the Son. And the final Heh (*Heh final*) is Assiah, the element of earth, the Daughter. Together, these four "family members" make up the composite "whole" of existence, and therefore, "God" as we understand Him/Her/Them.

QABALAH AND TAROT

At this point, I'm betting that you've probably begun putting together that there are intriguing commonalities between Qabalah and tarot (at least I *hope* that you have begun seeing a few connections between them). The easiest connection to point out is the elements. Fire, water, air, and earth correspond to the Qabalistic worlds and the members of the YHVH "family." Thus, right away we know that the four Qabalistic worlds correspond to the suits and court cards in tarot.

The concept of a family—of a Father, Mother, Son, and Daughter—brings to mind the court cards: Knight, Queen, Prince, and Princess. The Court cards in each suit correspond to other things that come in fours—elements, magickal powers, directions, the Qabalistic worlds, and anything else that is four-fold.

Next, recall the number of pathways between the sephiroth, 22, the same as the number of cards in the major arcana of the tarot. Each pathway on the Tree of Life corresponds to a specific major arcana card.

There are ten sephiroth on the Tree, and ten small cards (Ace through 10) in each suit. Each small card resides in the sephira that shares its number.

I could go on and on, but instead, I'll show you with the rest of the book how these two systems (not to mention astrology, numerology, and every other system of magick) connect to one another. The fact is, the tarot is a perfect pictorial representation of the Qabalah—one that you can interact with on an intimate and immediate personal level. Like the Qabalah, the tarot is a working model of the Universe, containing within it the building blocks of anything you can experience, perceive, think of, or create. The two systems are beautifully succinct in their own rights, but put them together, and you hold the keys to mastering your own reality.

There! That's it. I hope it wasn't too painful, and I hope you've found these past two chapters helpful, or at least not completely bewildering. I've done my best to give you the quick and dirty explanations of basics, purely for the sake of setting a meaningful stage for us to work on as we explore Keenan's music through the lens of tarot. My hope is that you'll use this as a jumping-off point for further explorations.

If you're already intrigued, you can gain a more in-depth understanding of all that we've covered here and more with Lon Milo DuQuette's most excellent *Understanding Aleister Crowley's Thoth Tarot*. In the opening chapters of this must-have book for *Thoth* enthusiasts, Mr. DuQuette provides the most straightforward, easy-to-follow guide to these topics that I've ever come across, plus a whole lot more on everything you ever wanted to know about the *Thoth* deck.

I should note here that I'm not directing you immediately to Crowley's original book on the deck, because...well, Crowley was not known for writing anything that could remotely be called "light reading." If *Thoth* is your calling, DuQuette's *Understanding...* is the book to start with, and it will make getting through Crowley's original *Book of Thoth* much more bearable and infinitely more meaningful later.

And now, with these basics under our collective belt, let us truly begin.

CHAPTER 4

SEPHIROTH AND ALBUMS

The easiest place to begin exploring how Maynard James Keenan's music can serve as a giant mnemonic device for learning tarot is with the sephiroth on the Tree of Life. As you may recall from the previous chapter, each sephira is something of a world of its own, not unlike an album. Every album by any artist has a mood, a theme, and associated lessons and experiences that accompany it. Understanding the lyrics of a given album is a large piece of the process of receiving the artist's intended message.

This is where the puzzle began for me, when it first occurred to me that, thematically, A Perfect Circle's debut album could be considered something of an anima exploration for Keenan. *Mer de Noms* followed immediately after Tool's *Ænima*, when Keenan's lyrics first explore Carl Jung's idea of the feminine side of men (the anima) and the masculine side of women (the animus). And in terms of Qabalah, I would argue that the concept of an internal feminine archetype corresponds to Binah, the Supernal Mother, the endless black sea of form and gestation. Coincidentally, *Mer de Noms* translates to "sea of names," which is another interesting tie-in with Binah's enduring comparison to an infinite black sea.

With that first puzzle piece in place, the other albums seemed to slot themselves in effortlessly. The resulting arrangement that follows utilizes nearly all of Keenan's full-length, original albums to date, with Tool occupying the middle pillar, Puscifer on the Pillar of Mercy, and A Perfect Circle on the Pillar of Severity. This arrangement emphasizes Tool's development over time into a project that achieves balance by exploring both the light and the dark, starting with *10,000 Days'* descriptions of daily life and societal issues in Malkuth and rising up to *Fear Inoculum's* explorations of divine unity in Kether. A Perfect Circle's albums dive deep into emotional and physical experiences and limitations on the Pillar of Severity, while Puscifer gives expansive treatment to ideas, philosophy, and possibility on the Pillar of Mercy.

1. **Kether (Crown)** – corresponds to Source – *Fear Inoculum* – The light of Source lives in Kether; this sephira represents the sum total, the All, clarity, and unity. Tool's latest album and masterpiece is rich in spiritual metaphor and themes of unity among humanity and with the Divine, and draws further on the metaphysical themes first explored in *Lateralus.*

2. **Chokmah (Wisdom)** – corresponds to the Zodiac – *Money Shot* – The second sephira is the Other to Kether's Self. Here is where we find themes of applied wisdom, balance, and duality. Puscifer's third full-length offering fits this theme well, with wise life experience informing explorations of spirituality, parenting and family life, science, work, and politics.

3. **Binah (Understanding)** – corresponds to Saturn – *Mer de Noms* – The third sephira is the black sea of formation and the seat of the supernal feminine, the anima, which A Perfect Circle's debut album so masterfully illustrates. This album's tracks are mostly named for people, representing a multitude of forms, emotional

connections, and relationships. Here, Keenan explores maternal power, heartbreak, sexual connection, and healing.

4. **Da'ath (Knowledge)** – also known as The Abyss or the False Sephira – *Ænima* – Da'ath is the hidden or secret sephira located between Kether and Tiphareth, in the realm typically referred to as The Abyss. Da'ath's knowledge separates the Supernals from the lower sephiroth of matter and manifestation. Tool's second full-length album's entire theme is the discovery that there is more than meets the casual eye. This album faithfully explores how accumulated knowledge can lead to new doors of perception, but the ultimate question is, can you escape your mind?

5. **Chesed (Mercy)** – corresponds to Jupiter – *Conditions of My Parole* – The fourth sephira is the first one that falls below the Abyss, and it marks the entryway of spirit into matter. Like the gifts that spring from the Divine Paternal, Puscifer's *Conditions of My Parole* extols the virtues of material experience, growth, harvest, abundance, and even death.

6. **Geburah (Severity)** – corresponds to Mars – *Thirtheenth Step* – This sephira on the Pillar of Form focuses on all things conflict and dis-ease, which are aptly described on A Perfect Circle's second album. Addiction and all its attendant issues are the picture of battle and conflict, both internal and external.[1]

7. **Tiphareth (Beauty)** – corresponds to the Sun – *Lateralus* – The sixth sephira is the center of the Tree of Life. It represents the heart-center, the Christ Consciousness, the Holy Guardian Angel, and the evolving human spirit. Tool's third original full-length album made the leap from themes of darkness to light, introducing fans to a new, metaphysical way of looking at the world.

8. **Netzach (Victory)** – corresponds to Venus – *"V" is for Vagina* – Sephira seven encompasses all things earthly feminine, fertile, and abundant. This is the feminine rooted in the body as opposed to the spirit, and Puscifer's debut album deliciously goes there. Full of exhilarating sexual romps and bodily fulfillment, *"V" is for Vagina* sparks and satiates desire.

9. **Hod (Glory)** – corresponds to Mercury – *Eat the Elephant* – The eighth sephira corresponds to communication, technology, and speed. A Perfect Circle's most recent album masterfully explores modern American life, concentrating on themes of propaganda, weaponized data, information overload, and intellectual overwhelm.

10. **Yesod (Foundation)** – corresponds to the Moon – *Undertow* – The ninth sephira finds us stretching up toward the heavens. Yesod is the first sephira we reach when we push beyond our own mundane perceptions of the world around us in Malkuth. Here is where we encounter religion, spirituality, and psychism, but because it's also far down the Tree and under the authority of the Moon, so there's plenty of room for dark creepiness and mental breakdowns. Tool's first full-length album, named for a phenomenon caused by the Moon's magnetic pull upon the earth, dove deep into the dark side of Yesod, struggling with addiction, religion, and faith, as well as exploring themes of darkly altered consciousness that drags us downward.

11. **Malkuth (Kingdom)** – corresponds to Earth – *10,000 Days* – The final sephira is our daily home, the world around us that we interact with via our five physical senses. Tool's 2006 release is likewise concerned with mundane life experiences, including family life, modern media, popular culture, religion, and sociopolitical issues.

Viewing the Tree of Life in this way, with albums serving as the markers of major themes on the path to enlightenment, helps us to get a bearing on the placement of card-song matches from this point forward. The sephiroth and albums are the broadest categories of information, while the cards and songs are the details that live inside these broader topics. The pathways between the sephiroth are represented by their corresponding major arcana tarot cards and matched songs, while the minor arcana tarot cards and their songs find their homes inside individual sephiroth.

As you may have already noticed, on every album there are one or two songs that don't necessarily match the basic theme of the album and the sephira (a prime example is the mundane and confrontational "Ticks and Leeches" appearing on the metaphysical *Lateralus* album). That's OK, as far as I'm concerned. The point is that the overarching theme of the album matches the sephira.

Likewise, not all of the minor arcana cards are matched with songs that come from the album assigned to that sephira. For example, Geburah—the sephira of war that I have matched with A Perfect Circle's *Thirteenth Step*—encompasses within it the 5s of Wands, Cups, Swords, and Disks, but these cards' song matches do not all come from *Thirteenth Step*. Instead, I made matches based on which song best illustrates the card, regardless of who, where, or when they were released. As I mentioned in the introduction, I made every effort to preserve the integrity of the esoteric teachings I'm working with, and resisted shoving square pegs in round holes for the sake of simplicity.

One final point before moving on: the structure, definitions, and correspondences pertaining to the Qabalistic Tree of Life, the sephiroth, the pathways, tarot cards, astrology, deities, and numerology that I'm using here are pre-determined by the last 125 years of metaphysical and occult teachings. The pieces that are "mine" are the overlay of Keenan's works onto this broader structure, my interpretations and commentary on the music, and my explanations of how my interpretations of the music match the information contained in the occult systems I reference herein.

You may disagree with any number of aspects of what I've done here—in fact I hope you do! I encourage everyone reading this book to create their own model to help them understand and learn the tarot—in fact, every occultist is expected to design their own tarot deck as a matter of course and a rite of passage. Choose the medium that you like best—ink, pencil, charcoal, crayons, glitter—whatever tickles your fancy. Or, for those who use words as their artistic medium like I do, perhaps you'll create a system like this one with your own poetry or lyrics. The Universe opens its arms to you! Create as a god, for that is what we each are!

CHAPTER 5

PATHWAYS ON THE TREE

THE MAJOR ARCANA

T he major arcana or "greater mysteries" of the tarot consists of twenty-two cards that begin with 0, The Fool, and conclude with XXI, The Universe. These cards represent the Path to Enlightenment or the evolution of the soul, with The Fool representing the querent and the cards numbered I – XXI representing stations along the journey. For a bit of fun and to show you the archetypes of this half of the tarot, let's take a look at The Fool's journey from the perspective of a fairy tale...

THE FOOL'S JOURNEY

In the faintly yellow atmosphere of a lucid dream, The Fool steps off the ledge of surety in the material world, and into the limitless fall of the unknown. As air rushes through his hair and clothing, separating him from all he has known or owned, he has no knowledge of who he is or what is to come. He only knows that he must take a chance and trust that he'll find his way on this soon-to-be-revealed grand adventure of mystical initiation. Down and down, he tumbles, freefalling in the wormhole, twisting and turning through multiple realities, until at last he lands on new ground.

The Fool stands and brushes himself off, and finds himself before a table covered in a simple yellow cloth, displaying several strange and magickal objects. Unsure of what to do, he picks up the one thing he does recognize, a stylus, which he dips in a nearby inkwell. Parchment appears before him, and he is unable to resist the impulse to write his name. But...what *is* his name? He can't remember, but the word that appears on the parchment at the end of his stylus is *Magus*. Before the ink on the *s* has dried, all of the objects on the table —a wand, a cup, a sword, and a disk—have leapt from the table and settled themselves about him. Here at Atu (Key) I, The Magus, our hero discovers himself—or rather, he discovers that he IS a self. It is the station of self-identification, where he learns that he is powerful beyond measure, able to create anything he desires, and imbued with self-determination. He leaves this place well-armed, feeling the bliss of the ego and the limitlessness of Spirit.

Unsure of where to go, he wanders about this strange, dreamlike world until he comes to Atu II, The Priestess, a woman sitting upon a moonlit throne, her impossibly blue eyes and silent lips peeking out from her blue hooded robe.

Unable to look away from this silvery vision of loveliness, the hero catches a glimpse behind The Priestess' Veil of Enlightenment and first fathoms the depths of the mysteries of the Universe. He spontaneously understands that he truly knows very little, but he's enamored with this fleeting vision of divinity and wants desperately to remain in The Priestess's place of inner peace and knowing.

Though she says nothing and doesn't reach out to touch him, The Fool knows he is deeply connected to The Priestess. Our hero contemplates staying in The Priestess' silent sanctuary forever, but his own voice of inner knowing clearly tells him he must leave now, so he tears himself away and carries on.

After some time, The Fool arrives at an emerald green, rolling meadow of wild flowers. Atu III, The Empress, is resting there with her babes near a babbling creek. She reaches out a warm, soft hand to The Fool, and as he grasps it, he instantly experiences the energy of The Mother and the wonders of earthly creation, nurturance, fertility, and abundance. The Fool watches as the Empress miraculously fills garden upon garden with all manner of beautiful flora and fauna, which she loves and cherishes. He finds himself aching to be in the arms of this consummate mother, like the infant at her breast —safe, nurtured, and loved. And even as he recognizes this desire, it is fulfilled, so that he stumbles away half-drunk with maternal love and devotion.

As he reaches the edge of the meadow, The Fool discovers a worn footpath. He steps on the path and feels a cadence beneath his feet, a soft drumming that coalesces and builds, until it becomes a regimented march. Onward he goes, exuberant in matching his footfalls to the beats, as the dirt path gives way to pavement. After some time, our hero finally comes face to face with the scarlet countenance of The Emperor, Atu IV. The Emperor appraises The Fool's airy, whimsical nature, and seems resigned to teaching this joker a thing or two. He sets off, leading The Fool on a tour of instruction on how to manicure the beautiful gardens The Empress Mother has birthed. On and on, the tour continues until The Fool has thoroughly learned the benefits of order, systems, and measurement in the process of growth and evolution, as guided by the principles of the Father.

With his tour of duty complete, The Emperor hands The Fool off to the next level of order and authority: Atu V, The Hierophant. The Hierophant's red-orange robes cut an imposing figure, and his fine stole, sacred key, and papal crown intimidate The Fool in his own simple attire. Stunningly, The Hierophant reaches out and inserts his key into The Fool's heart, and turns it. The heavens open up before The Fool's eyes. Stars rejoice, the planets sing, and The Fool knows— just what, he cannot say, for words fail the majesty of the vision The Hierophant has provided him. But The Fool knows beyond the shadow of doubt that The Emperor's gardens reflect the order of the heavens above, and he rests safely in that knowledge. Here, in this new-found relationship with even larger systems of civilization and divine order, the teachings of which create culture and society as we know it, The Hierophant teaches The Fool cosmic law as morals and values.

Properly trained and raised up now, The Fool departs from the foot of The Hierophant and continues on his way. At Atu VI, The Lovers, our hero's growth is recognized and rewarded. He is now ready to choose his mate. His options are many, but he knows he should not make his decision lightly! This is the station of choices and decisions, duality and longing, partnership and love. Here is the pairing of opposites and the confirmation of freewill and choice. The Fool makes his choice of beloved, and the two are cleansed, conse-crated, and married in the sight of the Divine.

Now fully armed with a sense of self and a place in the world, The Fool and his twin are ready to join the race! The next stop, Atu VII, The Chariot, represents commitments, honor, duty—the accountabilities that come on the road to privilege and abundance. What's at the finish line? No one knows for sure, but everyone seems to have their favorite fantasies about the rich rewards waiting there. There's nothing left to do but begin the hard work of running!

But the journey is getting harder, and the path grows ever more difficult to make out. The running of the race is chaotic, and in the effort to pull ahead of the crowd, things sometimes get out of hand. The Fool realizes he has long ago left the path and forgotten every-thing and everyone he has gained along the way, and that course corrections are now necessary.

Instantly, he arrives at Atu VIII, Adjustment, where a blindfolded woman balances on the tip of a sword, holding the pans of a giant scale in each arm. The Fool places himself on one side of the scale and discovers his balance is indeed off, and the spirit of justice shows our hero how to bring moral equanimity back to his journey.

Determined to make good on what he has just learned, our hero is in desperate need of a retreat to think and re-examine his perspec-tive. Thus, he finds himself at the mouth of a cave on the side of a lonely mountain. This is Atu IX, home of The Hermit. In this place of solitude, the hero has all the time and silence he needs to reflect on what he has learned on the journey so far. He spends many days and nights in deep meditation and prayer, reading, studying, and writing. After some time, a philosophy begins to come together, and The Fool finds that he, like The Hierophant, has much to share with others by way of teaching, too. Our Fool is now a wise man.

He may have learned much, but there is still far more to go. Our hero can't spend the rest of eternity hiding out in his cave, after all, for the world keeps on turning. He finally leaves The Hermit's hideout to discover that everything has changed! Even though The Fool has been hiding out for a time, the ever-turning wheel has continued right along, spinning new yarns, weaving new worlds, and launching new ideas out into the Universe. The Fool glances down to see that he rides the rim of the Wheel of Fortune, Atu X. Over and over, the wheel turns; sometimes The Fool is on top, riding high above chaos and confusion. Sometimes he is crushed beneath the weight of the grinding rim. Everything is temporary, but as sure as he rises, he eventually falls, and rises again. The Fool wonders at the majesty of change, the Universe's only constant.

After some time riding the ups and downs of the Wheel of Fortune, The Fool climbs down and continues his explorations until he comes to Atu XI, where he finds the delicious figure of the one they call Lust. For so long, The Fool has been living in his mind, at the expense of his body and its needs. But here, in the arms of sensuality embodied, he remembers what it's like to enjoy being incarnate. Our hero and his lusty companion tumble into bed together, where they spend untold days and nights in the cocoon of wild passion. He finds his hunger and thirst for Lust are insatiable, and he rejoices in this vigorous use of his body. In a flash of insight, The Fool remembers when he met The Magus so long ago, and he reconnects to his own power, virility, and capability.

Energized and motivated to continue on, The Fool takes his leave of Lust and journeys to the next station, Atu XII. Here, a curious man dangling upside down from one foot greets The Fool with silence. Try as he might, our hero is unable to get The Hanged Man to answer his questions, so he does the only thing he can think to do—he sits down and waits. Time passes, and nothing changes. The Fool begins to get impatient and fear that he's losing his way by staying here. He knows he's supposed to learn something at each stop, but here, he's waiting for seemingly nothing. Hours become days, and the silence becomes deafening. Still, The Fool waits and The Hanged Man is silent. Finally, inspiration strikes, and The Fool declares, "I cannot make you talk to me, but I'm willing to sacrifice all I have to learn your wisdom." The curious upside-down man says nothing, but The Fool thinks he sees him wink, signaling The Fool's freedom to go. The Fool glances down to find that the few possessions he's accumulated along the way have vanished, his price to pass this station now paid.

The lesson of sacrifice learned, The Fool's next stop, Atu XIII, is Death. Our empty-handed hero comes face to face with the Reaper—the faceless, hooded one, with breath like ice and a scythe sharpened to an infinite edge. The hooded figure of Death says naught, but snatches our hero's breath from his throat, and The Fool instantly dies. The Fool's body drops where it once stood; it rots and decays, and when the season changes, something new—something miraculous—springs to life in his place. It is our hero, but he has transformed. By facing his mortality, The Fool has freed himself from the burdens of fear. He now knows that he can never truly die.

Marching on, reinvigorated in his quest for enlightenment, The Fool begins the final leg of his journey. At the next stop, Atu XIV or Art, our sweet Fool discovers why he was resurrected. He approaches a curious figure with two faces standing over a roiling cauldron. One of the figure's hands pours water into the cauldron; the other adds fire to the brew. A new substance, steam, rises from the concoction. The Fool watches the steam rise from the alchemist's cauldron and finally understands his own purpose in this life. In a moment of dazzling self-realization, The Fool completely remakes himself from all his disparate bits and parts—reassembling them in a brand-new way—and becomes someone else entirely. The Fool is now dual-natured, having both masculine and feminine energies blended and balanced within him. Armed with his newfound purpose and form, he presses on.

In the next station, Atu XV, a new adversary appears. Unlike Death, whose only aim was to harvest and destroy, this adversary wants The Fool to LIVE. *Live it up! Indulge! Suck the marrow from life, kid!* The Devil's voiceless prodding echoes in our hero's mind. *It's all yours for the taking. Let's revel in the muck and shit together, like the dirty little pigs we are!* But The Fool feels vaguely threatened by all this talk about getting down in the mire. There is madness at the edges of The Devil's eyes as he holds out a skin of wine to The Fool, and The Fool finds The Devil's erect penis and cloven hooves downright disturbing. Reluctantly taking a swig from the pouch, our hero finds himself plunged beneath the waves of consciousness, torn between desire and futility, hunger and revulsion, pleasure and lunacy. His head swims as he stumbles away from The Devil, the demon's soundless laughter still ringing in The Fool's head.

Onward, our terrified hero runs. Blinded by panic, he finds and takes shelter in Atu XVI, The Tower. Running, running, running, The Fool climbs the stairwell to the very top of The Tower, where he feels safe and far, far away from visions of The Devil's craven addiction, psychosis, and horrors in the dark. A storm of near-pitch black clouds is brewing outside, and suddenly lightning strikes The Tower, blasting The Fool clear out of it. He awakens to find that the storm has destroyed nearly everything around him, yet he survives. The rubble of The Tower surrounds him, smoldering bits of wood, glass, and stone. The Fool picks himself up, dusts himself off, and trudges on in near total shock.

By this time, our friend The Fool has experienced all manner of thrills and chills. He has died and been reborn. He has skirted the edges of lunacy. He has lost and regained and lost again. Feeling defeated, he casts his eyes to the heavens on a now clear night. Atu

XVII, The Star, shines down on him. In the heavens, it seems he can just make out the figure of an unspeakably beautiful goddess pouring jugs of sacred, milky starlight upon the world below. Her crystalline light is dimmer than sunlight, but that doesn't matter to The Fool. All he knows is that he feels better somehow, more hopeful. He still doesn't know how all this will end, but he finds he has... something new...could it be...faith? Yes, faith. And in this moment, The Fool knows with absolute clarity that he's close to finally finding out What It's All About.

He's deeper into the night now, and all has grown darker. Atu XVIII, the full Moon, has risen above the land, but it casts only enough light for The Fool's eyes play tricks on him. Is what he's seeing real? He has no way of knowing, even as the visions become more outlandish, more dreamlike, more seductive and disturbing. His unease blossoms into paranoia, and The Fool becomes convinced that The Devil is still watching him, perhaps hiding nearby. Our hero picks up his pace and runs on through the night, watching for dawn, waiting to be released from this nightmare.

Dawn finally breaks many hours later, and Atu XIX, the gloriously blazing Sun, rises in a clear, blue sky. The Fool rejoices, for he is finally able to clearly see everything around him. The air is warm and fragrant with flowers, and the hero realizes he has found his way inside a beautiful, walled garden. With childlike glee, he sheds his clothes and runs naked and free, flower to flower, tree to tree, sniffing and tasting and frolicking. He realizes that, while the journey has been scary at times, it has brought him to some truly astounding places! But he's not finished yet. He must still complete his quest.

At the end of this beautiful day in The Sun, The Fool curls up, exhausted and utterly fulfilled. In his blissful state, he drifts off and dreams of himself in another dimension, a dream within the dream. Atu XX, The Aeon, is an astral place. All the previous stations on his journey flash in his mind's eye, one after another, lessons along the way. When he resurfaces from his vision, who knows how many hours or days later, he sees with a new clarity. He sees now that, at every stage along the way, he was meeting...himself. Was learning from himself. Was comforted by, frightened by, and loved by himself. In fact, with this new vision, he can only see himself. He notices he's beginning to have trouble discerning where he ends and the outside world begins. Befuddled, he half wanders through this new kaleidoscopic reality to find the final station on this magnificent journey.

Atu XXI, The Universe and the final station on the path, is completely silent. No one is there to greet The Fool when he arrives. There is no place to sit, no building to enter, no riddle to solve. In fact, our hero looks around in amazement as the physical reality he has always known completely dissolves, and he finds himself floating in infinity. His body, old and haggard with wear when he arrived here, is now fresh, young, and vaguely feminine. In this moment, only our hero exists. The Fool twirls about in space, laughing as stars spin out into existence from her fingertips in whirling waves. And it is obvious in this moment that there is only The Fool. That's all there ever was. And The Fool is God, and me, and you, and light, and time, and space, and All There Is.

The Fool smiles and sighs in his sleep before stirring and stretching, eyes opening to greet a new day. He sits up in bed, yawns, and exclaims, "What a fantastic dream!" Outside, the strange and wonderful path awaits his footsteps.

CHAPTER 6
0. THE FOOL: "GRAVITY," A PERFECT CIRCLE

Traditional Title: Spirit of the Æther
Planet/Element: Uranus/Air
Qabalistic Correspondence: Path 11, from Kether (1) to Chokmah (2)
Key Words: beginnings, learning, journey, potential, innocence

"Gravity"
A Perfect Circle
Thirteenth Step, 2003

Atu Line
"I am surrendering to gravity and the unknown"

Atu (or Key) 0 is The Fool. We will begin here with zero, a number void of value, shaped like an egg, and symbolic of pure possibility. It is from this moment of potential that all life emerges, and all of life is contained within the tarot, so here is a fitting place to start. The Fool corresponds to the element of Air, and is associated with beginnings, potential, learning, and journeys. The Fool's path on the Tree of Life leads from first sephira, Kether, to the second sephira, Chokmah. It is the first emanation from Kether, and as such, represents the Breath of the Divine.

This card is traditionally considered the beginning of the deck, but as its number is 0, it really can appear between any two cards as well as at the beginning or end. In a real sense, The Fool represents the querent, and all the cards in the deck are The Fool's (and the querent's) experiences on the way to enlightenment. As will be illustrated multiple times throughout this book, tarot is ultimately a cycle. Every ending yields a beginning, creating the spiral of consciousness.

As the trump card representing elemental Air, The Fool is also deeply tied to the air sign cards—The Lovers (Gemini), Adjustment (Libra), and The Star (Aquarius)—as well as to all the Swords.

THE SONG

The Fool steps off the ledge of solid ground in the "real world," to fall into the unknown, having no idea or expectation of what will come next. He just knows he needs to live, and in order to fully and completely live, he must stop attempting to control the world around him, stop numbing himself, and actually surrender to the experience of existence. A Perfect Circle's "Gravity" reflects the willingness to let go of the familiar and start over again, and The Fool is nothing if not willing to walk away from what he has always known.

While the particular narrative of "Gravity" is told in the context of addiction and recovery, it still holds truths in any situation in which we are dissolving a pattern to become something or someone new. There is rawness inherent in becoming this new thing, and in the lack of the armor perfected by years of coping, compensating, and self-protecting inside the pattern. The Fool is vulnerable in every sense, as we all are, and that vulnerability is all that can prepare him to ascend up the Tree of Life toward the Sun, which is another way of referencing the Universe/Source/Light.

TABULA MUNDI TAROT

In M.M. Meleen's *Tabula Mundi Tarot*, we see The Fool about to step into a wormhole, "a hypothetical topological feature of space-time, like a tunnel connecting two universes," as Meleen describes it.[1] Where he is and where he's going are unclear, but the indication is that he has the ability to move about in space-time, much like the card can be inserted anywhere in the pack.

The Fool's skin is tattooed with symbols of the Sun (masculine), Moon (feminine), and alchemical elements Mercury, Sulphur (masculine), and Salt (feminine)—keys to universal operations—and he is further accompanied by a tiger and a crocodile, also representations of the respective masculine and feminine balance of the

Universe. Into the wormhole stream both flames and water, yet more symbols of masculine/feminine balance. The figure is also surrounded by butterflies—symbols of transformation. Throughout this card's illustration are indications that The Fool is going on a journey that will ultimately lead to this balance. For those of us who are already familiar with the tarot, we know that the balancing of polarities leads to their integration into wholeness, represented here by the presence of alchemical Mercury.

THOTH TAROT

In general, we will note throughout the book that Crowley's perspective on the occult is summarily masculine in its focus and preferences. This biased and skewed outlook on the tarot and its mysteries is a result of several influences—not only the time period in which he was writing, but also his own personal spiritual journey as a male-identified individual. Meleen, on the other hand, tends to write from a more balanced approach, incorporating both masculine and feminine mysteries to create a perspective on the tarot that is distinctly modern and forward-looking. Say what we will about the historical man named Aleister Crowley, he was human, and as such, had his own foibles and hang-ups; the goal here is to keep and build upon the revelatory aspects of his teachings, using all we have learned in the intervening years since his passing, which is what Meleen has so wisely done with *Tabula Mundi*.

In the Crowley-Harris *Thoth Tarot*, The Fool card contains many of the same symbols, including the tiger, crocodile, butterfly, flames, and water. His physical posture seems to indicate freefall, with arms and feet outstretched. While Meleen's Fool is much more open about the integration of masculine and feminine, the *Thoth* Fool tends to focus on the masculine; Crowley's first sentence about this card notes that the card's "significance is primarily Phallic."[2] Yet this card also has indicators of the masculine-feminine balance in the symbols noted above, as well as symbols of the feminine in the dove and vulture, and the integrative, animating mercurial element in the rainbows, twin children, and the little dragonfly-like caduceus making a heart-shaped loop over The Fool's heart.

Crowley later acknowledges the necessity of both elements and that their complete amalgamation creates the Tetragrammaton, the four-fold model of God intelligible to the human mind.[3] He further explains that the masculine is mere impulse until conjoined with the formative feminine—that is to say, the masculine energy may come first in the order of operations, but it is impotent without the influence of the feminine to give the impulse form.

Thoth's Fool also shows us the tools he's carrying in his bag—all of the astrological signs and planets—a representation of all the various energies of the cosmos, which correspond to the sephirah of Chokmah; as the representation of the breath of God, The Fool treads the path between Kether and Chokmah. The color yellow also features prominently in this card, due to its correspondence to elemental Air.

READING THIS CARD

When Atu 0 appears in a reading, there is an opportunity to surrender control over some aspect of life, to let go and experience a journey into the unknown, and/or to trust that the experience ahead is one that will expand one's consciousness. The Fool is a common card to receive at the beginning of a momentous undertaking or unexpected twist in the plot of life. The "key" to surviving The Fool's journey is trusting in the Universe to catch and ultimately lift us back up toward wholeness, especially during interim moments of challenge, uncertainty, and even terror. Surrender your arrogance, admit that you know nothing, open your senses, and the mystery will reveal itself to you in due time. Approach this card's lessons with curiosity and wonder, and you will be rewarded with discovery, growth, and synchronicity.

Although we don't read reversals when reading *Thoth* tradition-ally, we can consider what this card looks like when ill-dignified: being unwilling to surrender against circumstances beyond our control, insisting on being in charge (especially when unwarranted or undeserved), delusions of grandeur, and stubbornness can all be ill-dignified expressions of The Fool.

CHAPTER 7

I. THE MAGUS: "LATERALUS," TOOL

Traditional Title: The Magician, The Magus of Power
Planet: Mercury
Qabalistic Correspondence: Path 12, from Kether (1) to Binah (3);
Sephira 8, Hod
Key Words: power, talent, skill, cunning, wit, intelligence, magick

"Lateralus"
Tool
Lateralus, 2001

Atu Line
"To swing on the spiral of our divinity and still be a human"

The Magus (aka The Magician) is Atu I of the major arcana, and it corresponds to the element and planet Mercury. There is so much to unpack in this archetype, as Mercury is associated with so many things. At once, Mercury rules over all systems of human knowledge; represents communication, technology, and data; embodies the trickster, the sage, and psychopomp (or guide in the underworld); is the undisputed Master of Magick; and so much more. Mercury rules both social and philosophical butterfly Gemini (The Lovers), as well as detail-oriented analyst and manifester Virgo (The Hermit). The Magus's path on the Tree of Life leads from Kether to Binah, and as the second emanation from Kether, He represents The Word, or Logos, of the Divine.

Because of these attributions, The Magus is multitalented and armed with all the tools necessary to shape his experienced reality to his will. Thus, he is pictured in the tarot with all the magickal tools in the deck: the Wand from the Ace of Wands (which represents the element of Fire), the Chalice from the Ace of Cups (which represents the element of Water), the Sword from the Ace of Swords (represents Air), and the Pantacle from the Ace of Disks (represents elemental Earth).

Crowley describes Mercury as both the principle of action as well as the fluid substance of it (p70). In the tradition of alchemy, Sulphur is the masculine element, Salt is the feminine, and Mercury is neither/both; Mercury is the principle of quickening that catalyzes and animates the masculine and feminine together. Although Crowley insists that the nature of planetary and deified Mercury (and therefore the Magus Card) would in fact be masculine/solar due to its orbit being so close to the sun, he also summarizes this card's alchemical element as being a third in addition to masculine and feminine; logic and lore posit that this element would indeed be neither or both polarities combined. After all, all of the deities associated here have androgynous aspects; Thoth is a lunar god (as opposed to the more common solar god or lunar goddess), and Mercury/Hermes was known for having the ability to appear as male or female.

THE SONG

Tool's "Lateralus" is the match for The Magus; the song describes the practice of magick by a master mage. The lyrics of this track famously incorporate the sacred geometric formula of the Fibonacci Sequence, a pattern that naturally occurs throughout nature and presents visually as a spiral. In the occult, the spiral is used as a metaphor for the spiritual evolution of the soul.

What is less noted is the fact that the lyrics also include references to all the elements, and thus The Magus's weapons...or tools. The word *will* is a reference to the magickal power To Will and a metaphor for Fire (the Wand), the fountain is a metaphor for the magickal power To Dare and the element of Water (the Cup), allusions to sensations on the skin and breath refer to the element of Air and the magickal power To Know (the Sword), and the reference to the ground represents Earth and its magickal power To Keep Silent (the Disk). Yes, indeed, all the Magus's tools are present and accounted for in "Lateralus."

Furthermore, the colors listed in the lyrics—black, white, red, and yellow—are also magickal, in that they are the color correspondences of the first four alchemical operations: calcination, dissolution, separation, conjunction.[1] These first four of the seven operations of alchemy allow the alchemist to create the Lesser Stone, "a state of consciousness in which the initiate is able to clearly discern what needs to be done to achieve lasting enlightenment,"[2] what Thelema calls the *Knowledge and Conversation of the Holy Guardian Angel*, and Carl Jung termed *individuation*. The magus/magickian is an alchemist, after all—he seeks to turn the lead of the common human into the gold of the enlightened one.

Thus, the lyrics of "Lateralus" describe the process of learning to practice magick, wherein we move beyond our understanding of the material and into experiencing psychic phenomena that cannot be explained with the rational mind, and cannot even be described, lest we cheapen them. This is an interesting idea when we consider The Magus as a symbol of the Logos, the Word, and the fact that Mercury rules over communication: any attempt at expressing the ineffable necessarily destroys IT, for IT is beyond human comprehension and therefore beyond human expression. We are compelled to communicate the divine, and words mock us. Perhaps that is why humanity so often turns to the arts to communicate all that we find to be holy.

The ultimate aim of the magickian is to connect to and sync with the larger rhythm of the Universe, to learn to rhyme our own song with that of the cosmos. The beauty is the understanding of what "As above, so below" truly means: that we are each simultaneously God, and a dust particle. As String Theory illustrates, we are each the largest thing in some system, the smallest in another, and in the middle in yet another. All things in existence are merely steps of an ever-repeating, spiraling fractal.

On the original tour in support of the Lateralus album, "Lateralus" was the final song of each evening. Before the song commenced, Keenan would address the audience directly, asking everyone to "take all of the feelings you've experienced here tonight, and create something positive with them." This is a perfect way to sum up the match between this song and this card, for the power to create is in the hands of The Magus—and thus also in the hands of each and every one of us.

TABULA MUNDI TAROT

Lightheartedly, *Tabula Mundi* depicts Lord Mercury as 'the DJ in the house," a wordplay on the Hebrew letter assigned to this card: *Beth*, which translates to *house*. Meleen has applied the metaphor to the card throughout, connecting the above of the Universe to the below of earthly music by incorporating all of The Magus' weapons and mercurial symbolism into the equipment the Magus is using to create his art. As Mercury rules over music and mathematics, this is such a fun and joyous illustration of magickal ability and creativity, and it is a more than apt depiction of Keenan, especially later in his career, as his music has become more electronic in nature.

When we consider all that Keenan has communicated, taught, and achieved through the vehicle of his music, The Magus (and this particular iteration most especially) is a delightful representation of Keenan's unique brand of artistic expression. When it came time to choose a cover for this book, it was the only image that would do to capture the power and magick of this modern-day alchemist.

THOTH TAROT

While the *Tabula Mundi* Magus is thoroughly modern, the *Thoth* Magus is a throwback to antiquity. A traditional Hermes figure is shown balancing on the cosmic egg of creation, his body incorporated into the caduceus that spans the entirety of the card. His elemental weapons and tools are shown floating about him, and the specter of Hermanubis or the Ape of Thoth is seen creeping up on him from the right side of the card, a reference to the fact that words —even The Word—are poor substitutes for the majesty of magickal and mystical experience and the perfection of naught.

READING THIS CARD

When this card is drawn, pay special attention to the capabilities of the querent, and how those strengths and talents are being developed and utilized. What systems of knowledge is the querent being invited to master and/or wield? Realize that the querent holds the control in the situation at hand, and it is up to them to exert their influence upon it, to manifest what they most desire. This is a card of magick and inspiration, of messages from the Divine, and of issues regarding communication. In all aspects, it is incumbent upon the querent to take responsibility for their part in the situation at hand and to use their power intentionally.

If The Magus is ill-dignified, the querent could be drawing on this archetype in a trickster or duplicitous way, whether used as a sales tool, an illusion of some kind, or political subterfuge. While there is no value judgment inherent in that—it is possible to use the power of will in these ways to positive effect—the querent should nonetheless be cognizant of the impact and likely repercussions of their actions.

CHAPTER 8

II. THE PRIESTESS: "PARABOLA," TOOL

Traditional Title: The High Priestess, The Priestess of the Silver Star
Planet: The Moon
Qabalistic Correspondences: Path 13, from Kether (1) to Tiphareth
(6); Sephira 9, Yesod
Key Words: intuition, knowing, The Mysteries, wisdom, divine femi-
nine, initiatrix

"Parabola"
Tool
Lateralus, 2001

Atu Line
"We are eternal, all this pain is an illusion"

T he Priestess, Atu II, is paradoxically mystic clarity and
comfort with ambiguity. She represents inner wisdom,
intuition, and sacred knowledge. Her realm is that of
esoteric knowledge: the secrets hidden from most of humanity by
the veil of everyday consciousness. Her correspondence is the Moon,
which is a symbol of the divine feminine. She embodies the energy of
the blessed Shekinah or Sophia, who knows all and keeps silent. The
Priestess can be said to represent the querent's inner wisdom, intuition, and connection to the Divine.

The Priestess' path begins in the first sephira of Kether and ends
in the sixth sephira of Tiphareth; it is the connection between the
light of source (God) and the light of the Sun (Son). This is fascinating in light of the Priestess's correspondence to the Moon, which
reflects the light of the Sun, which in turn is projecting the light
of All.

THE SONG

The highest human wisdom lies on the path of The Priestess,
because it is the only path directly across the Abyss, connecting the

Source (Kether) and the transcendent consciousness (Tiphareth). Perhaps one could look at "Parabol" as Kether (Godhead), and "Parabola" as Tiphareth (enlightened humanity). This pair of tracks together convey the ultimate wisdom of Keenan's work (and I would go so far as to say, of occult work in general), and they build on ideas explored in the Lateralus track.

Humans are simultaneously divine and fallen, and because of that, the human experience is itself divine and profane. "Parabol" is an alternate spelling of the word *parable*, which the Oxford Dictionary defines as "a simple story used to illustrate a moral or spiritual lesson, as told by Jesus in the Gospels." *Parabola* is a mathematical term used to describe a plane curve which is mirror-symmetrical and approximately U-shaped. The pair of songs together is a mirror image, a lesson taught via the symbolism of duality. Humans are in control and not, themselves and not, particle of the whole and still whole unto themselves.

We are products of the Divine's longing for itself. We are particles of Spirit that materialized into mortal form for the purpose of experiencing corporeal reality, in all its ups and downs. We came here to experience it all, but we forget that along the way, and the dualistic (good/bad, male/female, black/white) incarnate experience becomes the only reality we know.

Bill Hicks, the comic to whom Tool dedicated *Ænima*, wrote a beautiful bit called "It's Just a Ride" that I strongly encourage you to look up if you're not already familiar with it, because it is so perfectly, compassionately, and humorously expressive of the wisdom of this card as well as its song match. In the bit, Hicks describes how completely and thoroughly this human experience fools us into thinking that this reality is all there is. But this world we are living in—this set of stimuli we are interacting with—is just one facet of the infinite, and we can choose a different experience anytime we like. Everything we encounter, from the highest highs to the lowest lows, is an extremely convincing simulation that we originally chose to enter for thrills and kicks. None of it is "real" in any permanent sense. It's all just information for our use.

TABULA MUNDI TAROT

In this traditional rendition of Atu II, The Priestess stands as the Middle Pillar between the Pillar of Mercy (Jachin, force, masculine, light, solar) and the Pillar of Severity (Boaz, form, feminine, dark, lunar). Meleen's illustration draws deeply on Qabalistic and long-standing symbolism for this card, including the Moon, water (the element correspondent to the Moon), pomegranate seeds (associated with Persephone, the Greek goddess of the underworld, who connects the earthly realm and the afterlife), a bow/lyre (associated with the virginal Greek goddess of the hunt, Artemis). Her posture is one of comfort and openness, as if to reassure us that what lies beyond the veil is the balm for all sorrows: the Truth of our own infinite nature.

THOTH TAROT

Many have observed that Lady Frieda Harris' famously jaw-dropping depiction of The Priestess appears to be created from pure light. She is shown seated, the bottom half of her body carved from stone and covered in the net of material reality; the top half of her body, behind the net, is soft and luminous in veils of light. At her feet are crystals, flowers, and fruits of nascence, offering, and wisdom, as well as a camel, symbolic of the Hebrew letter *Gimel* (camel) assigned to this card. She is the mystical oasis that moves, that carries the soul across the desert of the Abyss to the enlightened City of Pyramids.

READING THIS CARD

When this card appears in a reading, the querent is being initiated in some way, particularly into wisdom that is not learned, but intuited.

There is a quiet voice inside each person that knows The Way. Trust and listen to your own intuition; it will lead you to your path. The Priestess is the virgin divine feminine, whole unto herself—she needs no outside influence or power; the same is true for the querent when this card appears. The time has come to be self-directed and to seek esoteric wisdom. The querent is being invited to study The Mysteries and lunar magick.

CHAPTER 9

III. THE EMPRESS: "ORESTES," A PERFECT CIRCLE

Traditional Title: The Daughter of the Mighty Ones
Planet: Venus
Qabalistic Correspondences: Path 14, from Chokmah (2) to Binah (3); Sephira 7, Netzach
Key Words: The Mother, fertility, growth, beauty, abundance, love, sensuality

"Orestes"
A Perfect Circle
Mer de Noms, 2000

Atu Line

The Empress, Atu III, is the card representing Venus, the archetype of the Mother. Venus rules both earthy, luxury-loving Taurus and beauty- and harmony-seeking Libra, and she is concerned with beauty, abundance, nurturance, and sensuality. The correspondent Hebrew letter is *Daleth* (door), and appropriately, this is the representation of the earthly mother, the door of life that acts as the conduit of existence in Malkuth, and maternity and motherhood in the everyday sense. She is symbolic of the journey of conception, gestation, birth, and nurturance that every person engages within the creation of absolutely anything at all. It's important to point out that the archetypes of the tarot are not relevant to only certain types of people; each of them applies to every life, regardless of gender in any way. At one time or another, we all play the mother to some kind of child.

THE SONG

Yes, "Orestes" is a decidedly dark take on the Mother. However, The Empress as an archetype can be quite dark Herself, as She is concerned only with growth for growth's sake. The Empress continually spins out permutations of life, more and more and more, without regard to any monster she might create. In doing so, She endlessly supplies the Emperor with a verdant garden to curate. She is the path between Chokmah's Force (inspiration and impetus) and Binah's Form (material existence), and as such, she is the wild, unruly growth of life. The next card, The Emperor, will shape this overgrown Eden into civilization with structure, rules, regulations, and yes, paternal colonialism—but that comes later. Here, we are lost in the thick and dark undergrowth of Her savage garden.

If you imagine a living engine that is constantly spurting out more vines, trees, weeds, flowers, insects, animals, and people, eventually there is no room. No space to breathe. No freedom of movement, and the garden must be cut back, or else everything will choke. This is the version of The Mother we see here in "Orestes". This track, of course, refers to the story of Orestes, who kills his own mother. All of us at one time or another have felt the desire to 'kill off' or individuate from the influence of our parents, particularly the overbearing, suffocating protection of our maternal figure.

As mentioned earlier, The Empress is the archetype of the human mother, and includes all issues surrounding pregnancy, child-bearing, child-rearing, and nurturance. Interestingly, there are a few lines in "Orestes" in which the narrator mentions killing the mother figure and pulling her down, which can be interpreted as dragging The Supernal Mother (Binah) down below the Abyss into material reality, defiling Her Holiness by making Her subject to material manifestation—where birth is painful and dangerous and the mother is subject to the rules of mortality, as our mothers in Malkuth are.

TABULA MUNDI TAROT

This modernized iteration of The Empress is rich with Venusian symbolism. Absolutely every element of Meleen's Empress card is representative of the maternal drive—from the female honey bees swarming out of the "door" of the Empress' honeyed heart, to Her position between lunar phases reminiscent of the womb's phases, to Her starry kerchief, white eagle wings, and lotus wand. Like the *Thoth Tarot's* Empress, this Empress also faces toward Her consort, The Emperor, the next card in the deck, positioned to Her left. The expression on Her face is one of strength, determination, and safe-guarding. All is rich, nurtured, and protected.

THOTH TAROT

While containing some of the same symbols as the *Tabula Mundi* Empress—the lotus wand, the moon phases, and the doorway encompassing the illustration—the *Thoth* Empress is certainly subdued by comparison. Harris' pastel blue, green, and pink domi-nate the card, evoking decidedly feminine feelings of nurturing comfort and calm. The card is packed with alchemical symbolism (including her posture in the shape of the glyph of alchemical Salt), and references to royalty, announcing The Empress as the queen of heaven and earth, and the gateway to life.

READING THIS CARD

When this card appears, questions of fertility, motherhood, recep-tiveness, gestation, and nurturance are at hand. Sometimes the card can indicate a literal pregnancy, and others it is indicating a metaphorical one. You might ask yourself how The Mother is active in your life at this time, or how she might show up in your life in the near future. The card may also represent an important female in the querent's life—mother, wife, caregiver, daughter, etc.

When ill-dignified, as The Empress is in "Orestes," issues around boundaries may be present. What is too much to expect of the situa-tion at hand? Where might the querent be over-stepping others' boundaries, or threatening to suffocate those they are in relationship with? Is there a boundary that needs to be set with a maternal figure?

Lastly, what is the querent's relationship to the motherhood question? Depending on the surrounding cards, there could be information regarding the querent's parenting path.

CHAPTER 10
IV. THE EMPEROR: "INVINCIBLE," TOOL

Traditional Title: Son of the Morning, Chief Among the Mighty
Sign: Aries
Planetary Ruler/Exaltation: Mars rules, Sun exalted
Date Range: March 21 – April 20
Qabalistic Correspondences: Path 28, Netzach (7) to Hod (8); Sephira 5, Geburah (via ruling planet Mars)
Key Words: The Father, power, dominance, order, civilization, rules

"Invincible"
Tool
Fear Inoculum, 2019

Atu Line

A tu IV, The Emperor, corresponds to the astrological sign of Aries (sign of the personality, self, beginnings, the head and face, identity), which is ruled by Mars (planet of war, aggression, dominance, and power). The Emperor is king of kings, Chief Among the Mighty.

He is the archetype of the father, the ruler, the warrior, and the counterpart of the Empress. Whereas she creates a wild and flourishing garden, he strives to order and arrange the garden into something that makes sense. The Emperor carves civilization from the raw wilderness of the earth—this is the card of civil engineers, legislators, explorers, and soldiers. It is also the source of Timothy Leary's oft-quoted observance about "authorities" who provide "order, rules, regulations, informing—forming in our minds—their view of reality."[1]

THE SONG

Tool's "Invincible," from *Fear Inoculum* is really an apt exploration of the masculine archetype of The Emperor, what with its descriptions of armor, weaponry, the aging warrior, the ruthless emperor Caligula, and the intrepid explorer Ponce de Leon.

Beyond just invoking those aspects of The Emperor archetype, "Invincible" describes the struggles with adhering to this archetype across the lifespan: to always be hardened, victorious, physically and mentally strong. As the phrase "weapon out and belly in" at different points in the song illustrate, this is easier done in youth than in old age. It's interesting to think about how 'weapon out and belly in' means something different in youth and advanced life. In youth, it is the discipline of a fighting stance—to tighten and flex well-developed musculature; later, it's more likely a reminder to suck in a soft and protruding belly in order to hide one's vulnerabilities.

While it's certainly true that the curse of youth and aging hits women hard—they are no longer considered attractive or useful when they are beyond child-bearing age, so they must hide signs of aging at all cost—the same can absolutely be said of men, who lose their power and relevance when they are no longer physically or mentally imposing. With time, both genders reach toward androgyny, men becoming softer, women losing their softness. Time is an unrelenting bitch.

It may be tempting to view this as a silly or trivial contemplation of such a powerful figure, but the very nature of this archetype is one of temporariness and change. Fire, the element associated with this card, will die once it burns through its fuel; people age and die; empires grow and collapse. Nothing lasts forever, and a wise ruler keeps their humility about them for this reason. So yes, beyond the sheer force of will and unadulterated power inherent in The Emperor's archetype, there is also fear, loss, grief, and change.

TABULA MUNDI TAROT

Meleen's *Tabula Mundi* Emperor is such a great illustration of the relentlessness of time's passage, and the way it erodes absolutely everything. Meleen describes the figure on the card as battle-weary, looking at a bee hive that is symbolic of The Empress. It's as though he is deeply contemplating the meaning and value of battle in defense of one's kingdom, progeny, and bloodline. Is all the pain, suffering, and loss worth it? What will become of this king of kings and his empire?

THOTH TAROT

Harris' Emperor adheres much more closely with the traditional color scale of reds, oranges, and yellows. He also gazes to his right, toward his wife The Empress, and he is seated in a stylized posture indicative of the glyph of alchemical Sulphur. Whereas Meleen's Emperor is a warrior-king, Harris' is more of a civic leader (though one should note that makes him no less capable of violence). Crowley notes that the lamb in the lower left corner of the *Thoth* card represents the tamed, docile, domesticated version of the wild, free, and indomitable rams that correspond to the card's sign of Aries. He further remarks that the transition from ram to lamb is the function and impact of governance.

READING THIS CARD

When this card appears in a spread, the concepts of structure, strength, power, control, and organization are being invoked. What is the querent's relationship to these forces in their life? What is in need of reigning in or challenging? How does the querent interact with the masculine archetype? Questions of fatherhood may be being considered at this juncture. Concepts surrounding fatherhood are also present, including guidance, protection, discipline, and provision. The card may also represent an important male in the querent's life: father, husband, employer, mentor, etc.

As mentioned in The Empress' explanation, she is responsible for birthing the world, and The Emperor is responsible for curating, organizing, and ruling over all that she has created. Thus, this card's presence in a reading also could point to organizational and/or leadership functions, especially such roles as chair, executive, project manager, architect, or engineer. The querent may be called to fulfill one or more of these roles, or else adopt their characteristics.

If The Emperor is ill-dignified, one could expect to see the less functional, toxic aspects of masculinity on display. This card can indicate overbearing, brutish, or arrogant behavior or philosophy. An unwillingness to compromise or be vulnerable could also be present. In short, an ill-dignified Emperor is all the things we expect to see from an abusive father, husband, or leader—someone who is most interested in amassing and wielding power, at any cost.

CHAPTER II
V. THE HIEROPHANT: "SOUR GRAPES," PUSCIFER

Traditional Title: The Magus of the Eternal
Sign: Taurus
Planetary Ruler/Exaltation: Venus/Moon
Date Range: April 21 – May 20
Qabalistic Correspondences: Path 16, Chokmah (2) to Chesed (4);
Sephira 7, Netzach (via ruling planet Venus)
Key Words: priesthood, exoteric wisdom, large social systems, tradition, initiator, teacher

"Sour Grapes"
Puscifer
V Is for Vagina, 2007

Atu Line

A tu V, The Hierophant, is many things: a representative of the Church, government, or other large system; a teacher of exoteric (public or nonhidden) knowledge; a priest; the son of God. His lesson is faith in the abundance of the universe. He is the bringer of light and knowledge to the masses, and as the card of the astrological sign of Taurus (ruled by Venus), he represents comfort on this material plane.

Many people struggle with The Hierophant, due to his associations with established religion. This is understandable, given all of the violence done by organized religion throughout human history. However, the card itself, when properly understood, dissolves this bitterness. The Hierophant teaches us that there is no such thing as "not enough," because the Universe is infinite. For a moment, set aside your beliefs about these organizations and consider: what can the Vatican not accomplish, obtain, own? Nothing. When the full force of the United States federal government is applied, what obstacle can it not remove? Nothing. These behemoths are but microcosmic reflections of the Universe at large.

THE SONG

It is difficult to distill the wisdom of Sour Grapes into a snippet of lines. The lyrics in their entirety are a sublime sermon. Every line imparts the wisdom of the Christ Consciousness as it was intended to be conveyed to the masses—at least from a gnostic or mystic Christian's perspective. There are no esoteric teachings here, but instead, what every believer should know and embody (the exoteric). Here, instead of The Church's teachings of fear, intolerance, and hatred, are the Gnostics' ideas of trust, love, and wisdom. There is balance between the masculine and feminine, what with all the references to Venus (again, ruler of Taurus!) as the morning angel and holy virgin. It refutes the notion of Satan or The Devil as the enemy of man, reminding us that what we conflate with evil (because 'evil' is one half of a dichotomy that, in truth, doesn't exist) lives in the hearts of humans. That the process of transformation is necessary and natural. That we are a reflection of the sky above us (remember, The Hierophant is also a Magus, and the Magus's motto is "as above, so below").

The act of "getting right with Jesus" is not in repentance; it is in its opposite: embracing our power and likeness to Him. *The grapes will sour as long as you believe that anyone or anything other than you is making the wine.* This is the sermon believers should be hearing— what would've been the result of Christ's teachings minus the corruption of power.

TABULA MUNDI TAROT

Meleen's Hierophant focuses equally on the priest as well as the goddess he worships, Venus, the ruler of Taurus. He is seated between the twin pillars, encompassed within the six-pointed star of the macrocosm (the cosmos). The five-pointed star of the microcosm (the earthly plane) is nailed to the hexagram, and golden solar (masculine) and silver lunar (feminine) keys also hang from the nail, representing his initiation into the holy mysteries of divine integration: the joining of polarities into unified wholeness and harmony.

THOTH TAROT

Thoth's Hierophant is a priest of the New Age, the Aeon of the Crowned and Conquering Child. He represents Osiris, as Isis in Her warrior aspect stands guard before him and the child Horus dances within the pentagram on his chest. As in Meleen's, this Hierophant also stands within a hexagram and his nails (the translation of the Hebrew letter *Vau*) affix the microcosm to the macrocosm.

READING THIS CARD

When this card appears, the querent's faith in and relationship to the abundance of the universe may be central to the question. How does the querent understand themselves as a micro reflection of the universe at large? Questions or struggles around tradition and breaks with it could be central to the reading. The querent may be called to serve as a guide or clergy in some capacity. Or they could be moving into a position within a large system—such as a job in government, a church, or a university—soon. Rise and take your place within the larger power structure.

When The Hierophant is ill-dignified, the holy priest becomes something much more toxic—power hungry, despotic, manipulative, domineering of others, judgmental, preying upon the weak, corrupt in every way. This dignity can indicate the querent's past or ongoing trauma at the hands of an organization, family members, religious community, workplace, university, hospital, or other large institution.

CHAPTER 12

VI. THE LOVERS: "SCHISM," TOOL

Traditional Title: The Children of the Voice, The Oracle of the
Mighty Gods
Sign: Gemini
Planetary Ruler/Exaltation: Mercury/Dragon's Head
Date Range: May 21 – June 20
Qabalistic Correspondences: Path 17, Binah (3) to Tiphareth (6);
Sephira 8, Hod (via ruling planet Mercury)
Key Words: duality, relationship, choices, communication, ideals

"Schism"
Tool
Lateralus, 2001

Atu Line

The Lovers, Atu VI, corresponds to the astrological sign of
Gemini, which is ruled by Mercury. The symbol of Gemini
is the twins; this sign is heavily concerned with pairs, duality, and choosing between options.

In order for there to be a relationship of any kind, there must be
at least two separate entities, which requires differentiation (e.g.,
male/female, light/dark). With differentiation comes the potential
for conversation, reflection, disagreement, and conflict. The sword
(The Hebrew letter associated with this card is *zain*, meaning sword)
of The Lovers card is used to separate opposites, acknowledging
their differences.

Communication and relationships between pairs naturally
includes both fluidity and conflict. Where there are two, a choice is
implied: two sides of the story, what is said vs. what is heard, etc. In
any relationship, there must be mutual respect and affection if the
relationship is to function and be healthy.

THE SONG

With references to pieces fitting together, lovers, brothers, and communication, of course Tool's "Schism" is matched with this card. The twins of Gemini are twin siblings, lovers, friends, general duality, internal conflict (i.e., being of two minds), adversaries, etc. Crowley points out that the card should be titled "The Brothers" instead of The Lovers,[1] emphasizing that this card is not about romantic love, but rather duality.

The lyrics of "Schism" reflect the impact of *solve* in the alchemical formula of *solve et coagula,* the larger process of distillation and combination that yields the Philosopher's Stone. In The Lovers, the twins are divided and the choice is made. Their reunification occurs in *coagula* (represented in the Art card, Atu XIV), where the distinctions between the two have been clearly defined, so that #1 and #2 combine to create #3—something new and wholly different from its parents.

Finally, the trio of lines that reference the circle and the square are referencing the unsolvable challenge of squaring the circle, the point being, making the two into one is not possible by merely reducing them to their commonalities. We must instead respect and appreciate their differences and leverage them accordingly.

TABULA MUNDI TAROT

Here we see the marriage of The Emperor and The Empress, presided over by a young Hermit, whom we'll meet shortly. The bride and groom both present as blends of their human and alchemical forms —the Red Lion Emperor and the White Eagle Empress—and all is encompassed within the royal hive, dripping with sweet, nourishing honey. The Sword of division and distillation (a reference to the Hebrew letter *Zain*) is plunged into the stone nearby, reminding us of the sacred duality these two embody.

THOTH TAROT

The *Thoth* rendition of The Lovers emphasizes duality above all else. The bride and groom are mirrored opposites in every way; Harris' use of gold/silver, black/white, lance/cup, and lion/eagle drive home the message that this is a marriage of opposites. To what effect? We'll see in Atu XIV, Art. Meanwhile, the hooded Hermit infinitely presides over this endless wedding, assisted by Cupid's arrow, which seems to be aimed to carry the benediction of unity from Kether to the wisdom of Chokmah.

READING THIS CARD

The appearance of The Lovers card in a reading draws attention to the querent's relationships or relationship in question, and how they participate in those relationships. Do they forge bonds of equity and compassion, or do they continue to participate in relationships in which one person is more valuable than the other? Are their relationships competitive or cooperative? The surrounding cards will figure heavily in determining whether the card represents a balanced or imbalanced relationship.

Alternatively, what choice is the querent facing? Sometimes this card can imply a choice that is being presented between two seemingly attractive alternatives. Cards on either side of The Lovers can stand in for the options presented, and their interpretations will be helpful in choosing between them.

Finally, this card can represent general duality, both as an external quality of the world around the querent, and as an internal shadow issue. The recognition of duality's presence in our thinking or relationship to the world around us ushers in growth, shifts in perspective, and the development of compassion, wisdom, and understanding.

CHAPTER 13

VII. THE CHARIOT: "PASSENGER," DEFTONES

Traditional Title: The Child of the Powers of the Waters, The Lord of the Triumph of Light
Sign: Cancer
Planetary Ruler/Exaltation: The Moon/Jupiter
Date Range: June 21 – July 21
Qabalistic Correspondences: Path 18, Binah (3) to Geburah (5); Sephira 9, Yesod (via ruling planet Moon)
Key Words: progress, The Grail, the two-in-one conveyed, protection, duty, honor

"Passenger"
Deftones
White Pony, 2000

Atu Line

<hr />

Atu VII is The Chariot, and it is the card of the astrological sign of Cancer. Ruled by the Moon, this fascinating sign is equal parts mystic and warrior, receptive to the surrounding unspoken currents while being fiercely protective of those they love. They are the armored exterior protecting the soft, squishy innards. There is often confusion about how The Chariot represents Cancer, but I think they absolutely make sense together, because the knight driving The Chariot is the protector and transporter of The Grail.

In the previous Atu, The Lovers, two opposites—light and dark, fire and water, wand and cup, male and female—are separated, purified, consecrated, and paired. After the marriage, of course, comes consummation, when bride and groom pour their distilled essences into The Grail, to mix and to eventually become something else entirely: a child.

This is the alchemical mixing we see in everyday life through brides and grooms the world over. And the grail holding their essences? The uterus, naturally. The uterus is contained in a body, which comports the grail and its contents from place to place. A pregnant woman is literally The Chariot, with its charioteer driving the transport and protecting the Grail. She's not the only example of the Chariot in real life, but she's the Original.

THE SONG

What better way to represent The Chariot than sex in a car??

Yes, please. Drive faster.

Deftones' "Passenger" is not only a deliciously erotic account told in a series of compelling images and symbols; it is also a great metaphor for the concept of the two-in-one conveyed. Who is the passenger in the song? Who is riding whom? Who is carrying something? Who is doing the driving? The configurations are wide and varied, but in the final analysis, it's apparent that the song goes far beyond two people and a car on a cool night.

TABULA MUNDI TAROT

Meleen's delightful take on The Chariot and the astrological sign of Cancer features a surfing charioteer bearing The Grail through a pipeline wave on the infinite ocean of Binah. In this nighttime Chariot card, the spray of the wave spins out the stars of Nuit's body in the night sky, connecting the macrocosmic Mother Nuit with Her microcosmic Daughter Babalon (the Grail). The charioteer's board is drawn by two hippocampi (half horse, half dolphin), representations of land and sea—further recalling water and earth, mother and daughter, the two feminine elements.

THOTH TAROT

Crowley and Harris' version of The Chariot is largely patterned after classical depictions of this archetype: a knight transports the Holy Grail in a chariot pulled by mythological creatures that symbolize the elements or forces of the microcosm. The canopy over the chariot represents the night sky of Nuit, and upon it is written *Abracadabra*, a misspelling of the magickal word *Abrahadabra*, which is commonly interpreted to mean, "as I speak, so I create." The card is overall a compelling illustration of the process of accomplishing the Great Work.

READING THIS CARD

When this card appears, progress, growth, promotion, or a quest of some kind is indicated. Since Cancer is frequently associated with hearth and home—as in, the crab takes his home with him wherever he goes—the growth or progress in usually tied to the household in some way. Whether through moving residence, having more resources to put into one's sanctuary of home, buying a new car (don't forget, The Chariot is a vehicle of transportation), or getting a promotion that elevates one's station, The Chariot is symbolic of the progress we make in life.

The card can also represent honor-bound duty, protection, and a willingness to use force if necessary in order to attain the objective—this card can indicate protectors of some kind, such as military or law enforcement personnel. Along the same lines, The Chariot can also be an indication of a vow or commitment made.

When ill-dignified, it can signify possessiveness, blind allegiance, an unwillingness to take on responsibility, or a perversion or lack of Cancer-like qualities such as compassion, protection, nurturance, or sensitivity. An ill-dignified Chariot can also indicate drowning in one's own intuitions or emotions, or an over-abundance of feminine or lunar energy.

CHAPTER 14
VIII. ADJUSTMENT: "GREEN VALLEY," PUSCIFER

Traditional Title: Justice, The Daughter of the Lords of Truth, The Ruler of the Balance
Sign: Libra
Planetary Ruler/Exaltation: Venus/Saturn
Date Range: September 23 – October 22
Qabalistic Correspondences: Path 22, Geburah (5) to Tiphareth (6); Sephira 7, Netzach (via ruling planet Venus)
Key Words: justice, balance, symmetry, harmony, fairness, beauty

"Green Valley"
Puscifer
Conditions of My Parole, 2011

Atu Line

Atu VIII, Adjustment (also known as Justice in many tarot decks), is the card of Libra, The Scales. Libra is ruled by Venus, who rules over all that is just through her love of harmony, symmetry, and balance. In the Thoth tradition, the card is called Adjustment as an acknowledgement that balance is not a static state, but a dynamic one. It is a card of minute tweaks and shifts to account for our perceptions of duality—not too far this way, nor that. The way is the middle path, which does not identify with either side of the coin but embraces both.

The old title, "Justice," implies that there is one true answer to every question: "What is just?" But the seeker eventually comes to realize that there are multiple true answers to any given question, and what is true can change. Perhaps the better question is, "What is just in this moment, in this situation?"

The wisdom of this card is the understanding that all things present in the cosmos belong. The feminine figure in the card balances the alpha and the omega, which don't just symbolize the

BEYOND AS ABOVE, SO BELOW

beginning and end, but also the macrocosm and the microcosm, The All That Is. All things present in the cosmos serve a purpose; the challenge is determining what is called for at a given point, which is why this card is associated with wise discernment.

THE SONG

Puscifer's "Green Valley" is matched to Adjustment for its themes of judgment of worthiness. Incidentally, Venus's main color is green, and green is also a prominent color on the Adjustment card for the same reason. *Verde*, of course, is the Spanish word for green.

Both the card and the track evoke the image of the Egyptian goddess Ma'at, who judged the souls of the dead. In addition to being the goddess of justice, Ma'at was also goddess of harmony, beauty, balance, truth, and morality. Descending through Judgement Valley is referencing the descent into the underworld for judgment, where Ma'at was known to place the departed's heart in a scale and weigh it against an ostrich feather.

The chorus describes this ritual of passing judgement. Those whose hearts are weighed and found to be worthy are allowed to pass into and stay in heaven. And if not, the journey is over—either way, all becomes known and one is no longer a stranger to the truth.

TABULA MUNDI TAROT

The TM Adjustment card emphasizes balance and harmony through an image of a young woman ice skating on a sword's edge. She is blindfolded, dressed in green, and adorned with peacock and parrot feathers (odes to air sign Libra). The harlequin pattern on her bodice identifies her as the feminine counterpart of The Fool, the card of potential and elemental air. She is a living, dancing scale, holding from her outstretched arms pans that contain a heart canopic jar, and an ostrich feather, maintaining grace and balance. The air is filled with music, another representation of balance, symmetry, and harmony that Venus and Libra are so known for.

THOTH TAROT

Harris adheres to the color scales precisely for this card (emerald green, blue, deep blue-green, and pale green), which depicts the goddess Ma'at, perfectly balanced on the *very tips* of Her toes and the *very tip* of the Ace of Swords' blade, held on edge between Her legs. The pans of Ma'at's scales descend from Her ostrich feather crown, and the pans contain the Greek symbols Alpha and Omega. The overall design of the card suggests a harlequin style theme, a nod to The Fool (see paragraph above).

READING THIS CARD

When Adjustment appears in a reading, themes of harmony, justice, symmetry, and balance—and of beauty as an outcome of these—are at work. The card may refer to court proceedings or a decision to be made (especially if someone else is the decision maker), a need for balance and fairness, or the presence or absence of beauty and harmony in the querent's life.

As one might guess, the surrounding cards impact Adjustment's dignity—that is to say, surrounding or adjacent cards with positive connotations and even numbers would be more likely to indicate justice and/or balance being achieved, and vice versa.

When reading this card, remember to watch for other literal information tarot sometimes provides: notice when there are same value cards on either side (two 7s for example), or when cards on either side share important similarities or differences. The greatest skill in reading tarot is learning to recognize these and other kinds of patterns in the cards, and learning to interpret the information they present.

CHAPTER 15

IX. THE HERMIT: "FORTY-SIX & 2," TOOL

Traditional Title: The Prophet of the Eternal, The Prophet of the Gods, The Magus of the Voice of Power
Sign: Virgo
Planetary Ruler/Exaltation: Mercury/Mercury
Date Range: August 23 – September 22
Qabalistic Correspondences: Path 20, Chesed (4) to Tiphareth (6); Sephira 8, Hod (via ruling planet Mercury)
Key Words: solitude, independence, learning, study, wisdom, introspection, Know Thyself

"Forty-Six & 2"
Tool
Ænima, 1996

Atu Line

T he Hermit, Atu IX, is the wise sage who seeks the secret seed within. He studies and thinks, leaving his hermitage only to bring the light of wisdom where it is needed. This is the card of Virgo, ruled by Mercury, and as such, it's closely related to the Magus. Crowley likens The Hermit to a wiser, higher expression of The Magus. He further describes The Hermit as its correspondent Hebrew letter, *Yod*,[1] calling it "the Father, who is Wisdom; he is the highest form of Mercury, and the Logos, the Creator of all worlds."[2] Finally, Crowley calls Mercury "the fluidic essence of Light" and "the secret fire."[3]

The Hermit didn't come by this knowledge or wisdom easily. He became the Creator of all worlds through endless receptivity to learning about himself, because He understands that the self is a microcosmic reflection of the universe. In order to fully learn and master the universe, he fully learns and masters himself; thus, his path is one of digging through the subconscious Shadow to bring it to conscious light. In traversing the dark corners of the psyche, one comes face to face with their greatest fears and flaws. Mastery is achieved when the conscious self (the "light" half, the masculine) and the shadow (the "dark" half, the feminine) are united and reconciled. The Hermit's relentless drive to understand the inner machinations of his own mind, personality, and life have made him wise to the world around him, too, because he is (naturally) the world in miniature, just as we all are.

THE SONG

For this reason, Forty-Six & 2 is the track that is matched to The Hermit. The lyrics here revolve around themes of solitary exploration, of going within for the answers we seek. "Shadow work," as this is often called, is neither gentle nor lighthearted, for it requires the aspirant to go deep within his or her own psyche to face their own unique demons and internal monsters. It is a necessary process in order to overcome patterns of dysfunction. "Until you make the unconscious conscious," wrote psychologist Carl Jung, "it will direct your life and you will call it fate."

Another interesting wrinkle in the match between this track and card is in the title of the song. Humans have forty-six chromosomes, although our closest primate relatives have forty-eight. Forty-Six & 2 is a reference to Drunvalo Melchizedek's theory that humans actually have forty-eight chromosomes, but the last two are ethereal instead of material. Melchizekdek's theory further states that humans will reach their next stage in evolution when the ethereal pair of chromosomes becomes material, something that can be achieved through correct meditation. Evolution from within is precisely what The Hermit is about, and The Hermit's willingness to go to any lengths necessary to advance the cause of consciousness is vividly conveyed in this track.

TABULA MUNDI TAROT

The Hermit is seen carrying his lantern down into a subterranean chamber, bringing the masculine light of the Sun down into the depths of the feminine earth. His lamp's flame is in the shape of a six-pointed star, symbolic not only of the Sun (remember Tiphareth, sephira of the Sun, is number 6), it's also symbolic of the micro- and macrocosm together, and the masculine and feminine combined. The hexagram also symbolizes one of the fundamental truths of the Emerald Tablet (as above, so below). This essential text of alchemy, hermeticism, and ceremonial magick is attributed to Hermes Trismegistus, himself a form of Mercury/Thoth, the god of magick. The lamp further signifies The Hermit's possession of the totality of occult knowledge, and his identity as Mercury-Hermes-Thoth.

THOTH TAROT

Mercury/Thoth studies the Cosmic Egg, symbolic of potential form, as he holds the lantern containing the Sun's light, symbolic of cosmic force. Standing amid stalks of wheat and accompanied by a sperm-like staff and the Hound of Hell, this is the picture of the work of uniting the light and the dark to create new life, illustrating what Crowley called "the entire mystery of Life in its most secret workings."[4]

READING THIS CARD

Those who draw or are drawn to The Hermit are attracted to or in need of solitude and time to think. The Hermit is the eternal scholar, researcher, and teacher. He is necessarily introverted, and while he's not antisocial, he does his best work alone. When this card appears, there are insights waiting to be had, if only the querent would slow down and spend some thoughtful time alone. Revelations are primed to download into the quiet mind.

CHAPTER 16

X. FORTUNE: "DELICIOUS," A PERFECT CIRCLE

Traditional Title: The Wheel of Fortune, The Lord of the Forces of Life
Planet: Jupiter
Qabalistic Correspondences: Path 21, Chesed (4) to Netzach (7); Sephira 4, Chesed
Key Words: karma, luck, change, The Wheel turns, flow, transformation, fortune

"Delicious"
A Perfect Circle
Eat the Elephant, 2018

Atu Line

The Wheel of Fortune (shortened to Fortune in the *Thoth* tradition), Atu X, corresponds to the greater beneficent, Jupiter, planet of growth and gifts. Crowley describes this card as luck, or "the incalculable factor."[1] The Wheel of Fortune continuously turns, and no one stays on top forever. No one stays at the bottom forever, either. And at one point or another, we're all grateful that both of those facts are true! This card represents the continually changing nature of the Universe and the chance for growth, prosperity, setbacks, and victory.

THE SONG

A Perfect Circle's "Delicious" is matched with the Fortune card, because it is describing just such a change in fortune. The narrator describes the schadenfreude of watching someone get their just deserts after behaving repugnantly. The track specifically references how the egotistical and impudent party made their bed and must now lie in it. Because the person was previously in a position of control (hoisting away their smug grenades regardless of collateral damage), the track further reminds us that fortune ever changes, so if you're on the receiving end of the explosives, it won't be awful forever.

Likewise, good times don't last forever either, so be sure to keep your own karmic front stoop clean and mind your own business, lest the consequences of your actions come back to haunt you. The Wheel turns, and those who've flaunted the balance will eventually answer their karma. The song is a delightful fit with the card, as the karma is the Sphinx (restoring balance), the arrogant party is the Typhon (who has been acting out of ignorance), and the narrator and his peers are Hermanubis (restlessness for comeuppance).

TABULA MUNDI TAROT

Meleen's Fortune card is a spinning wheel drawing out the thread of fate, woven into the tapestry of life by a four-pronged vajra (symbolic of Jupiter and Chesed, correspondent to the number 4) as the shuttle. On the right side of the card, the woven tapestry is visible, with the strands of the warp corresponding to the planets and the weft strand being shuttled through by the vajra dorja. Her version of the figures stationed along the rim of the Wheel producing the weft thread include a three-eyed owl representing the wise masculine, the hand-serpent of Typhon writing the Greek letter Phi (symbolizing the golden ratio) as the understanding feminine, and a crowned ring-tail lemur as the androgynous mercurial force. Together, these three figures and seven planetary energies create the universe, in all its beauty and terror.

THOTH TAROT

The Thoth Fortune card shows three figures positioned around the rim of the Wheel: the Sphinx, representing masculine "calm, intelligence, lucidity and balance" sits atop holding a sword; to the right and moving to the bottom is Typhon, the crocodile god representing feminine "darkness, inertia, sloth, ignorance, death and the like;" and on the left moving toward the top of The Wheel is Hermanubis, a form of Thoth, representing "energy, excitement, fire, brilliance, restlessness."[2] No figure remains at the top of the wheel for long—the constant change and movement of the universe prevents stagnation and encourages adaptability.

READING THIS CARD

Admittedly, since it is the card of Jupiter and represents the path between the sephira of Jupiter (Chesed) and lovely Venus (Netzach), this card usually represents a turn of luck for the better, simply because most people consult the tarot in times of discord and/or confusion. For instance, though the lyrics of "Delicious" mostly focus on the asshat who is now paying for their arrogance, luck has certainly changed for the better for the narrator, as he and everyone else gets to watch the wrongdoer reap the consequences of insolent behavior.

When this card appears in a reading, luck in an uncertain situation should improve, but now is not the time to get haughty. Watch for happy surprises and opportunities to expand, grow, learn, and improve. When the time comes, relinquish what is no longer yours with grace, and welcome the next gift coming your way. The Wheel of Fortune always, always, always turns—those who are too attached, who attempt to stifle its revolution, find themselves broken and torn by the spokes of the Catherine Wheel.

CHAPTER 17

XI. LUST: "QUEEN B,"
PUSCIFER

Traditional Title: Strength, The Daughter of the Flaming Sword, Leader of the Lion

Sign: Leo

Planetary Ruler/Exaltation: Sun/Uranus

Date Range: July 22 – August 22

Qabalistic Correspondences: Path 19, Chesed (4) to Geburah (6); Sephira 6, Tiphareth (via rulership by Sun)

Key Words: lust, strength, sex magick, Babalon and Beast, vigor, lust for life

"Queen B"

Puscifer

V Is for Vagina, 2007

Atu Line

Atu XI, Lust, represents the sign of Leo, which is ruled by the Sun and is often compared to the Christ Consciousness. Called "Strength" in non-Thoth based decks, this card historically shows a woman subduing a beastly lion. She is shown standing or sitting next to the lion, holding its mouth open, or controlling it in some way. The underlying interpretation is that she masters brutality with the strength of peace, Christian love, and compassion.

However, in Thoth-based decks, the card is called Lust, and the influence of Crowley's religion of Thelema comes through clearly. The woman on the card is identified as Babalon, the Holy Whore, who receives all in ecstatic sexual communion and denies no one. The lion with the serpent tail that she is shown riding is The Great Beast referenced in Revelations, and their pairing here is a blatant symbol of sex magick in pursuit of enlightenment.

It is true that Crowley adapted the symbol of The Beast to represent himself (Leo, The Lion, was his rising sign and he loved to refer to himself as The Beast 666). Crowley also called all of his lovers with whom he performed sex magick Scarlet Women. However, The Beast on the Lust card can represent any human seeking enlightenment, as well as the virile divine masculine principle. The depiction is of course intended to be highly erotic in nature, as the rapture of orgasm has been described as the closest common human experience to spiritual ascension. This comparison is so frequent that the French euphemism *la petite mort*, or "the little death," is commonly used to describe orgasm.

THE SONG

As tempting as it may be to match "Rev. 22:20" with Lust because of its juicier, more detailed depiction of Babalon, "Queen B" is the song for Lust because it describes the actual conjoining of Babalon and The Beast as shown on the card, the image of Her "riding" Him. After all, the card is called Lust due to an act that requires the presence of them both. Don't worry, Babalon gets all the explicit attention she deserves when we meet the Queen of Wands.

This song and card are such a great match because of the lyrics' repeated references to hell (Thelema quite turns the story of Revelations and The Whore of Babylon on its head), the goddess's fearlessness, and the salacious descriptions of her voluptuous physique and wanton willingness. The lyrics are especially fixated on her voluminous ass, which is pretty amusing, considering that Uranus is exalted in Leo—and the lusty teenager in all of us can't help but snicker.

TABULA MUNDI TAROT

The Mother of Abominations looks us brazenly in the eye as she erotically grasps the tail of Her Beast with Her left hand, and lifts Her golden Chalice filled with the blood of saints with Her right, in a gesture of triumphant glory. The solar influence pervades this card, and She is the reflection of this power, just as the moon reflects the sun's light to us on earth. Everywhere we see the fertility that arises from conjoining of opposites—the unification of the separate into the One—from the conjoined sun and moon in the sky, to the wheat stalks and sunflowers that surround the sacred pair, to the lemniscate that crowns the Chalice and the scene as a whole.

THOTH TAROT

Harris' Lust card is infamously daring, especially for the time in which it was painted. We see a naked, luminously golden woman astride a likewise golden, seven-headed beast. In one hand, Babalon holds the reins that control Her consort, and in the other, She holds aloft the Cup of Abominations, filled with the life essence of all who have returned to Her. Beneath the paws of the Beast are the trampled bodies of the saints who've given their all in worship of Her; above are the sephiroth of the Tree of Life, scattered and in need of order as the old Aeon falls away. Above Her Cup, we see order restored in the new Aeon, the age in which all people individually understand and embrace their likeness to the divine.

READING THIS CARD

When the Lust card comes up in a reading, it's an indicator of sex magick, lust for life, feminine sexuality and allure, the time period of Leo, and all of Leo's characteristics. Extravagant, generous, center-of-attention Leo is unafraid to be seen and worshipped, and Leo loves to perform and shine like the Sun that rules it. You are being called to the spotlight for your chance to be seen. How are you harnessing your strength, vigor, and lust to create the life you yearn for?

If ill-dignified, Lust can indicate using sex as a weapon, viewing sex from a perspective of shame or defilement, or an unwillingness to allow oneself to experience the joy of vigorous exercise of the body. Lust is foremost the joy of having a physical body, so an ill-dignified Lust card can indicate a deliberate severing of the connection between the upper and lower energy centers and a preference for living in one's mind and spirit over the body. This division of the ethereal body separates us from our life force, and drains us of the ability to manifest our desires.

CHAPTER 18

XII. THE HANGED MAN: "REFLECTION," TOOL

Traditional Title: The Spirit of the Mighty Waters
Planet/Element: Neptune/Water
Qabalistic Correspondences: Path 23, Geburah (5) to Hod (8)
Key Words: sacrifice, patience, wisdom gained, surrender, destiny,
change in perspective

"Reflection"
Tool
Lateralus, 2001

Atu Line

T he Hanged Man, Atu XII, represents the element of Water as well as Neptune, the planet that rules Pisces in contemporary astrology. This card symbolizes surrender and sacrifice. It is the card of letting go of the illusion of control, of waiting patiently for what comes next. This feat requires stillness, faith, and humility. Following its directive, we come to see the bigger picture and gain wisdom beyond our limited understanding of the world as we experience it via our meatsuit bodies and miniscule human awareness.

Qabalistically, The Hanged Man is the Hebrew letter Mem, which means water. In many decks, he's shown dangling by his foot above a pool. By virtue of his element, he's related to every other water-related card in the deck—including water signs Cancer (The Chariot), Scorpio (Death), and Pisces (The Moon). The Hanged Man as elemental Water is also related to the planetary Moon (The Priestess); the Moon has always been associated with Water due to its effect on the tides as well as the similarities between the waxing and waning of the Moon and that of the womb. The feminine is inextricably tied to the element of water. Pregnancy and the amniotic sac,

101

the monthly blood (often called Blood of the Moon), intuition, and emotionality are all connected to the Moon and Water.

THE SONG

Reflection as an activity is a common interpretation of The Hanged Man card and a variety of myths from around the world regarding the path to attaining enlightenment. Odin hung on the sacred tree Yggdrasil for nine days to gain wisdom. Christ was hung on the cross to attain redemption of his followers and to ascend to heaven. The Buddha sat beneath the Bodhi tree to achieve enlightenment. Multiple mythologies describe gods who willingly sacrificed themselves through introspection and Shadow work to attain true enlightenment. These humans who remembered their divinity decided, once and for all, to reach up toward the Light and abandon their egos.

For these reasons and more, Tool's "Reflection" is the track best matched with The Hanged Man. Inherent in this track are the symbols of mirrors, water (the original mirror), introspection, and humility. "Reflection" pushes us deep within ourselves, to examine the hold our egos have on our perceptions, to reflect on the ways we fool ourselves into believing our limitations, to get comfortable with our flaws and sniff out our misperceptions.

As indicated earlier, this card has a special relationship with the Moon. The planetary Moon is represented in the tarot deck by The Priestess, who you may recall is matched with "Parabol" and "Parabola." In "Reflection," we hear that The Moon tells The Hanged Man a secret. But it's not just any secret, it's the secret of All: that we as spiritual beings are unending and that our trials here in Malkuth are mere illusions that we ourselves create just so we can experience them.

The knowledge of this holy secret leads The Hanged Man to the enlightenment he has so patiently awaited, wherein he finally understands that one supreme energy—one Light—animates all beings, and that energy is better known as Love. We all descend from the light of Kether as tiny particles of divinity, and as reflections of that ultimate Light, we are invincible and infinitely powerful.

"Reflection" also contains multiple references to light and its reflection, that we do not contain light of our own, but are reflections of the one light, the source (Kether). The moon has no light of its own, but acts as a messenger reflecting the light of the sun, the center of our solar system. Remember, the Moon (The Priestess) is the only path across the Abyss, back to Source, so without her wisdom and guidance, we truly are lost and hopeless.

TABULA MUNDI TAROT

Odin hangs from Yggdrasil, a brilliant blue background emphasizing the watery nature of this card. Beneath him is the pool of Mimir's Well, reflecting the eye that Odin has sacrificed to gain access to his psychic powers. The water dragon Necksa, King of the Undines, slips from the waters and winds up the tree and Odin's body. Unfolded cubes flank the tree, revealing Tau of The Universe card and Mem of The Hanged Man as the secret feminine doctrine of the Daughter becoming the Mother, and of Odin's baptism in the salt water of the feminine to achieve gnosis.

THOTH TAROT

A male figure is suspended in the same posture as is seen on the *Tabula Mundi* Hanged Man, creating an upside-down glyph of alchemical Sulphur, as well as the upright glyph of light's descent into matter. He is suspended above the pool of the Abyss by one foot, which is hooked inside an inverted ankh and secured there by the coils of a serpent. In the background is a grid comprised of all the Elemental Tablets, on a field of Venusian green. In the pool below, another serpent, representing new life, awakens.

READING THIS CARD

When The Hanged Man appears in a reading, it's time to recognize that the Universe does not run on human timetables. The desire to have what the ego wants, no matter how strong that desire may be, does not force the All into submission. It's time to sacrifice egotistical desires, get quiet, and listen. This card can indicate delays beyond our control, especially in obtaining something we really want. It can also indicate a need for meditation or spiritual retreat, or a dramatic shift in perspective. Hypnosis is an effective method to work with this card.

If the card is ill-dignified it can represent martyrdom or loss. Crowley points out in *The Book of Thoth* that the traditional interpretation of The Hanged Man is obsolete in the New Aeon, because we no longer are beholden to systems of scientific ignorance, pious guilt, and internalized shame. In the new paradigm, the sacrifice is of ego separateness in order to remember and teach others that we are all One. Thus, an ill-dignified Hanged Man may present as a person who uses poor-me attitudes and martyrdom as a crown of thorns to manipulate others or to soothe their own ego, or a person who is making unnecessary sacrifices.

CHAPTER 19
XIII. DEATH:
"HORIZONS," PUSCIFER

Traditional Title: The Lord of the Gates of Death, The Child of the Great Transformers
Sign: Scorpio
Planetary Ruler/Exaltation: Mars/Pluto
Date Range: October 23 – November 22
Qabalistic Correspondences: Path 24, Tiphareth (6) to Netzach (7); Sephira 5, Geburah (via ruling planet Mars)
Key Words: transition, transformation, fertilization, putrefaction, rebirth

"Horizons"
Puscifer
Conditions of My Parole, 2011

Atu Line

Death, Atu XIII, is the card of transformation. And as every professional tarot reader since the beginning of time has said, Death does not necessarily mean literal death. There. :)

Now that we've gotten that out of the way, Death can sometimes mean literal death. But most often it just means a metaphorical death, like the death of a certain role or part of one's life. We undergo many deaths in life before reaching the final one, do we not?

The card is associated with Scorpio, the dark water sign with a wicked sense of humor that is comfortable—even pleased—with all things taboo: death, money, and sex. The dirtier the better, Scorpio says!

No matter how uncomfortable this card and the subject of its title may make us feel, this is an absolutely imperative stage of life. If energy is neither created nor destroyed, then every birth must be preceded by some kind of death, and every death must herald a birth of some kind. If we want to bring something new into our lives, we must let go of something to make room for it. So far in this reality as we know it, the fact of birth makes death a certainty.

THE SONG

My intention with this book is to discuss songs as stand-alone narratives, not assuming Keenan is the narrator unless there is ample public knowledge of a song's origin within his life events. This is one such track, describing the spreading of Keenan's mother's ashes among the vines of his vineyard's most prized block, which is hand-farmed and produces some of his most cherished wines.

Keenan's mother, Judith, died after a long and terrible illness. As such, her death was not unexpected, and even in some ways was welcomed as an end of her suffering. However, the finality of burial, or in this case, the spreading of ashes, represents a moment of coming to absolute terms with the reality of the death of any loved one. The gravity of this event is magnified when it is a parent, and "Horizons" reflects this.

In *The Book of Thoth*, Crowley writes that Death is the completion of Lust in the Formula of the Cup of Babalon.[1] After surrendering all of the ego to our lust for union with Babalon and Beast, the initiate dies—orgasmically, psychologically, or literally—and is reborn in the City of Pyramids to join the ranks of the enlightened. The person is said to have given every last drop of blood to be mingled with the blood of the saints. In a very real sense, "Horizons" marks the acknowledgement of an earthly mother transforming and merging into the Great Mother, the completion of the Great Work. It is an incredibly intimate portrait of this card's archetype.

The title of this track also calls to mind the term 'event horizon,' the point of an event beyond which an observer cannot see. Like the black holes to which this term is so often applied, we cannot know what lies on the other side of the Great Transformation until we experience it for ourselves.

TABULA MUNDI TAROT

In the companion book to the deck, *Book M: Liber Mundi*, Meleen notes, "They say Death rides a pale horse; I say Death rides a feathered serpent."[2] Indeed, the central figure of the card is a magnificent creature composed of the defining characteristics of scorpion, serpent, and eagle, which represent the three-fold, transformative nature of Scorpio. Upon this feathered serpent rides Death, in the skeletal form of the risen Osirus, who stirs new life from the waters below. Another striking element of this card is its dramatic color palette of browns, greens, and blues—the color scale correspondent to the Death card, as well as associated with Scorpio. All symbolism in this card speaks to death as transformation, and specifically as a gateway to new life.

THOTH TAROT

The *Thoth* Death card features a skeletal reaper wearing the crown of Osirus. With his scythe, he is not cutting down life on land, but rather stirring up life from the putrefaction at the bottom of the sea. A trail of bubbles carries these new possibilities to the surface, and graceful lines trace the reaper's dancelike movements across the sea floor. All of Scorpio's forms appear on the card, as well as the fish indicated by the Hebrew letter *Nun*.

READING THIS CARD

When Death appears in a reading, there is a part of the querent's life that is ready to transition. Know that there can be no new growth without shedding what no longer fits. Allow the transformation to occur, and from the ashes of the departed will arise new growth, new hope, new direction. Remember that with life, comes death: the two are a package deal. Can indicate the end of a cycle, or putrefaction leading to new life.

CHAPTER 20

XIV. ART: "AGOSTINA," PUSCIFER

Traditional Title: Temperance, The Daughter of the Reconcilers, The Bringer Forth of Life

Sign: Sagittarius

Planetary Ruler/Exaltation: Jupiter/Dragon's Tail

Date Range: November 23 – December 20

Qabalistic Correspondences: Path 25, Tiphareth (6) to Yesod (9); Sephira 4, Chesed (via ruling planet Jupiter)

Key Words: creation, alchemy, perfection, purification, transmutation, synthesis

"Agostina"

Puscifer

Money Shot, 2015

Atu Line

Atu XIV, Art, is called Temperance in non-Thoth decks. As M.M. Meleen notes in *Book M: Liber Mundi*, Crowley renamed this card to highlight the art of alchemy.[1] Art represents the second phase of *solve et coagula*, when the combined fluids of the Bride-Mother and Groom-Father coagulate to yield a new entity that is neither of them: The Child. In alchemical terms, this child is the Philosopher's Stone, the purified transformational substance that can turn lead into gold. The Child represents new life —all possibility, all potentiality—perfect, pure, and closer to Source than either of its parents. The importance of this archetype and its represented event cannot be overstated, as it is the process of the birth of every new particle, idea, person, animal, plant, and star in the Universe.

Idea (Force, The Supernal Father) + Raw Materials (Form, The Supernal Mother) = Offspring.

Every child receives aspects of both parents, but no child is an exact replica of either parent. The child is its own, a unique expression of the alchemical Universe.

The Art card depicts the mixing of opposites, in this case Fire (Father/Knight) and Water (Mother/Queen), to obtain a new element, Air (Son/Prince), in the form of steam. The card is associated with the astrological sign of Sagittarius, the archer, and on the Tree of Life, Art's path runs between the masculine Sun in Tiphareth and the feminine Moon in Yesod, speaking to the card's balance between these two forces. It is satisfyingly symmetrical in every way.

As M.M. Meleen notes in *Book M*, the title of this card in non-Thoth decks is Temperance, not because of a requirement of moderation, but rather in the creative sense of the word. To temper something is to expose it to extremes in order to strengthen it. She uses the example of tempering the blade of a sword (such as the sword, *Zain*, in the Lovers card that represents Sagittarius' opposite sign Gemini) by repeatedly exposing it to extreme heat and then extreme cold. Through this process, the metal is solidified into something suitably strong enough to use as a trustworthy weapon. What began with the Lovers is perfected with Art.

Likewise, the Art card is also referencing the processes a new creation endures to become the final product. Like the gestation of a baby, all of the steps involved are necessary and useful in yielding the best possible outcome, and the dedication and precision with which the steps are carried out determines the success of the operation.

THE SONG

Puscifer's "Agostina" is the match for Art, *The Bringer Forth of Life*, because it so perfectly captures that most sacred alchemical and magickal act of creation in all its mystery, intention, labor, and dedication. The song commemorates the birth of Maynard and Lei Li's daughter, and captures the awe and joy of bringing forth new life into the world. The narrator, ostensibly Keenan himself in this case, wonders at the myriad synchronicities that were required to take place to result in this one particular and sacred event: from the infinite circumstances that brought him together with Lei Li, to the infinite circumstances that culminated in the development of a brand-new human being, who will now experience life for herself as well as impact the world around her. Elements purified, brought together, combined, and gestated over the course of time to create new life is an operation of the most divine of sciences, itself a form of alchemy.

Love, for both the mother and child, are evident in the lyrics here, as are gratitude, ecstasy, and contentment. This is the song of a magickian who has once again participated in a magickal achievement (for every birth, every creation, every change we effectuate in the environment around us is indeed magick), in the same way as those who came before him have done and those who will come to be after he is gone will do, until the end of humanity.

TABULA MUNDI TAROT

The archer, half human and half green lion of alchemy (a.k.a. the Philosophers Stone, a.k.a. V.I.T.R.I.O.L.), draws a fiery arrow with a bow of water, aiming for the center of the orphic egg with the blended and balanced elements of water and fire, the feminine and masculine. The elements combine to breathe life into the possibility of the egg, and also symbolize the Tree of Life path of the Art card, from the Sun's sephira Tiphareth to the Moon's sephira Yesod. There is a sense of synergy about this card.

THOTH TAROT

Harris' card focuses on symmetry and balance between opposites, much like what is seen in the Lovers card, which is fitting as Art is the next step in The Lovers' journey. The bride and groom are now joined as one being, mixing and blending their masculine and feminine characteristics, crossing streams and growing in strength. They combine their elements of water and fire to produce a rainbow, symbolic of the Son element of air. Behind the conjoined pair is the outline of the orphic egg, upon which the formula for V.I.T.R.I.O.L. appears: "Visit the interior of the earth, and by rectifying you will find the hidden stone."

READING THIS CARD

When this card appears in a reading, the miracles of creation are upon you. You are being called to create something that does not currently exist, either out of the raw materials of yourself or other raw materials. There is an opportunity to re-make something to be better, to channel divinity into something tangible, or to bring about new life, metaphorically or literally. Themes of creativity, regeneration, birth and rebirth, and synergy abound here.

If the Art card is ill-dignified, there is some barrier to evolution present. The process of creation is dammed up in some way, the person in question is refusing to allow change, or perhaps the querent is afraid of what the transformation could bring or mean. It is also possible to examine the cards next to Art for clues as to what is being combined and thus transmuted.

CHAPTER 21
XV. THE DEVIL: "BREATHE," PUSCIFER

Traditional Title: The Lord of the Gates of Matter, The Child of the Forces of Time
Sign: Capricorn
Planetary Ruler/Exaltation: Saturn/Mars
Date Range: 12/21 – 1/19
Qabalistic Correspondences: Path 26, Tiphareth (6) to Hod (8); Sephira 3, Binah (via ruling planet Saturn)
Key Words: determination, virility, drive, physicality, addiction, mental illness, shrewdness

"Breathe"
Puscifer
Donkey Punch the Night, 2013

Atu Line

———————————————

One of the Hermetic titles of The Devil is The Lord of the Gates of Matter. He represents the drive and determination to materialize at any cost. As such, He is tied to and exalts in all things material and tangible, including the mortal body, money, and resources, in all their positive and negative forms. He is often closely associated with addiction, mental illness, disease, and pure carnality; however, he is also the keeper of business savviness and success, physical resources, male virility and fertility, and determination.

The Devil is the card of the sign of Capricorn, which is befitting, considering that the goat is driven to climb the mountain and is undeterred by its height or dangers. Furthermore, Capricorn is ruled by Saturn and Mars is exalted there, resulting in a deeply masculine, driven energy for this card.

THE SONG

Puscifer's "Breathe" emphasizes the physicality of the human experience, in all its cravings and neediness, strength and endurance. References to feeding and breathing throughout are used to reframe activities (such as fucking) that are often viewed as weak, shameful, or dirty in Western society as activities that are, in fact, necessary to life. All animals breathe, eat, excrete, and breed; they are each a necessary process that ensures survival. "Breathe" not only removes the shame from these biological processes, it actively celebrates them. This attitude and understanding are the very foundation of The Devil, an archetype that is constructed on the basest, most primal, and most shadow-driven aspects of nature.

This track is unabashedly sexual and hunger-driven. Lyrics referring to the material body and strangers especially draw attention to the unleashed libido—the desire to rut and fuck everyone and everything—which the vast majority of us live our lives keeping tightly in check. "Breathe" is a perfect representation of the energy of Pan, the horny, goat-footed Greek god who is the All-Begetter and Pan-Progenitor. Meleen points out in *Book M* that this is a god known by many names, among them: Satan, Saturn, Set, Baal, Beezlebub, Baphomet.

TABULA MUNDI TAROT

Meleen's take on The Devil is a beautiful and rather virile depiction of Pan, evoking multiple facets of this archetype, including Saturn, Baphomet, and the Green Man Cernunnos. From His third eye streams a continuous DNA strand, which ensnares the Emperor and Empress at the bottom of the card. An hour glass appears at the end of a stream of Saturns on The Devil's other side, a reminder of the chronological, mortal limitations of material reality, in addition to limitations of the flesh. Paradoxically, He also represents the continuation of human DNA across millennia.

THOTH TAROT

One of the most blatant cards of this deck, *Thoth's* Devil card bothers little to disguise the erect penis and testicles that literally dominate the card. It is the very depiction of male virility. The card is also heavily dominated by the three eyed Himalayan goat standing in front of the penis "tree." Finally, the testicle "roots" contain male and female forms dancing, symbolic of the life-giving potential present in the act of copulation. The particularly masculine hunger for carnality is palpable in this card.

READING THIS CARD

The Devil is highly dependent on the dignities of its surrounding cards—perhaps even more so than normal. Since the card is primarily concerned with the carnal, it can manifest in both deeply constructive and destructive ways.

When surrounded by positive cards, the interpretation is typically more focused through the determination, business, fertility, and virility lenses. It's industriousness, effectiveness, and power.

However, when surrounded by negative cards, the shadow side of The Devil is being invoked. Concerns about such issues as addiction and other mental illnesses can come into play, as well as destructive tendencies such as over-working (driven) or over-indulging (carnal).

When this card appears in a reading, it's also time to pay attention to what is happening on the physical, even carnal, level. Sleep, diet, exercise, sex—every aspect of human hygiene should be considered.

CHAPTER 22
XVI. THE TOWER: "ÆNEMA," TOOL

Traditional Title: The Lord of the Hosts of the Mighty, House of God
Planet: Mars
Qabalistic Correspondences: Path 27, Netzach (7) to Hod (8); Sephira
5, Geburah (ruled by Mars)
Key Words: crisis, war, surprise collapse, destruction of falsehood,
Tower of Babylon, wrath of God

"Ænema"
Tool
Ænima, 1996

Atu Line

A tu XVI, The Tower, is the card that corresponds to Mars, the planet of war and aggression. The card evokes the story of the Tower of Babylon in the Bible, which was struck down by God as punishment for man's arrogance. This card typically depicts a tower being struck by lightning and falling in a shower of flames and bodies. It's a disturbing, violent card, full of wrath and foreboding, and usually not a welcome sight in a reading.

However.

When something that was built in falsehood is destroyed, there presents an opportunity to rebuild in truth, to attempt to correct what went wrong before, and to act from a place of earnest honesty. In reality, any destruction is simply making way for construction to come.

Such is the opportunity presented by The Tower. It's a chance to change paths, change your mind, make a different choice, and potentially be significantly happier and better than before.

THE SONG

Perhaps the most apt track for The Tower card ever written, "Ænema"[1] is, at its core, a desire to clean the slate and start over. It just happens to express this desire along with a heavy hit of absolutely scathing social commentary. "Ænema" disparages all that southern California has become, in its consumerism, materialism, superficiality, and callousness. As described by the lyrics, Los Angeles has become its own Tower of Babylon: a place which, like the Jewish people's perceptions of their oppressive Babylonian captors in the Bible,[2] is an oppressive symbol of all that is wrong with society and culture at large. It's something that needs to be torn down.

The Tower', Mars, rules both Aries and Scorpio (in the classical tradition). Most Tower cards heavily feature fire, the element commonly associated with Mars. This makes sense, as fire is tightly associated with Mars via destruction, war, and force, and Aries is a fire sign.

However, in "Ænema," Keenan uses a less frequently associated —but no less destructive—element in his description of the wishful destruction of Southern California: water. Water may seem like an ill match for a Mars card; however, Scorpio is ruled by Mars and is a water sign—the darkest of them. Those born under the sign of Scorpio are often described as emotionally dark, brooding personalities who are unafraid to seek vengeance when wronged. The death and destruction implied by the song certainly fit the Scorpionic bill, and the frequent usage of the word flush further illustrates the narrator's exceedingly low opinion of the state of L.A.: as a shitty toilet that is overdue for a flushing.

Near the end of the track, the narrator implores the listener to not simply write him off as bitter—there is more to his message than just vengeful destruction. One would do well to remember the whole vision of The Tower, in that the destruction serves a purpose: it tears down what no longer serves the higher calling, so that something useful and true can be raised in its stead. It offers the opportunity for recovery, health, and sanity in the future. The Tower tears corruption and illusion out by the roots to make the ground ready to start over.

TABULA MUNDI TAROT

The correspondent Hebrew letter for The Tower is *Peh* (mouth). In both the *Tabula Mundi* and *Thoth* decks, the destruction of The Tower comes from the mouth of Hell below. The TM Tower is contains only creatures, so the mouth of Hell is the mouth of a boar, and the figures falling from the Tower are various mythological creatures. In the background is the All-Seeing Eye of God, and the "lightning of shamanic initiation" simultaneously strikes the crumbling structure.

THOTH TAROT

In this we see the inspiration for Meleen's treatment. A Tower, blown down by fire from the mouth of Hell below; people falling from the Tower as lightning simultaneously strikes it; the All-Seeing Eye witnesses the entire scene. The Dove and Serpent-Lion, representing the two forms of Love (of life/death? male/female? light/dark?), appear as well, indicating a choice to be made moving forward.

READING THIS CARD

When The Tower appears in a reading, the querent has had the proverbial rug jerked out from under them, or is soon to have this experience. Some aspect of the querent's life, which they may have thought was stable or clear, is suddenly on volatile ground. If the collapse is large or shocking enough, the querent may feel like they "don't know anything anymore." They may be in a state of shock, crisis, or aftermath. The important thing to emphasize is that the destruction is ultimately for the best, and will serve the querent's growth and development in the long run, even if that it doesn't feel that way yet.

Like the tried-and-true cliché about the Chinese symbol for crisis being a combination of the symbols for danger and opportunity, the querent now has the opportunity to start with a clean slate and re-build the area of life that has collapsed in a new, more beneficial, manner. Learning to see the situation in this optimistic light will serve the querent well. Don your warrior's helmet and forge onward and upward!

CHAPTER 23

XVII. THE STAR: "GRAND CANYON," PUSCIFER

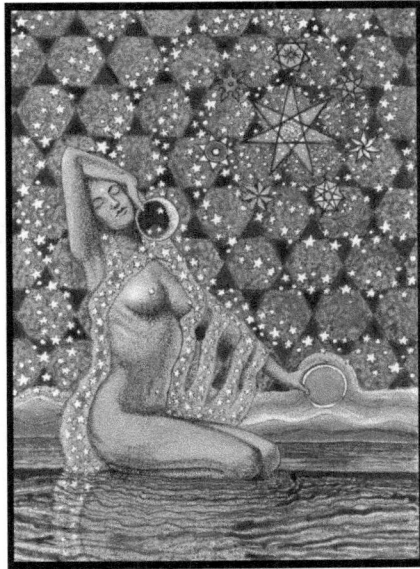

Traditional Title: The Daughter of the Firmament, The Dweller Between the Waters
Sign: Aquarius
Planetary Ruler/Exaltation: Saturn/Neptune
Date Range: 1/20 – 2/18
Qabalistic Correspondences: Path 15, Chokmah (2) to Tiphareth (6); Sephira 3, Binah (via ruling planet Saturn)
Key Words: hope, vision, clarity, faith, beauty, Babalon, Nuit

"Grand Canyon"
Puscifer
Money Shot, 2015

Atu Line

The very essence of The Star card, Atu XVII, is hope. The Star is the card of faith, vision, compassion, and hope beyond measure. This card depicts Nuit, the Egyptian mother goddess of the sky, who is also an aspect of Babalon the Beautiful. Ancient Egyptians envisioned the Milky Way as Nuit, her body arched over the earth. In Thelemic teachings, Nuit's consort, Hadit, is the finite point in the center of existence, and Nuit is the infinity of space surrounding us. Crowley describes her as pouring the divine milk of starlight from her chalices as she kneels in the Abyss between land and sea, and that her principal nature is Love.[1]

The Star's path on the Tree of Life stretches from Chokmah to Tiphareth, skirting the edge of the Abyss, which humans must cross in order to reunite with the Source, the All, the Godhead. Although The Star is not The Priestess, and thus doesn't provide a direct pathway across the terrifying nothingness, The Star does provide a vision and hope for attaining connection with The Source via that visionary path from the Christ Consciousness in Tiphareth to the wisdom of the Supernal Father in Chokmah.

There can be no better description of the goddess in The Star card than Crowley's own, so rather than feebly try to recreate the wheel, here instead are some of the most moving lines from Nuit contained in the *Book of the Law*. This is a much clearer way to understand the nature of this card:

> *"I give unimaginable joys on earth: certainty, not faith, while in life, upon death; peace unutterable, rest, ecstasy; nor do I demand aught in sacrifice....*
>
> *"But to love me is better than all things: if under the night-stars in the desert thou presently burnest mine incense before me, invoking me with a pure heart, and the Serpent flame therein, thou shalt come a little to lie in my bosom....*
>
> *"Sing the rapturous love-song unto me! Burn to me perfumes! Wear to me jewels! Drink to me, for I love you! I love you!*
>
> *"I am the blue-lidded daughter of Sunset; I am the naked brilliance of the voluptuous night-sky.*
>
> *"To me! To me!"*[2]

THE SONG

Puscifer's "Grand Canyon" is, of course, the match for this card, because the song embodies the hope and wonder associated with Nuit and The Star card's unspeakably beautiful goddess. The narrator addresses the Supernal Mother with reverence and awe, love and faith, and the lyrics make a stunning match to the words and tone of Nuit's words in *Book of the Law*. Furthermore, the narrator's description of standing on the edge of the Canyon is an appropriate description for The Star's Qabalistic path on the edge of the Abyss, and the lyrics also speak to infinity of the Universe and each individual's microscopic, yet vital, role in it.

The Grand Canyon, as a geographical location, is an ideal place to experience the wonders of the night sky (recall the Egyptian Nuit, goddess of the sky, who stretches above the earth as a starry maternal shield each night), as well as the breadth and diversity of the creations of "Mother Nature," to say nothing of the impact the sheer expanse of the Canyon has on the observer's psyche. Anyone who has stood on the edge of the Grand Canyon is immediately reminded of how small and insignificant the trivialities of our lives truly are. It's a match worthy of the Queen of Heaven.

TABULA MUNDI TAROT

This brilliant blue, exquisite depiction of the goddess Nuit as The Star is among the most visually stunning cards in the deck. The goddess is surrounded by starlight, stars, galaxies, and large seven-pointed stars representing Babalon and the planetary energies. The goddess holds the Sun and Moon, cosmic representations of the traditional golden and silver chalices.

THOTH TAROT

The goddess Nuit pours liquid starlight in the form of milk, blood, and wine over Herself, as well as pours it over the meeting of land and sea. She is the goddess of Love, synonymous with Babalon, Inanna, Ishtar, and Venus, Queen of Heaven, source of hope and faith. She is the mother principle in the Tetragrammaton.

READING THIS CARD

When this card appears in a reading, put away cynicism and surrender to hope and faith. Now is the time to invest in your dreams, envisioning and acting upon them as reality. The Lady watches over us all, blesses us all, loves us all. Unanticipated help comes to the aid of the querent. Spiritual insights abound. The divine connection you are seeking is seeking you.

CHAPTER 24

XVIII. THE MOON: "CULLING VOICES," TOOL

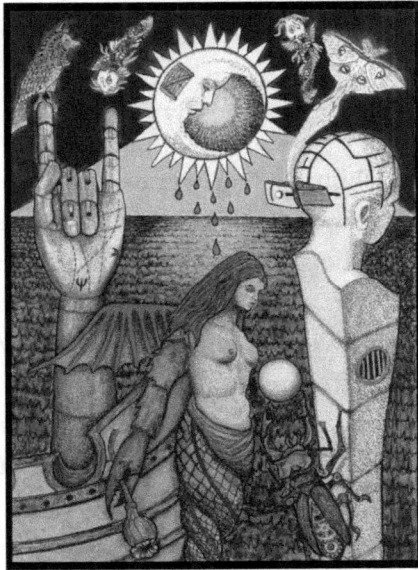

Traditional Title: The Ruler of Flux and Reflux, The Child of the Sons of the Mighty
Sign: Pisces
Planetary Ruler/Exaltation: Jupiter (Classical), Neptune (Modern)/Venus
Date Range: 2/19 – 3/20
Qabalistic Correspondences: Path 29, Netzach (7) to Malkuth (10); Sephira 4, Chesed (via ruling planet Jupiter)
Key Words: confusion, illusion, shadow, madness, witchcraft, darkness

"Culling Voices"
Tool
Fear Inoculum, 2019

Atu Line

The ever-changing moon waxes and wanes in a never-ending cycle. She grows, becomes full, shrinks down to nothing, and begins again anew. The Moon card, Atu XVIII, represents the confusion and lack of clarity that comes with examining things by figurative moonlight. Since the Moon's face (and therefore the light that it reflects) continually changes from our perspective here on earth, the card represents such things as dreams, psychedelic experiences, an unreliable narrator, illusions, psychopathy (lunacy), and psychological abuse.

Its path on the Tree of Life is a great illustration of The Moon's off-kilter nature, flowing down one side of the Tree from Venus's rule in Netzach down to the earth in Malkuth. It's far down the Tree, one-sided, and heavily influenced by the darker, feminine energies. Crowley associated this card with "witchcraft and abominable deeds,"[1] which DuQuette later clarified the use of "witchcraft" as being of the general tone of the panic that accompanied the witch hunts, rather than the modern, neopagan understanding of the term.[2]

This card is associated with the astrological sign of Pisces. Because of its position as the final sign of the zodiac, and because it is the mutable sign in the most malleable element, Pisces is not only extremely sensitive to everything around them, but is also wise... often seemingly beyond reason. The sign is deeply psychic, even if it is often overwhelmed by what it 'sees.'

The Hebrew letter for The Moon is *Qoph*, which translates to "back of the head," symbolic of the subconscious and unconscious mind. No question, this card deals with all that is buried in the dark recesses of the psyche.

THE SONG

The match for The Moon is "Culling Voices" from Tool's *Fear Inoculum*, and the match could scarcely be more literal. This track vividly describes various indicators of mental distress, including paranoia, auditory hallucination (hearing voices), anxiety, and delusional thinking. These are also often experienced during crises of the soul, those long dark nights of grief, longing, and horror. The track could not be more on-point with the archetype of the card in this pairing.

TABULA MUNDI TAROT

Meleen creates a disturbingly beautiful dreamscape in pitch night. The card adheres to the traditional structure and many of the traditional elements (the Moon dripping blood between the pillars, water below, the scrab beetle pushing the solar disk), and she also incorporates new symbols that represent psychosis, the subconscious, witchcraft, legends of monsters, and tales of madness. This collection of 'off' items appeal to the modern mind, and communicate the true range of madness that is this archetype.

THOTH TAROT

A traditional Moon card, showing the moon dripping blood into a body of water between two pillars that represent the gate of reality, prophecy, consciousness, etc. Twin Anubis figures with twin jackals stand on either side of the gate, guarding the way. Below, a scarab beetle rolls the sun through the night of the underworld, patiently and silently delivering it again to the morning.

READING THIS CARD

The Moon card, despite any attachments we may have to lunar deities or to the satellite itself, is intended to cause unease. It is intended to recall in the reader the sense that nothing is what it seems; even under the light of the full moon, our eyes can and do play tricks on us. We do not know and are loathe to imagine what is hiding in the shadows.

This card often comes up during "the dark night of the soul," when there is important information the querent is not privy to or doesn't have yet, when things are in a state of flux, and/or when the situation is developing and not "set" yet. When this card appears in a reading, the querent must reconsider what they think they know, acknowledge that not every passing thought is true or deserves to be believed in, and re-evaluate their conclusions.

CHAPTER 25

XIX. THE SUN: "PNEUMA," TOOL

Traditional Title: The Lord of the Fire of the World
Planet: Sun
Qabalistic Correspondences: Path 30, Hod (8) to Yesod (9); Sephira 6, Tiphareth (ruled by the Sun)
Key Words: the self, reputation, freedom, light, glory, triumph, pleasure, growth

"Pneuma"
Tool
Fear Inoculum, 2019

Atu Line

The Sun card corresponds to the path between the sephira of Mercury (Hod), and the sephira of the Moon (Yesod). It also associated with Tiphareth, the sephira of the Holy Guardian Angel and the Christ Consciousness in the center of the Tree of Life, connecting humanity in the lower half of the Tree to divinity above.

The Sun is our very own source of life, symbolic of the Light of All. The warmth and light of our star is the center and animating force of our solar system, and without it, this planet would be completely barren. And yet, it is so unimaginably powerful that it would kill us all if the earth were any closer to it.

The Thelemic tradition is, for these reasons and more, a predominantly solar (and also masculine-oriented) philosophy, in which all people are viewed as stars—microcosmic reflections of the macrocosmic Sun. We are the reflections of divinity, and as above, so below. The path that this card occupies, between Hod and Yesod, represents the connection between logic and intuition, between the rational mind and the mystic mind. The Sun card symbolizes truth, freedom, growth, and enlightenment inherent in standing in one's total power as a whole and unapologetically powerful being.

THE SONG

Tool's "Pneuma" is about the journey of every human to reunite with The Source, The All, The Ineffable Godhead. According to *Oxford Languages*, the Greek word *pneuma* means vital spirit, soul, or creative force; it literally translates to "that which is breathed or blown." In the Beginning, the Ineffable inhales One Breath (an action that corresponds to the path from Kether to Chokmah, the path of The Fool). The exhalation of that breath produces the One Word or Logos (which corresponds to the path from Kether to Binah, that of The Magus). Another way of explaining pneuma is to say it is a word for the universal animating energy of the Divine, the Breath of God that brings life.

The point of all religious practice is to bring a mortal human into alignment, concord, and relationship with the Divine, to reconcile one's own energy to that of the energy of the Divine. In magickal practice, the point is to remember on a cellular level that we are part of the Godhead, never separate from It. The entire point of religious observance is to become pneuma, pure and simple.

In the earliest stages of life, we are pure, "innocent" energy, completely aligned with God. As we age, we lose that connection, and many of us spend the rest of our lives trying to regain it. Tool's "Pneuma" discusses that journey, the struggle to return to the Godhead, to truly remember with every atom of our being who and what we are.

This song is matched with The Sun because our sun is the single most important piece of our reality in Malkuth—without it we could not survive. Its never-ending, self-contained, self-sustained fire literally powers everything in our solar system, from controlling the orbits of the planets and celestial bodies, to growing our food. It is our very own star, so integral to our existence that it has been worshipped as God throughout human history, both literally and figuratively. Early humans ascribed divine status to the celestial body itself, and in later human history, the most powerful gods have been tied to solar influence, including Ra, Jesus, Surya, Mithra, Shamash, Apollo, Helios, Sol, and dozens more. By recognizing ourselves as vehicles of pneuma, we are merging with God, becoming a star like the Sun.

TABULA MUNDI TAROT

The *Tabula Mundi* Sun card is a beautiful compendium of symbolism praising the Sun and its connection to humanity. The solar disk is winged, a reference to Hadit, the masculine, ever-contracting point that is the counterpart of Nuit, Who is feminine, ever-expanding space. The solar disk is detailed with the signs of the zodiac and their decans; and a mobius strip of the signs sits below it, emphasizing the infinite light of our star. Below, the human eye, pineal gland, and heart are combined with a crescent moon, symbolizing humanity's reflection of the Sun. Finally, twin serpents (like the ones found on the caduceus or wand of Mercury) appear on either side, representing the rising life force of Kundalini. We are awakened to our divine state, rising to meet the light of the Sun.

THOTH TAROT

In the Thoth deck, twin children representing the masculine and feminine dance outside the walls of a hilltop garden. Above them, the brilliant Sun lights the entire solar system (symbolized by the zodiac surrounding the scene). All is rainbows, sunshine, and joy. The Sun represents the truth of the New Age, that "every man and woman is a star" and that God lives within each person, rather than in some separate and unreachable entity.[1] The debut of this new information directly leads to the paradigm shift of the next card, The Aeon.

READING THIS CARD

When this card appears in a reading, the light of the Sun shines upon the situation at hand, bringing truth, visibility, blessings, growth, and triumph. Freedom comes to the querent or the situation. The dawn of a new age or stage, improvement, enlightenment, monetary gain, and/or an increase in positive regard are all indicated.

It's hard to conceive of a way that this card can be ill-dignified, simply because it is such a powerfully positive archetype. Perhaps the most obvious negative expression is focusing too hard or shining too much light on something, effectively burning it up with our attention. This could look like "outing" or "doxxing" someone, pressing for information, or forcing a situation that is not ready to blossom yet. Occasionally, The Sun can indicate someone being emancipated from their earthly body—a sudden return to Source. But on the whole, The Sun brings with it the promise of fresh starts, opportunities to shine, and real growth.

CHAPTER 26

XX. THE AEON: "GALILEO," PUSCIFER

Traditional Title: Judgment, The Last Judgment, Spirit of the Primal Fire,
Planet/Element: Pluto, Elemental Fire/Spirit
Qabalistic Correspondences: Path 31, Hod (8) to Malkuth (10)
Key Words: paradigm shift, awakening, purification, decision made, move forward, new age

"Galileo"
Puscifer
Money Shot, 2015

Atu Line

If The Tower represents wiping the slate clean and rebuilding, The Aeon is destroying the fucking slate and truly starting over. All assumptions are released and we start from scratch. Also known as Judgement or The Apocalypse in other decks, The Aeon card represents a complete break with life as we know it, and the development of a new understanding of "reality." The Thoth tradition has a radically different approach to this trump card than other systems like Rider-Waite, namely in that the Judgement card is about the return of Christ to earth and the Rapture, and this card specifically refutes the mythology of the dying and resurrected God entirely.

The Aeon corresponds to elemental fire, and thus is closely related to all the other fire cards in the deck, including The Emperor (Aries), Lust (Leo), and Art (Sagittarius) and all of the Wands. It also does double-duty as the correspondence for elemental spirit—that undefinable fifth element in addition to fire, water, air, and earth. If this seems confusing, consider that fire is the first emanation of the Godhead, and what would Godhead be, if not Spirit? The likening between fire and spirit is an old and enduring connection in the human consciousness.

The Hebrew letter associated here is Shin, meaning tooth, and it is one of the three mother letters (along with airy Aleph and watery Mem). If Aleph (The Fool) is the jumping off point on this journey, and Mem (The Hanged Man) is the middle point of crisis or sacrifice, then Shin (The Aeon) represents that moment of enlightenment exploding in the consciousness of the sojourner and heralding the approach of the final destination.

To make the most sense of this card and its departure from the traditional Judgement card, it's helpful to consider the Thelemic pantheon and worldview. From that perspective, humanity's understanding of their relationship to the divine has progressed over time, thanks to advances in scientific understanding of the world around us. In the first Aeon, humans understood God as The Mother (Isis, early paganism and goddess worship), because life came inexplicably and unpredictably from the Mother, represented by the inconstant moon. Spirituality was focused on encouraging the fertility of the divine Mother, who produced an abundance of children, crops, and animals—all the raw resources of early human life. Importance was placed on the earth, the body, and the material supports of our survival.

By the second Aeon, we had discovered the role of the Father in fertility, which led to a pendulum swing from God the Mother to God the Father (the sun, Osiris, the rise of monotheistic and Abrahamic religions). We now understood that the paternal "contribution" preceded pregnancy, so it was assumed that the "important" aspect was the father's spirit injected into the mother's body. Because our ancestors had also observed that God's representation, the sun, "dies" at the end of each day (the sun sets) and at the end of harvest season (sunlight gets weaker after the autumnal equinox), worship became focused on encouraging the sun's rebirth over and over.

We are now living in the dawn of a new age, in which God is The Crowned and Conquering Child—Horus/Heru-Ra-Ha—neither feminine nor masculine, the androgenous seed or spark of spirit located within each of us. Every human is a particle of God and made of the same stuff, i.e., "made in the image of God."

THE SONG

Puscifer's "Galileo" is an irresistibly apt illustration of this card. Galileo Galilei has been called the father of observational astronomy, modern physics, the scientific method, and modern science. He was a champion of heliocentrism, the theory that the Sun is the center of a system around which earth, the other planets, and their satellites revolve—an opinion that ran counter to the teachings of the church, and for which he paid dearly for much of his career.

Galileo's support of this theory was an act of courageous refusal to kowtow to religious dogma in the face of scientific evidence contrary, and it has led directly to the majority of our modern understanding of science and the physical laws of the universe. His heresy literally feeds us all today via the technology he made possible, and that heresy also protects us from our ancestors' fears of the Sun dying each night and conceivably not being reborn one morning or one spring.

We now live in an age in which we completely understand the Sun is a constant, never-ending[1] source of life sustaining energy. We now understand that the daily and seasonal changes in how we experience the Sun are cyclical. Just as we understand that life and death and the energy that makes up everything in existence (including us) is cyclical and neither created nor destroyed, we now understand that we are protected from the fear of death that has driven humans for millennia via the unseen forces of physics and universal law.

Beyond his role in influencing and supporting nearly every scientific discovery and invention for the past 400+ years, a simple search of Galileo's name turns up several quotes that also fit with the themes of The Aeon, as well as contain subjects that would possibly pique Keenan's interest and inspire him as an alchemist and wine maker:[2]

- "I do not feel obliged to believe that the same God who has endowed us with sense, reason, and intellect has intended us to forgo their use."
- "Wine is sunlight, held together by water."
- "The sun, with all those planets revolving around it and dependent on it, can still ripen a bunch of grapes as if it had nothing else in the universe to do."

TABULA MUNDI TAROT

Meleen depicts the dawning of the New Aeon as a Solstice dawn at Stonehenge. Nuit and Hadit, the maternal and paternal deities of Thelema, oversee the birth of the Sun, their Son Horus, the deity of the New Aeon. He appears here as a fiery ouroboros dragon resulting from an alchemical reaction, and with that, the ending of one age ushers in the start of the new one. To the left is the orphic egg of potentiality balanced on the glyph of Pisces (the end of the zodiac); on the right, a hatched and sprouting egg sits atop the glyph of Aries (the beginning of the zodiac).

THOTH TAROT

The *Thoth Tarot* completely explodes the traditional Judgement card, changing it to The Aeon as an acknowledgement that the old card belongs to the old Aeon, when we believed God to be continuously dying and resurrecting. Instead of the scene of the Last Judgement, we see instead the Holy Family, composed of cosmic Mother Nuit, cosmic Father Hadit, and their dual-natured son, Heru-Ra-Ha, in both His passive and active aspects. In the New Age, we understand that, not only is God unending and immortal, but God is neither and both masculine and feminine, and the spark of God resides in each and every human. We are children of God, and this is the Age of the Crowned and Conquering Child—the age of humanity's triumph over death and separateness.

READING THIS CARD

When this card appears, the querent is being reborn in some significant way. The worldview or guiding philosophy is being re-made completely. There could be a major shift in identity. It may feel like resurfacing or returning to the light. Religion, politics, philosophy, career, sexuality...all are fair game for a major overhaul—for the better. This card can also indicate that a decision has been made and the querent should accept the choice and move forward.

When ill-dignified, The Aeon can signal that the truth will set you free by first burning down absolutely everything you knew. Not that this isn't included in a well-dignified Aeon! But it could indicate a struggle to accept new information, new realities, or make necessary changes. Instead of a graceful shift in paradigm, an ill-dignified Aeon can look like the apocalypse. But as DuQuette points out in *Understanding*, "It only looks like the end of the world to those who cannot accept the possibility that old spiritual points of view can ever be replaced by new ones."

CHAPTER 27

XXI. THE UNIVERSE: "THE GRUDGE," TOOL

Traditional Title: The World, The Great One of the Night of Time
Planet/Element: Saturn/Earth
Qabalistic Correspondences: Path 32, Yesod (9) to Malkuth (10);
Sephira 3, Binah (ruled by Saturn) and Sephira 10, Malkuth (Earth, or
the Kingdom)
Key Words: completion, evolution, lessons, the ending of a cycle is
the beginning of another, endings, fruition

"The Grudge"
Tool
Lateralus, 2001

Atu Line

Atu XXI, The Universe, is the final card of the major arcana, and it's impossible to over-state its importance. Known as The World in other decks, The Universe represents the culmination of the human journey, the completion of the cycle and the Great Work, and as M.M. Meleen describes it in *Book M: Liber Mundi*, The Universe represents "the crystallization and fulfillment of the whole matter involved."[1]

Naturally, the ending of one cycle is the beginning of another, because nothing in tarot or Qabalah or astrology—or any other metaphysical system—is linear. Everything is cyclical and linked like daisy chains...or spirals, if you prefer. Every ending is the jumping off point for the next adventure, lesson, cycle, etc. As such, The Universe is inextricably linked to The Fool at the beginning of the major arcana. Recall our brief foray into Qabalah in the Qabalah Basics chapter, and you may remember that every Malkuth is the Kether of the Tree below it, and every Kether is the Malkuth of the Tree above.

The Universe corresponds to the planet Saturn, and thus is tied to Binah, the sephira of Saturn and the Mother Heh in YHVH. Likewise, the card also corresponds to that other Heh, the Daughter counterpart to Binah's role as Mother: the tenth sephira of Malkuth, the earthly plane and thus elemental earth. On the Tree of Life, we find this card's pathway between Malkuth and Yesod.

THE SONG

Easily among Tool's masterpieces, The Grudge is full of qabalistic references, as well as literary, alchemical, and astrological references, to boot. The density of symbolism layered throughout Keenan's lyrics here is almost dizzying. I've read many a fan interpretation of "The Grudge," and haven't come across any that touch on all the symbolic references contained therein, so I suppose that just means it's my turn to give it a go.

With the basic description of the card above, there are several lyrical symbols that need to be explained in short order, to bring the meaning of this song pairing into focus.

First, Saturn. Saturn is the planet of limitations, lessons, and responsibilities. It was given these associations because, when astrology as a discipline was first created, Saturn was the outermost planet in our known solar system—Saturn was the limit, the boundary, after which there was no more. Saturn kept us in-bounds, so to speak. That is why there are only 7 "planets" associated with Qabalah and classical astrology.[2] Likewise, that is also why the Universe represents both Saturn and Earth—we begin our journey on Earth and end it at the outer bounds of space—because the beginning and the ending, the micro and macro, are actually correspondent in metaphysics. As above, so below.

Saturn's orbit around the Sun is roughly 28 years. In each ~28-year cycle of a person's life, they have the opportunity to work through the "lessons" they are here to learn at Saturn's behest. Each cycle concludes when Saturn returns to the point it occupied when the person was born; this is known as their Saturn return. If we are fortunate, we get three of these in our lifetimes.

During a Saturn return, a person has the opportunity to fully integrate what they've learned over the past nearly three decades. If they've been paying attention and have properly learned, they ascend to the "next level" of consciousness, and a new set of lessons. If not, well, Saturn attempts to teach us again, and this time less gently. Saturn returns are frequently fraught with either horror stories about everything in life falling apart, or harmonious visions of things finally falling into place. Do you face your issues and dissolve them, or do you preserve and wear them like a badge of honor? The choice is yours, and what you experience when Saturn comes 'round again is purely up to you and your willingness to do 'the work' of healing, growing, and progressing.

The next major concept in the building blocks of The Grudge are the numbers one and ten. As you read earlier in the Qabalah Basics section, there are ten sephiroth on the Tree of Life. The first (highest) is Kether, the pure light of the godhead; the last (lowest) is Malkuth, the literal material manifestation of Earth and our everyday existence. And at the risk of stating the obvious, Kether is known as one and Malkuth is ten in typical Qabalah discourse. Between them lie every permutation of existence in the Universe, with the common understanding that the higher up the Tree, the purer the energy, and the lower down the Tree, the slower and muddier the vibrations become until they slow to the point of forming matter.

It is possible to "travel" up and down the Tree, from Malkuth to Kether and every sephira between, via meditation and other exercises of the Spirit. The pathway rising up from Malkuth to Kether is known as the Serpent's Path and is the path of initiation and evolution; the pathway down from Kether to Malkuth is the path of the Flaming Sword and it is the path of divine inspiration leading to manifestation.

Third, the concept of transmuting lead to gold is the fundamental basis of the discipline of alchemy, and arguably the basis for all of Western esotericism and occult knowledge. In addition to being a literal goal of transmuting a ubiquitous and worthless substance (lead) to a rare, priceless one (gold), alchemy sought the same in the hearts and souls of humanity. Through an understanding of correspondences, it was thought that if one could discover how to turn lead into gold, he could thereby learn to transform himself from basic to enlightened.

"Scarlet lettermen" is a reference to Nathaniel Hawthorne's *The Scarlet Letter*, a novel centered on themes of puritanical judgmentalism. In a colonial Massachusetts village, those who flout the laws of purity, chastity, and other Puritan Christian values are forced to wear a red letter on their chest at all times, forever marking and shaming them for their sins.

The stone is the symbol for all that is emotionally and spiritually heavy—our wounds, our hang-ups, our issues, our grudges, our never-ending need to control everything. The stone is the spiritual and psychological weight or baggage we carry with us for years when we nurture and protect our pain and self-righteousness at all cost, instead of healing and releasing it.

Put it all together and what do you get? The most perfect description of The Universe card ever. The Grudge is about relinquishing that which holds us down—the slights, the trauma, the wrongs done to us by others, as well as our compulsive need to pass judgment on others for their wrongdoings. What began as a self-protective coping mechanism—to punish those who hurt others and to re-affirm over and over that which is righteous and that which is shameful (and especially our own membership in the righteous club)—becomes a full-time job of misery and indignation. No good comes of it, and we sink deeper into hatefulness instead of rising toward the light. The longer we hang on to this way of being, the more suffering it brings, and yet the harder it is to change, for fear of having been wrong all along, and thus, 'bad.'

To throw off the chains and lay down the stone is to stop carrying the weight of the responsibility for judging souls and leave that to God, the Universe, Spirit, Kether. In so doing, our own wounds are healed and we are 'reborn' in a spiritual sense—shiny and new like a child. Letting go frees us to be happy, to love, to enjoy our fleeting time here, and it is well-worth the effort to heal ourselves of that original hurt. Through letting go of the stone, and learning the lesson, we are free to ascend.

TABULA MUNDI TAROT

The finale of *Tabula Mundi's* major arcana is among the most traditional of the pack. Meleen keeps the general vesica piscis structure of the card, as well as the Kerubic beasts in the corners. The background is that of deep space, and the Universal maiden, Daughter of Babalon, bursts from the wormhole, only moments after The Fool took his fateful step into the other end. The vesica is an ouroboros, the symbol of infinity.

THOTH TAROT

This card is likewise very traditional in its general vesica structure with the beasts in the corners, but Harris' brilliance shines in the dazzling use of color to create the sense of action and vigor in the card. The Universal maiden is dancing on the head of a serpent. With one hand She holds the serpent's tail, and with the other she appears to be piercing the Eye of God with a scythe. Behind Her, a mobius of three twists continuously morphs, the wheel of Fortune ever turning and rotating power between the masculine, the feminine, and the mercurial.

READING THIS CARD

When The Universe appears in a reading, one chapter is closing and another is opening. The querent has "leveled up" and is on the way to the next lesson in life, via the completion of a major stage. These are momentous times, when children become adults, adults become parents, parents become empty nesters, and the elderly pass on to the next world. This card often accompanies significant life events such as births, graduations, marriages, divorces—and also crises, such that life is forever redefined to 'before' and 'after'—any major event that brings massive change and ushers us into a new stage of life. The old is crystalized and set; only the new is malleable now, and it lies ahead.

Frequently The Universe appears when a person is approaching or experiencing a very particular kind of chapter ending: a Saturn return.[3] If the querent is near any of these ages and this card appears, the cards surrounding The Universe will draw attention to what this Saturn return will highlight in the querent's life, things to pay attention to, tools they can use to help themselves during this intense period, and so on.

The Universe is also particularly concerned with healing in order to truly let go and move forward. The cards surrounding the Universe can often indicate what needs to be healed, and/or what pattern, habit, or narrative needs to be released in order to move on.

CHAPTER 28

RESIDENTS IN THE SEPHIROTH

THE MINOR ARCANA

Now that we have fully explored the major arcana, which represent the overarching archetypes of the human experience, we'll move on to the minor arcana, which deals with day-to-day life situations, choices, and interactions. These 56 "small" cards provide detail in readings; they help answer the questions of who, where, when, and why, while the majors take care of the big-picture question of what. Here's a brief description of the layout of the minor arcana side of the deck.

STRUCTURE OF THE MINOR ARCANA

The minor cards can be broken down into four sets of fourteen, each consisting of: Ace (which theoretically 'contains' all of the rest of the cards in its suit), Knight, Queen, Prince, Princess, and Two through Ten. Each set of 14 constitutes a suit, which is tied to an element:

- Wands – fire, creativity, inspiration, spirituality, sexuality, force, spring, Yod, masculine

- Cups – water, connection, emotion, intuition, relationships, form, summer, Heh, feminine
- Swords – air, intellect, reason, belief, identity, psychology, conflict, autumn, Vau, masculine
- Disks – earth, materiality, security, abundance, stability, resources, work, winter, Heh, feminine

Likewise, the members of the Court families also are each tied to an element:

- Knights – Fire, powerful, impulsive, forceful, paternal
- Queens – Water, practical, intuitive, protective, maternal
- Princes – Air, intellectual, technological, rational, virile
- Princesses – Earth, productive, creative, receptive, fertile

The combination of the four suits and four court members yields sixteen general personality archetypes. The Knights, Queens, and Princes of the suits are correspondent to astrological signs, and the Princesses correspond to cardinal directions or quarters.

And as mentioned earlier in the Qabalah introduction chapter, the entire minor arcana can also be broken down among the sephiroth on the Tree of Life:

1. Kether (Crown) – Aces
2. Chokmah (Wisdom) – Knights and Twos
3. Binah (Understanding) – Queens and Threes
4. Chesed (Mercy) – Fours
5. Geburah (Severity) – Fives
6. Tiphareth (Beauty) – Princes and Sixes
7. Netzach (Victory) – Sevens
8. Hod (Glory) – Eights
9. Yesod (Foundation) – Nines
10. Malkuth (Kingdom) – Princesses and Tens

Understanding the basic themes of each station on the Tree of Life gives us a starting point when interpreting cards of each suit—particularly the numbered aspect of the cards. In learning these Qabalistic basics, we can clearly trace the path of energy as it leaves godhead and makes its way down toward us in our everyday lives, and in so doing, we gain an understanding of the energy of each number.

You will also notice that the small cards 2 through 10 contain planetary and astrological symbols. These represent the influences of the *decan* that each card represents. Decans are subdivisions of each sign; the heavens surrounding us can be divided into the twelve houses of the zodiac, 30 degrees per sign (360 degrees divided by 12 is 30 degrees each). Each sign can be further divided into three ten-degree decans, which act somewhat as lenses for the energy of the sign. Decans are each ruled by a planet, and that planet has a definitive impact on the expression of the energy (and thus the meaning) of the card. This is another example of the sublimely tidy system of the tarot: in each suit, the 2, 3, and 4 are the cards of the cardinal sign of the element, the 5, 6, and 7 belong to the fixed sign of the element, the 8, 9, and 10 correspond to the mutable sign, and the Ace contains them all, as the card of the element itself.

A great way to see the concept of decans in action is to consider any two people you know who have the same sun sign. Ever wondered how they can be so alike, and yet so different from one another? Much of that is due to the placement of all the other planets at the time of their birth, but they will differ even in their sun sign attributes if they were born in different decans.

For example, a first-decan Pisces (who is represented by the Knight of Cups and the 8 of Cups "Indolence") is nothing like a third-decan Pisces (represented by the Queen of Wands and the 10 of Cups "Satiety"), because one is deeply impacted by Saturn's limiting forces, while the other is heavily influenced by Mars' aggressive tendencies.

This is why getting familiar with basic astrological aspects will help you learn the intricacies of tarot, and will support your ability to differentiate between the cards. Even if you have temporarily forgotten the usual interpretation of a card, if you know basics about astrological signs and planetary energy, you will be able to add that to your understanding of the suit's element and the card's number's basic characteristics, and therefore piece together the meaning of the card.

If all of this seems to be about as clear as mud, have no fear! Let's dive in together to see all of this glorious madness in action.

CHAPTER 29

ACE OF WANDS:
"INTENSION," TOOL

Traditional Title: Root of the Powers of Fire
Element: Fire
Qabalistic Correspondences: Kether of Atziluth
Key Words: creativity, inspiration, natural (as opposed to invoked) power

"Intension"
Tool
10,000 Days, 2006

Atu Line

A ces are the seeds of their element. They are not yet manifest in any form we recognize. In them exist the *possibility* of the things we associate with their element. In the Ace of Wands, the conditions are right for fire and fiery things—the seed is there—but we don't see it manifest into anything recognizable until the next card, the 2 of Wands. Elements may not be manifest as something we can perceive yet in the Aces, but do not be fooled into thinking the Aces are weak. They are the purest, most potent form of their element, straight from the godhead of Kether, and like any great power, the test is in how they are wielded.

The first of the Wands cards, the Ace of Wands, contains all of the potentiality of fire, as well as everything that fire could ever create (force, creativity, sexuality, inspiration, courage, etc.). It is the Magus' Wand, a representation of the magickal power To Will, and the container of all the Wands cards.

THE SONG

As the first elemental emanation, fire is nearly pure energy, hence the match of its Ace with Tool's "Intension" and its descriptions of pure beginnings. The Will, the Wand, is the naturally existing power of spontaneous inspiration and self-direction. "Intension" highlights that the intentional creation of tools, and the use of fire in particular as a tool, had both positive and negative impacts on humanity.

Likewise, the Ace of Wands carries its own tension. The fiery wand can be wielded positively or negatively, to construct or destroy. We can use fire to see at night, to warm our homes, to cook our food...and we can use it to destroy and to cause physical pain. The flame that cooks our food burns the flesh of absolutely everything it touches, and it takes a skilled, experienced hand to properly use and control such a powerful force of energy.

TABULA MUNDI TAROT

Lightning strikes an old growth tree, sparking flames that erupt in the form of the sephiroth on the Tree of Life; behind the tree is the upright triangle, glyph of elemental fire, lit in blue flames.

THOTH TAROT

The lightening flash of inspiration strikes wood that erupts in combustion. Ten flames emanate from the wooden torch, arranged as the sephiroth on the Tree of Life; this card is aflame with the colors of fire: yellows, oranges, and reds set off by green flashes of lighting.

READING THIS CARD

When the Ace of Wands appears in a reading, it refers to a source of power. This could be the beginnings of a new creative project, the seed of faith, or a source of magick, creativity, sexuality, or force. The makings are present for any of these, it just needs to be taken up and used. The Wand is an instrument (and therefore a symbol) of one's creative Will.

CHAPTER 30

KNIGHT OF WANDS: "EULOGY," TOOL

Traditional Title: King of Wands, Lord of the Flame and the Lightning, King of the Spirits of Fire, King of the Salamanders
Element/Sign: Fire of Fire, first two decans of Sagittarius (last decan of Scorpio)
Planetary Ruler: Jupiter
Date Range: November 13 – December 12
Qabalistic Correspondences: Chokmah of Atziluth
Key Words: active, prideful, impulsive, explosive

"Eulogy"
Tool
Ænima, 1996

Atu Line

K night of Wands represents the fiery part of fire. Fire is the first element, energy emanating directly from Spirit. It is destructive, and yet also purifying. Knights are the highest-ranking court cards, the father in the royal family. Taken together, the Knight of Wands represents the Father letter of Yod in YHVH, in the Father element of Fire. This particular Knight mostly represents the sign of Sagittarius,[1] whose key phrase is "I EXPLORE."

THE SONG

This uber-masculine card is aggressive, dominating, fast moving, and all consuming. He embodies the naked masculine energy of the warrior, the conqueror, the emperor. Tool's "Eulogy" describes this Man's Man as a religious leader who stands in judgement and condemnation of others, whose shouting speaks of hellfire and brimstone, who is so sure of his righteousness. And yet, he is also charismatic, his crackling and undulating flames mesmerizing the crowds that surround him wherever he goes.

Interestingly, for all his natural speed and power, Crowley says this Knight is a one-shot kinda guy.[2] He prides himself on being first to act, and he puts everything he's got in to the single, giant fireball he launches. And if he misses, he's not usually able to rally and try again. The lines consoling this (likely self-proclaimed) martyr hint at this idea, as well. Hey, at least he tried...

TABULA MUNDI TAROT

The Emperor appears here as the Knight of Fire upon his black steed, charging into battle. He bears the Ace of Wands, a torch of flames, a bow and arrow (symbolic of Sagittarius, The Archer), and a shield that bears symbols of the small cards that belong to him: 7 of Cups (the last Scorpio card), 8 of Wands, and 9 of Wands (the first two Sagittarius cards).

THOTH TAROT

The Knight of Flames is shown leading the charge into battle, his black steed rearing up on hind legs. He aims the Ace of Wands ahead, showing the way, while his cape of fire becomes the column of energy that propels him forward.

READING THIS CARD

Court cards are notoriously hard to read, because they can represent so much! They can represent people, time periods, places, attitudes, and themes, to name a few. A great deal of learning how to read tarot is mastering the art of choosing the proper interpretation of a card when it appears in a particular spread, and the only way to do that is to learn the various meanings a card can have and then experimenting with their applications.

Court cards in the Wands suit are wielders of giant cocks, because that's exactly what Wands are: pulsing, electrified tools of force and power, energetic phalluses discharging cosmic semen wherever they're aimed—and sometimes where they aren't! The fact that every member of this family has a giant (literal or figurative) cock comes through in their personalities. They are big, showy, forceful, arrogant, and horny—eager to fuck in every sense of the word.

The Knight of Wands' appearance in a reading can suggest a person who is born between November 13 and December 12, or a person whose personality is similar to the description of the Knight of Wands. It can represent a part of the querent's personality, or how he or she is feeling or acting in the situation at hand. The Knight of Wands can also indicate the timing of an event between November 13 and December 12, or an extremely volatile situation.

CHAPTER 31
QUEEN OF WANDS: "REV. 22:20," PUSCIFER

Traditional Title: Queen of Wands, Queen of the Thrones of Flame, Queen of the Salamanders

Element/Sign: Water of Fire, first two decans Aries (last decan Pisces)

Planetary Ruler/Exaltation: Mars rules, Sun exalted

Date Range: March 11 – April 10

Qabalistic Correspondences: Binah of Atziluth

Key Words: transformation, seduction, independence

"Rev. 22:20"
Puscifer
V Is for Vagina, 2007

Atu Line

Queen of Wands represents the watery part of fire. As you'll recall, Fire is the destructive/purifying first element, energy emanating directly from Spirit. Queens are the highest-ranking female court cards, the mother in the royal family. Taken together, the Queen of Wands represents the Mother letter of Heh Primal in YHVH in the masculine element of fire. She corresponds to a small piece of the Pisces season, but she is mostly the sign of Aries, which heralds the birth of the self and a new year of growth ahead by bursting out with the dawn of spring, and whose key phrase is (what else?) I AM.

The essence of this card is transfiguration. Many decks' depiction of the Queen of Wands includes a spotted big cat, whose spots represent the cat's ongoing transition from lion to panther, or vice versa. She is the Queen of Fire, the meeting of water and fire that creates steam. Unabashedly erotic, she combines the most dramatic aspects of her elements to yield and wield the sexual magick that creates the universe.

THE SONG

The Book of Revelations, which is referenced in the title of this matched Puscifer track, details the end of the world and the return of Christ, the final judgement, and all of the conditions that will fall into place leading up to this finality. Revelations 22:20 is the second-to-last verse of the final chapter of the final book of the Bible. The verse reads, "He who testifies to these things says, 'Yes, I am coming soon.' Amen. Come, Lord Jesus." Of course, Keenan's use of this chapter as the title of the song would be nothing less than a play on the alternative meaning of the word 'come.'

The majority of "Rev. 22:20" describes the object of sexual obsession as Babylon Herself: in the Bible she is named "the Mystery, the Great, the Mother of Prostitutes and of the Abominations of the Earth." In the Christian context, *Babylon* is both the city as well as likened to a woman. In Crowley's Thelema, she is a principal deity, *Babalon*, Our Lady the Scarlet Woman, the Mother of Abominations and the Bride of Chaos.

Babalon's role in the achievement of enlightenment is to receive all and deny none. All those who give all of themselves over in worship of Her are drained out of themselves and into Her cup of abominations—sucked dry in a fit of carnal ecstasy, if you will—where their blood mixes with the blood of the saints, that they then may enter the City of Pyramids (a.k.a. the Supernal Triad) beyond the Abyss in the Tree of Life.

All of this "mixing with the blood of saints" business is just a metaphor for the death and rebirth experience that accompanies ego surrender, which every prophet, saint, and savior achieves in order to reach enlightenment. Babalon is the vehicle for return to the whole, the source, the All. The whole of Babalon's teachings are couched in an allegory of sexual relations, because orgasm is a tiny death—a sacred, transcendental experience that gives mere mortals a glimpse into the ineffable, infinite light of source.

So here you have a "dirty" song describing a sacred metamorphosis, an archetype of defiantly female sexual impurity heralding transformation and evolution, once again emphasizing that the sacred and profane are one and the same. As a person, the Queen of Wands is inspiring, motivating, alluring, passionate, magickal, and creative.

Incidentally, "Rev. 22:20" was originally considered for the Lust card, but ultimately passed over in favor of "Queen B." Though the choice was a hard one, it was ultimately made because the Lust card is Babalon and the Beast *conjoined*, and "Queen B's" lyrics describe the sexual union of the two as Babalon straddles and rides the Beast. On the other hand, "Rev 22:20" focuses more on the Scarlet Woman Herself, and the Queen of Wands is the perfect portrayal of Our Lady of Abominations.

TABULA MUNDI TAROT

The enthroned Queen of Wands wears an armored and bejeweled bodice dress with a long, flowing red skirt. She is crowned with a diadem of flame, to her left is her scepter topped with a flaming pine cone (a reference to the human pineal gland, believed to be the seat of the "soul"), and to her right is her leopard familiar, symbolic of her ability to transform.

THOTH TAROT

The Queen's throne, clothing, and hair are the flames of the fire she represents. Her crown projects twelve rays of light, symbolic of the sun's light permeating the heavens. She bears a pine cone-topped scepter, and her giant cat familiar appears to be shifting from yellow to black, or perhaps vice versa.

READING THIS CARD

Court cards can represent people, time periods, places, attitudes, and themes—the sheer diversity of information included in them is truly astounding sometimes. The Queen of Wands' appearance in a reading can suggest a person who is born between March 11 and April 10, or a person whose personality is similar to the description of the Queen of Wands. It can represent a part of the querent's personality, or how he or she is feeling or acting in the situation at hand. The Queen of Wands can also indicate the timing of an event between March 11 or April 10, or a sexually charged situation.

CHAPTER 32

PRINCE OF WANDS:
"HOOKER WITH A PENIS,"
TOOL

Traditional Title: Knight of Wands, Prince of the Chariot of Fire, Prince and Emperor of the Salamanders
Element/Sign: Air of Fire, first two decans of Leo (last decan of Cancer)
Planetary Ruler: Sun
Date Range: July 12 – August 11
Qabalistic Correspondences: Tiphareth of Atziluth
Key Words: extravagance, generosity, exuberance, courage, ego

"Hooker with a Penis"
Tool
Ænima, 1996

Atu Line

P rince of Wands is the airy part of fire. Princes are the son of the royal family, said to combine the active, inspired, fiery properties of the Knight and the stable, wise, watery aspects of the Queen into an intelligent, rational element of air. The Prince of Wands represents the son letter of Vau in YHVH in the father element of fire. His airy and fiery nature makes him vulnerable to conceit and arrogance, not to mention showmanship and general attention seeking. All of this a rather apt description of the sign of Leo, which this Prince mostly represents. His key phrase is I WILL, using the active, rather than futuristic, form of the verb—as in "I will it to be so," as opposed to "I will do this one day."

The Prince of Wands is the picture of adolescent and young adult male impetuousness. He is gregarious, fearless, passionate, proud, cocksure, and arrogant. He is also magnanimous, generous, brave beyond measure, and undeniably horny. He's a punk—love him or hate him, whatever. It makes zero difference to him and what he's doing.

THE SONG

Keenan effectively captures this character in Tool's "Hooker with a Penis"—the young man's arrogance is made from the combination of brash fire and know-it-all air. And, too, this card represents Leo personalities, who are known for both their drive to "look the part" and their one-upmanship. This is not to say that the Prince of Wands only ever exhibits this uncouth attitude, but it is to say that Keenan is known for his dark take on people and situations.

On the positive side of this personality, Prince of Wands is a natural performer and is lion-hearted. Like the ultimate Gryffindor of the court cards, he is courageous, kind, and compassionate— when he looks before he leaps. Sadly, the fast-moving, masculine, decisive nature of airy fire doesn't always lend itself to deliberation or discipline, which often gets him into trouble.

TABULA MUNDI TAROT

The Prince, dressed as a Roman soldier and holding the phoenix wand of the Second Adept, focuses as he drives a chariot pulled by the lion of Leo. The path of the chariot follows the flow of lava spilling from a volcano in the background of the card.

THOTH TAROT

This prince bursts out of flames, driving a chariot pulled by Leo's lion. He is not actively steering the beast, but rather extends his arms out and drapes the reigns over one wrist; he trusts the beast to know the way. This card is symbolic of Crowley as The Beast, due to the fact that Crowley's rising sign was Leo; thus, this Prince bears Crowley's personal sigil upon his chest.

READING THIS CARD

Court cards are some of the most diverse cards in the pack in terms of their possible interpretations—they can represent people, time periods, places, attitudes, and themes. The Prince of Wands' appearance in a reading can suggest a person who is born between July 12 and August 11, or a person whose personality is similar to the description of the Prince of Wands. It can represent a part of the querent's personality, or how he or she is feeling or acting in the role at question in the reading. The Prince of Wands can also indicate the timing of an event between July 12 and August 11, or a situation in which impulsivity, performance, or arrogance abounds.

CHAPTER 33

PRINCESS OF WANDS: "THE OUTSIDER," A PERFECT CIRCLE

Traditional Title: Page of Wands, Princess of the Shining Flame, The Rose of the Palace of Fire, Princess and Empress of the Salamanders, Throne of the Ace of Wands

Element/Sign: Earth of Fire, rules quadrant of earth under the constellations of Cancer-Leo-Virgo

Qabalistic Correspondences: Malkuth of Atziluth

Key Words: impetuousness, indomitability, creative inspiration, spontaneity

"The Outsider"
A Perfect Circle
Thirteenth Step, 2003

Atu Line

Princesses are the daughter of the royal family, and they are the "thrones," or homes, of their Aces. They represent the earthy aspects of their suits, so naturally they reside in Malkuth. While the Knights are active, the Queens are practical, and the Princes are intelligent, the Princesses are pure potential; they are the second Heh in YHVH formula. And unlike Knights, Queens, and Princes, who represent slices of time, Princesses represent space and geographic locations.

In this case, the Princess of Wands is the earthy part of fire, and she is the "throne" or home of the Ace of Wands. As this Princess lives in the Malkuth of the Atziluth tree, she embodies all the possibilities of fire here on earth—in all their creative and destructive glory. The Princess of Wands corresponds to the Cancer-Leo-Virgo quadrant of space above Earth, over Asia. This Princess is a free, creative spirit—she is utterly indomitable and irresistible. She can be at turns inspirational and insufferably self-centered, but there can be no debating her exuberance or lust for life.

THE SONG

The song matched with the Princess of Wands is A Perfect Circle's "The Outsider" from *Thirteenth Step*. The titular character is the epitome of the "Girls Gone Wild" stereotype—overly indulged, entitled, selfish, self-destructive, conceited, and shallow. She loves being the center of attention, and will do whatever it takes to garner the attention she wants. Her behavior is dangerous, her attitude explosive, her appearance half train-wreck, half daydream. In short, she is magnetized destruction.

In true Keenan fashion, "The Outsider" is a dark view of this particular personality or energy, but still apt. The essence of the Princess of Wands is wildness and craving represented by the fire of her suit, combined with the darkness of dense material reality represented by her association with the earth element. This Princess is full of youthful impetuousness like her brother, but her roots in the material world are what allow her to contain all of fire's potentiality.

Admittedly, "The Outsider" is not the most complete view of the Princess of Wands, but there is no denying her explosive, destructive potential. She is beautiful, beguiling, but able to do so much damage. This Princess, like all the other cards in the deck, is not all negative or positive; she could choose to be an iconoclast, a pioneer—destructive, but the ends which the destruction serves are open to interpretation.

TABULA MUNDI TAROT

The Princess stands, warrior-like, in front of the Ace of Wands tree, holding the flaming club of her suit. An altar of fire stands before her, the front face of which bears a rose, a reference to this Princess' title, "The Rose of the Palace of Fire." She is bare-breasted, wearing a helmet topped with a plume of flames, red cape, and short flowing red skirt reminiscent of her mother, The Queen of Wands', long red skirt.

THOTH TAROT

The wild, free, and nude Princess of Wands dances in flames before her altar. Upon the surface of the altar are red roses set aflame, also a reference to her title of Rose of the Palace of Fire. She is crowned with ostrich feathers, holds a scepter topped with the sun, and has caught a fully grown (seemingly unsuspecting and bewildered) tiger by the tail. All of these items are merely props in her ecstatic dance of joy, for her indomitable energy undeniably controls them.

READING THIS CARD

Court cards are some of the most diverse cards in the pack in terms of their possible interpretations—they can represent people, time periods, places, attitudes, and themes. The Princess of Wands' appearance in a reading can suggest an event that occurs in summer (Cancer through Virgo), or a person whose personality is similar to the description of the Princess of Wands. It can represent a part of the querent's personality, or how he or she is feeling or acting in the role at question in the reading. The Princess of Wands can also indicate a situation in which creative freedom yields tangible results, positive or negative.

CHAPTER 34

2 OF WANDS: "THINKING OF YOU," A PERFECT CIRCLE

Thoth Title: Dominion
Planet/Sign: Mars in Aries
Planetary Ruler/Exaltation: Mars rules, Sun exalted
Date Range: March 21 - 30
Qabalistic Correspondences: Chokmah of Atziluth
Key Words: aggression, dominance, leadership, rulership, ownership

"Thinking of You"
A Perfect Circle
Mer de Noms, 2000

Atu Line

The 2 of Wands is Mars (planet of aggression, war, dominance) in the first decan of Aries (sign of beginnings, the head, the self, and the personality; ruled by Mars). The combination of these two energies, along with the wisdom of the second sephira Chokmah, yields Dominion. People and situations indicated by this card have both the intelligence and raw power necessary to control. This card is among the most masculine in the deck—it is Mars in a Mars-ruled sign, after all—and it brings to mind all of the traditional associations with masculinity, for better and worse. Command and control, possession, domination, and conquest are all attributes of this card.

THE SONG

In *The Book of Thoth*,[1] Crowley writes that the 2 of Wands encompasses the destruction that precedes creation, with the initial fear and repulsion in response to destruction giving way to understanding and then surrender, making A Perfect Circle's "Thinking of You" an ideal track to associate here.

The narrator describes (presumably) his control over a sexual encounter, acting as the initiator into the sexual mysteries, leading a reluctant or reserved partner to new heights, showing the partner how gratifying sex can be. Again, hypermasculine—leading, directing, controlling, guiding the innocent, and being turned on by that, as illustrated by lines that infer masturbation[2] and sexual fantasy. What could be more masculine than a man masturbating to the fantasy of controlling and molding a less-experienced partner— dominating? It's fierce, dramatic, and definitely hot in every sense.

TABULA MUNDI TAROT

Meleen's rendition of this card showcases multiple symbols of masculine rulership, including the dual-headed falcon representing all-encompassing rule, the globe and equal-armed cross of dominion over the earth, the Egyptian crook and flail symbolic of protection and punishment, and in the background, a fiery Mars glyph. Like its inspiration, *Thoth Tarot*, the colors here are in keeping with the appropriate scales.

THOTH TAROT

Two dorjes, representations of lightning bolts and the masculine element, are crossed over a background of six flames representing the influence of the solar/phallic influence of this card. The colors are directly taken from the color scales: soft blue for the number 2 in the King/Wands scale, and all the reds of The Emperor and The Tower.

READING THIS CARD

The 2 of Wands carries connotations of control and dominance. Depending on the topic of the reading and the other cards surrounding it, this card can indicate leadership or tyranny, guidance or abuse, protection or possession. The 2 of Wands is also the first decan of Aries, so it can indicate spring, the vernal equinox, or the beginnings of something. In the context of something non-sexual, such as work, it could mean kicking ass and taking names, or kicking off a new project or initiative with a bang.

CHAPTER 35

3 OF WANDS: "SIMULTANEOUS," PUSCIFER

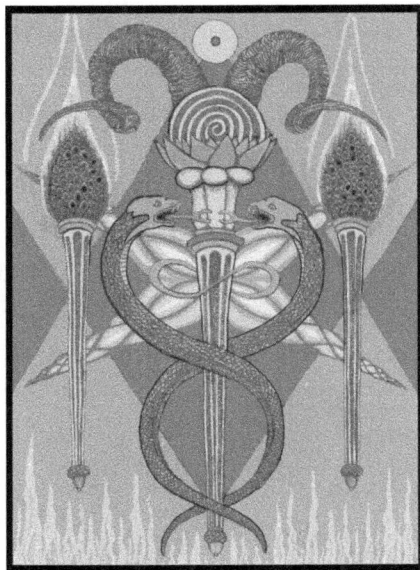

Thoth Title: Virtue
Planet/Sign: Sun in Aries
Planetary Ruler/Exaltation: Mars rules, Sun exalted
Date Range: March 31 – April 10
Qabalistic Correspondences: Binah of Atziluth
Key Words: awareness, character (as in character building), influence

"Simultaneous"
Puscifer
Money Shot, 2015

Atu Line

<hr>

The 3 of Wands is Sun (planet of growth, freedom, and independence) in Aries (sign of beginnings, the head, the self, and the personality, ruled by Mars), in the middle decan of Aries, and the 3 also associates this card with the third sephira, Binah or Understanding. With the title Virtue, this card is synonymous with all the "virtues" like honesty and integrity, as well as new awareness (thanks to Binah's influence) and a positive reputation. Virtues are beliefs, values, and mores given form via our actions. Those represented by this card are well-regarded by others around them, and are known to be effective, brilliant, and capable of learning and growing.

THE SONG

Puscifer's "Simultaneous" is a quirky and entertaining track that has far deeper themes than a casual first listen would reveal. What starts out as an in-depth description of an encounter with an eccentric, presumably indigent man at a town festival ultimately ends up as an appeal to our highest selves and common well-being. The narrator, in the chaos around him, has seemingly arbitrarily chosen to focus his attention on one person who arguably needs help. It's almost as though our virtues need a muse to inspire us to act on them. Long-time fans should be unsurprised by all of this meaning buried in mirth, because this is the artist Keenan has repeatedly shown himself to be—a trickster who hides deep philosophical meanings inside seemingly trivial, comedic one-off tracks.

Threes are the cards of focus, work, and dedication, of putting structure around an idea in order to bring it into fruition. Wands are the suit of divine inspiration, creativity, sexuality, action, and spiritual ascension. The 3 of Wands, Sun in Aries, is focused on spiritual work, such that in moments of crisis, our virtue shines through and we rise to meet the challenges to our humanity. Wisdom, new ideas, and inspiration can come from unexpected places, and in this case, it was kindness that yielded the narrator's epiphany.

"Simultaneous" speaks to the determination to overcome the flaws that hold us back as a species. No word is wasted here, nothing is accidental. In identifying the means to overcome the obstacles we face, we use our own divine spark and the three dimensions of this plane to solve spiritual conundrums and rise above the Malkuthian muck, reaching toward our divine origins.

Ultimately, the decision that lies before each of us is to use the resources we have here on this earth to rise above the problems we collectively face. The lyrics not only speak to our deeds on a global scale, but on a deeply personal, local level, too—as in choosing to have interaction and relationship with our fellow suffering human on the street. Not looking away from others' suffering, but engaging with it, and doing whatever we can to alleviate it, is our obligation to one another—it is our work on this plane.

TABULA MUNDI TAROT

Three wands are arranged on a field of flames. The central wand is a solar caduceus topped with ram's horns, and the two wands flanking it are topped with fiery pine cones that symbolize the pineal gland.

THOTH TAROT

Three wands on a fiery-orange background, two crossed in saltire fashion across the larger, central wand. Ten licking flames burst from their connecting point.

READING THIS CARD

In a reading, the 3 of Wands points to the positive attributes of the person or situation at hand. It's an encouraging sign that better natures will prevail, but it is incumbent on those involved to summon and put forward their best selves. Those who are rewarded are justly so. When this card is ill-dignified, it indicates the insufferable aspects of the human spirit, characteristics like arrogance, conceit, self-praise, and selfishness.

CHAPTER 36

4 OF WANDS: "GET THE LEAD OUT," A PERFECT CIRCLE

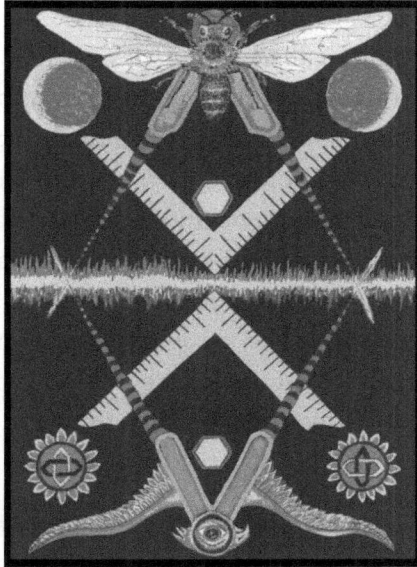

Thoth Title: Completion
Planet/Sign: Venus in Aries
Planetary Ruler/Exaltation: Mars rules, Sun exalted
Date Range: April 11 - 20
Qabalistic Correspondences: Chesed of Atziluth
Key Words: small cycle complete, accomplishment, achievement, good fortune from hard work

"Get the Lead Out"
A Perfect Circle
Eat the Elephant, 2018

Atu Line

———————————————————

The 4 of Wands, called Completion in the Crowley tradition, is Venus (planet of maternal instinct, nurturance, beauty, and fertility) in Aries (sign of beginnings, the head, the self, and the personality, ruled by Mars). Because it is a four and thus tied with Chesed—the first sephira below the Abyss and the first sephira of tangible materialism—this is a card of manifestation, often associated with celebratory moments such as weddings and graduations. It's a place to briefly pause and recognize the progress made so far, but it is not the final stop on the journey. Don't get too comfortable here; there's work to be done, places to go, things ahead to achieve.

THE SONG

The presence of Venus in the sign of Aries ruled by Mars means both the Mother and Father are at work here, getting things done through the combination of their strengths, creating, manifesting, activating new alchemical processes. Speaking of alchemical processes, I would be missing an important opportunity if I didn't recognize the significance of the title "Get the Lead Out," a nod to the overarching mission of alchemy: turning lead into gold.

This card and its matching song stress the essential nature of time in all that we are able to accomplish in this human life; although time is a human mental construct, our perception of it is fleeting, and we'd do well to not squander any of this precious and irreplaceable resource. We can accomplish this by learning to push the boundaries of time to its fullest through spiritual practices that put us "in the zone," including creating, meditating, astral travel, and other magickal exercises.

Of special note, this is the small card correspondent to Keenan's natal Sun in Aries. In effect, the 4 of Wands seems to capture something of his general outlook on life, and perhaps could explain how he seemingly has endless energy for the myriad and diverse projects that fill his days. The person represented by this card is always looking ahead to the next rise in the road, eager to get there and beyond.

TABULA MUNDI TAROT

The combination of Venus and Mars (the ruler of this card's sign, Aries) is evident here. The illustration is a mirror image of a lunar and a solar set of compass and square. All is balanced between the two polarities: the solar disks, the squares, and the eagle represent Mars/Aries, and the lunar disks, the compasses, and the bee represent Venus. Together, the two complete all the cycles of the world, and create all there is.

THOTH TAROT

This card's design recalls the Wheel of Fortune (known as Fortune in *Thoth*). The central design is an arrangement of four wands across a wheel; flames emanate from their intersection. Each wand bears a ram's head (Aries) on one end, and dove (Venus) on the other, and they are arranged so as to be alternating. The yellow, red, and orange of the card corresponds to Aries, and the verdant green background to Venus.

READING THIS CARD

The 4 of Wands is a welcome sight in a reading—it heralds a time to pause and celebrate all that has been achieved so far, as well as rest up for the next leg of the journey. Weddings, graduations, births, and other milestones are often indicated by this card, especially if the milestone precedes the next working stage (after the wedding is the marriage; after the graduation comes job hunting; after birth is the work of raising the child). The mix of work and pleasure here is a positive one, encouraging us to enjoy not only the fruits of our labor, but also our plans and the labor itself.

CHAPTER 37

5 OF WANDS: "PRISON SEX," TOOL

Thoth Title: Strife
Planet/Sign: Saturn in Leo
Planetary Ruler: Sun
Date Range: July 22 – Aug 1
Qabalistic Correspondences: Geburah of Atziluth
Key Words: repression, stifled growth, rebellion against tyranny, volcanic pressure

"Prison Sex"
Tool
Undertow, 1993

Atu Line

T he 5 of Wands is Saturn (planet of limitations, lessons, discipline, and time) in Leo (sign of courage, generosity, exuberance and performance; ruled by the Sun) in the 5th sephira of Geburah (sephira of conflict and war, ruled by Mars). Truthfully, this is a difficult card. Recall that 4 of Wands was a resting place—a brief pause to enjoy the stability we've built—before continuing on in the journey. Fours are always stability, reminiscent of the four legs of a table, but the addition of a fifth throws that balance off and inevitably leads to conflict.

Fives are always about the struggle, and 5 of Wands is a prime example of that. The juxtaposition of Saturn's limiting and Leo's expansive natures perfectly demonstrates Strife, as these two forces fight for control of the person or situation at hand. The id's desire to expand to meet its own needs and desires combine with the super-ego's duty to confine and limit describe the struggle with the Shadow. Leo just wants to be its usual self, shiny and happy and beautiful like a child, but the oppressive force of Saturn holds it down and kills its joy. The opposition of these two forces creates volcanic pressure that builds to the brink of explosion, which is where we find ourselves in this card.

THE SONG

There is no argument that "Prison Sex" describes difficult and unsettling concepts of child abuse, rape, and psychological torture. The cycles of sex abuse are at the forefront here in this truly chilling narrative of a child-victim growing up to become the adult-abuser, the cyclical nature of trauma, and how the absence of healing can lead one to become the monster they most fear. The title also evokes ideas about dynamics of sexual power and control between participants in any given act—who is active and who is passive and what is consensual versus nonconsensual—and it also points out that the strife is not just caused by sexual acts perpetrated against another person, but also the mental prison that unhealthy and dysfunctional sexual predilections can be for the person who is driven by them.

Conversely, one could also examine how this track references the child-victim as "lamb and martyr," which are symbols of Christ, and Leo is frequently associated with Jesus Christ through its ruler, the Sun (a homonym for the Son). Meanwhile, lyrical references to blood, flesh, body parts, and skin evoke the boundaries and limitations (Saturn) of the human body.[1] Again, expansion versus limitation: the expansiveness of an innocent child striving against the limitations of a cruel abuser.

TABULA MUNDI TAROT

The ancient Persian deity Zruvān, here shown as a composite of the Kerubic guardians (lion, bull, eagle, man), stands upon the sphere of the world perched in the lava flow of the exploding volcano in the background. Two of the four wands behind him are scythes, symbolic of Saturn, and he holds the fifth, topped with a Tau (Hebrew letter correspondent to The Universe, Saturn's card). He is confined by a serpent coiling up his body, and his fists are clenched; both indicate mounting pressure of compressed energy in need of release.

THOTH TAROT

Two wands of the Minor Adept and two of the Major Adept are crossed in an interlacing saltire fashion behind a central wand of the Chief Adept. Crowley's personal seal appears between the wings atop the Chief wand. Fire issues from the five wands' intersection, symbolic of the growing pressure of force contained.

READING THIS CARD

Of course, sex crimes are far from the only way that 5 of Wands manifests—this card comes up in any conflict in which one side wants to expand and grow, while the other side applies pressure to keep the situation contained and small. When this card appears, the reader should consider who or what is representing these two sides, and give an honest appraisal of which side should be in control. Generally, this is a card in which the side of expansion is poised to throw off confining chains in order to shine, although it is not guaranteed; check the surrounding cards for dignity.

CHAPTER 38

6 OF WANDS: "10,000 DAYS (WINGS, PT. 2)," TOOL

Thoth Title: Victory
Planet/Sign: Sun in Leo
Planetary Ruler: Sun
Date Range: August 2 - 11
Qabalistic Correspondences: Tiphareth of Atziluth
Key Words: decisive win, compassion, connection to the divine, glory, harmony, triumph

"10,000 Days (Wings, Pt. 2)"
Tool
10,000 Days, 2006

Atu Line

The 6 of Wands, Sun (planet of growth, freedom, independence and life) in Leo (sign of courage, generosity, exuberance and performance; ruled by the Sun), is complete and total Victory, quashing any and all opposition easily. Here, the Sun is in the sign and sephira of its rulership, magnifying its blessings and strength. Furthermore, Wands are the suit of Fire, the first emanation from the Godhead, and 6 is the number of Tiphareth—the sephira at the center of the Tree, the representation of the Holy Guardian Angel communicating between Kether and Malkuth, and the seat of the Christ consciousness. Sixes are blessed and in the company of angels. They exude compassion, and speak to the heart—in the case of this particular card, the heart of Will.

THE SONG

Tool's "10,000 Days (Wings, Pt. 2)" is one half of Keenan's opus to his mother, who suffered a terrible long-term illness that left her paralyzed and in pain, all the while never wavering in her Christian faith. The course of Keenan's career chronicles his difficult relationship with Christianity, from derision and suspicion, to bitterness and resentment, and finally to acceptance and peace.

When one listens to A Perfect Circle's "Judith" (which we will examine later as the Queen of Disks), and then to this track, it may at first be difficult to reconcile the dissonance in attitude toward his mother and her religion between the two. However, it's important to note that "Judith" was written before her death, while "Wings for Marie, Pt. 1" and "10,000 Days (Wings, Pt. 2)" were written after. The death of a parent often sets off an incredible journey of inner transformation that can include breakthroughs in healing and understanding, and this may have been true for Keenan's relationship with his mother and her religion. While he doesn't go so far as to embrace Christianity for himself, he finally reaches a place of respect for his mother's practice of her faith.

In so doing, Wings for Marie/10,000 Days represents his tribute to all that she taught him about faith, magick, the divine, and spiritual practice. He uses his own spiritual practice and expression—his own "little light"—to honor and protect her and to castigate those in her congregation who neglected, derided, and harmed her. The lyrics further paint the picture of a woman harshly tested by the cruelties of life in a mortal body, and found to be of sound character and strong heart—a model of faith that most people can only aspire to.

The 6 of Wands as a representation of the heart of Will is an ideal way to describe Judith's force of faith. Her strength was not in her physical body, but in her sheer will to continue on, ever faithful that the best is yet to come. It is a testament to massive strength in the face of adversity, a true crowning glory. This card match represents her Victory, and in its own way, Keenan's own revelation of the Christ consciousness.

TABULA MUNDI TAROT

Sixes are composed of two trinities, symbolic of the combination of the perfected masculine with the perfected feminine to yield the balanced whole. Meleen highlights this formula on the 6 of Wands card with the interlaced wands creating a series of triangles connecting the sun and moon. Beneath this arrangement are the lion and white owl of alchemy, representing the masculine and feminine elements respectively; between them are the infinite lemniscate and a golden-yellow rose symbolizing great value or worth.

THOTH

Harris' illustration of Victory is an arrangement of two each of the Minor, Major, and Chief Adept wands crossing one another in a hash-mark-type formation set on the diagonal. A flame kindles at each intersection, and the background is the purple of royalty—the combination of masculine fire's red and feminine water's blue.

READING THIS CARD

When this card appears in a reading, success and righteous victory are indicated, especially in regards to endeavors of a spiritual or personal nature. It can indicate winning a conflict, an award, a promotion, a role in a production, or some other highly visible prize through more than just luck. The world celebrates you! Use this opportunity to lift up the good, to be generous with your winnings, and to be a blessing to those around you. This is one that's difficult to dampen, even when surrounded by ill-dignifying cards.

CHAPTER 39
7 OF WANDS: "PASSIVE," A PERFECT CIRCLE

Thoth Title: Valour
Planet/Sign: Mars in Leo
Planetary Ruler: Sun
Date Range: August 12 - 22
Qabalistic Correspondences: Netzach of Atziluth
Key Words: victory after a long struggle, keep the faith, courage in the face of opposition

"Passive"
A Perfect Circle
eMOTIVe, 2004

Atu Line

―――――――――――――――――――――――

The 7 of Wands is Mars (planet of dominance, aggression, war, the masculine) in Leo (sign of courage, generosity, exuberance and performance; ruled by the Sun) in Netzach (sephira of Venus, the planet of the feminine, nurturance, beauty, fertility). The mixture of fierce Mars and Leo energy in the sphere of Venus is overwhelming to Her, and this card reflects the struggle to prevail over a formidable force or adversary.

Sevens, like fives, are off-balance from the even number that precedes them, so they accompany situations that are also off-kilter. Where fives herald conflict, sevens point to discrepancies, usually in the form of dishonesty, division, or scattered focus. In the case of the 7 of Wands, it's scattered effort and a flagging will on the verge of being snuffed out by the opposition that are being pointedly highlighted.

THE SONG

The match for 7 of Wands is the cover of Tapeworm's "Passive" on A Perfect Circle's *eMOTIVe* album, a collection of protest, anti-war, and peace songs recorded in response to the launch of the wars in Iraq and Afghanistan. This time period was one of the more noticeably political phases in Keenan's career, and this album in particular revealed a man obviously disgusted and disappointed with the actions and policies of the G.W. Bush administration in the early 2000s following the terrorist attacks on 9/11/01.

The 7 of Wands, like "Passive," points out situations of political and personal weakness, lack of political will, and willfully surrendering when victory is still possible. They are descriptions of passively standing by while your party or country is hijacked—of abdicating control. Like the 7 of Wands, "Passive" admonishes Americans and Republicans in particular: *be a worthy adversary! Where is your grit? Your integrity? Wake up!* As Crowley points out in this card's description in *The Book of Thoth*, "Patriotism, so to speak, is not enough."[1]

TABULA MUNDI TAROT

Meleen's expression of this card highlights the loss of victory when cooperation devolves to competition between equally necessary elements. A dragon and tiger (symbolic of the masculine and feminine) face off against one another in battle, the background between them revealing the blasted Tower, on fire and threatening to crumble. Beneath them are six crossed wands overlayed by a single larger wand, symbolic of all the opposition aligned against the querent.

THOTH TAROT

Six wands clash against a larger, primitive central wand. Sparks issue from the intersections of the wands, apparently caused by the clashes between them. The force seems evenly matched for the moment, but how long can the rudimentary club-wand hold off 6 polished wands of adepthood? The buoyant purple background of the 6 is now a dark and stormy indigo in the 7, symbolic of the situation's dire turbulence.

READING THIS CARD

When this card is present in a reading, it's a challenge to rise to the occasion, to face difficult trials and daunting opponents on the battlefield head-on, and to act with valor. The bad news is, there's no cavalry coming to your rescue; if you want to come out on the other side of this, it will be by your own fire in the belly. The less-bad news is that you can rally and potentially prevail, but absent a summoning of your best strength and fortitude, defeat is nearly certain. It's really up to you and your own resourcefulness, grit, and fire—raise that berserker scream and charge!

This is a card that is heavily dependent on dignity—look to the surrounding cards to give you an idea of whether the querent is successful in making their stand. Cups and negative cards don't bode well, while Swords, Disks, and positive cards are helpful and can indicate the querent prevailing against the odds.

CHAPTER 40

8 OF WANDS: "GREY AREA," PUSCIFER

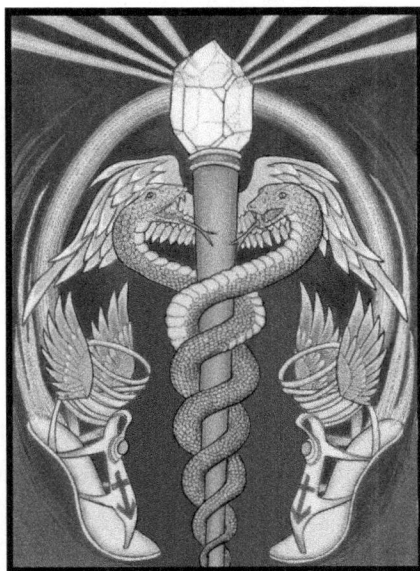

Thoth Title: Swiftness
Planet/Sign: Mercury in Sagittarius
Planetary Ruler: Jupiter
Date Range: November 23 – December 2
Qabalistic Correspondences: Hod of Atziluth
Key Words: rapid change or development, unexpected communications, electronic information

"Grey Area"
Puscifer
Existential Reckoning, 2020

Atu Line

The 8 of Wands is entitled "Swiftness," and it is ruled by the energy of Mercury (planet of communications, commerce, systems, speed) in Sagittarius (sign of higher thought, philosophy, travel, spontaneity), while residing in Mercury's home sephira of Hod. Mercury's airy, fast moving, intellectual nature is only made more insubstantial by Sagittarius's mutable fire. Sagittarius is the sign of the philosopher, student, and teacher, ruling over higher education, publishing, systems of law, and other higher intelligence functions. During the first half of the twentieth century, preceding the development of the computer, Crowley characterized this card as representing "energy of high velocity, such as furnished the master-key to modern mathematical physics."[1]

Today, we see this card through the distinctly different eyes of modern users of technology, and we have a new appreciation of the mutability of information—any piece of data can be used to prove a conclusion *and its opposite*—as well the speed with which data can be communicated. 8 of Wands' Sagittarius is symbolic of the infinite nature of our access to information, and the impact of Mercury is to blur the boundaries between fact and fiction. Therefore, we are able to understand this card differently than our forebearers, as representing the fast-moving developments of the digital information age, where change is constant, though not necessarily permanent. 8 of Wands is a glittering, electrical current—a tool that we can use, or be used by.

THE SONG

Puscifer's "Grey Area" really captures the trickster energy of this card. What happens when the lines between fact and fiction blur so much that they disappear? What becomes of information, when it is no longer objectively true nor false? These are the questions we collectively face in today's information era. The sheer volume of information, and the speed with which it enters our consciousness, are beyond the brain's ability to properly organize and integrate. Our systems of judgement are overwhelmed, and everything becomes a meaningless sea of binary zeroes and ones.

Interestingly, this realm of absolute relativity is the dominion of Lord Mercury; the nature of mercurial energy is uncategorizable, neither here nor there, but everywhere. This is the element of quickening, of energy carried on the wind, of electricity, of the impulse of attraction between opposing poles. The fire of Sagittarius is just adding a further spark to touch off an explosive chemical reaction.

The symbolism of the color grey is also important to the match here, for several reasons. First, it emphasizes the ambiguity of information, knowledge, and change (it's not black and white, as the saying goes). A grey area is one in which the rules or boundaries are unclear.

Secondly, silver (and its less shiny cousin, grey) is one of the colors associated with Mercury for this reason, as well as the for the color of the physical element. Due to its characteristic mixture of black and white, grey also symbolizes Chokmah and Baphomet for their blended and balanced qualities between absolutes.

Finally, grey is often used to refer to the brain (i.e., grey matter). In teaching others about magick, I often talk about how, more than being a system for contacting supernatural elements, magick is about learning how to "hack" or re-program our own brains, our own grey matter. The 8 of Wands is also a card that deals heavily with the mind and its programming—particularly how we experience and leverage change, novelty, and chaos.

TABULA MUNDI TAROT

The *Tabula Mundi* 8 of Wands showcases Mercury's winged sandals (stamped with the glyph of Sagittarius) and caduceus wand as symbols of speed and ethereality. Atop the wand is a clear quartz crystal transmitting energy in eight directions, and a rainbow connects the sandals and wand to create an egg shape, symbolic of the potentiality contained in the continuously morphing energy of both Mercury and Sagittarius.

THOTH TAROT

It is interesting to note that the *Thoth* version of this card shows the eight wands as arrows of energy arranged in the form of the chaos magick sigil. Chaos magick, like the technology it so frequently makes use of, also solidified in our consciousness after Crowley's lifetime, and yet this symbolism is completely congruent with the modern experience of the world and the card. The rainbow and multi-color geometric shapes in the background of the card further support the elusive, yet all-inclusive, nature of the card.

READING THIS CARD

When the 8 of Wands appears in a reading, the winds of change are blowing, and the querent will likely receive new information regarding the situation at hand (look to surrounding cards to get an idea of the content of the message and its impact). Electronic communications bring unexpected news, situations change swiftly with little warning, and new developments may or may not be enduring. Flow with the information for now, try not to make any permanent changes just yet—reserve your judgment and action until circumstances become more solidified.

CHAPTER 41

9 OF WANDS: "ROSE," A PERFECT CIRCLE

Thoth Title: Strength
Planet/Sign: Moon in Sagittarius
Planetary Ruler: Jupiter
Date Range: December 3 - 12
Qabalistic Correspondences: Yesod of Atziluth
Key Words: flexibility, defense, adaptability as strength, standing up for oneself

"Rose"
A Perfect Circle
Mer de Noms, 2000

Atu Line

T he 9 of Wands, Moon (planet of mystery, cycles, and all things psychic) in Sagittarius (sign of higher thought, philosophy, travel, spontaneity) in the Moon's sephira of Yesod, reminds us to be flexible. To be released from the electronic confusion trap of the 8 of Wands, we must cultivate a strength and flexibility of Will, as is found in this card, called Strength in the Crowley tradition. Like the Moon Herself, the 9 of Wands is ever-changing, and Sagittarius lends its fiery nature to the cause, making this the card of being able to bend when necessary, and to be fully aware of when it's not. It's this knowledge of how to bend and not break that leads to the full expression of the Will, the culmination of the suit of Wands at the height of its essence.

THE SONG

A Perfect Circle's "Rose" is the chosen match for this card, and the song's lyrical simplicity brings a finality and surety to its interpretation. The narrator describes a moment of transformation, in which they become unwilling to continue appeasing their oppressor (whoever or whatever that may be) any longer. They have consciously chosen to interrupt their "freeze" response to fear, and to make a stand. They finally know that his ability to bend and compromise can be used to fight back, and not just to surrender.

Interestingly, Keenan chose to use the word *rose* to illustrate this moment of transition. The flower known as a rose has a universal connotation of delicacy, of weakness and fragility. But the verb *rose*, past tense of rise, conjures intense images of uprisings, standing tall, building momentum, and reversal of position. It's as though the delicate flower finally remembered it has thorns...and knows how to use them!

This is a classic paradox in terms of energy and intention, and a fine tie-in with the Moon's double influence on this card. The Moon is typically considered to be feminine in nature, with its monthly cycle mimicking both menstruation and pregnancy, and thus this luminary is often viewed from the perspective of fragility, receptivity, and weakness.

But anyone who has ever watched a woman's body swell and flex and split to facilitate the entry of another person into the world knows beyond the shadow of doubt that there is nothing delicate about the mother principle, which not only accomplishes this feat, but survives it over and over again. Likewise, this song and card duo remind us how critically important flexibility is to strength—that we learn to bend and not break—not to withstand abuse, but to duck it, to turn it on itself, to channel that force into reflective and defensive strategies.

TABULA MUNDI TAROT

Nine arrows are nocked on a bow that closely resembles the ones found in The Priestess and Art (the cards for the Moon and Sagittarius). The arrows are collectively aimed at the Sun eclipsed by the Moon, a reference to the related majors and the fact that The

Priestess and Art pathways connect Kether, Tiphareth, and Yesod, as well as a symbol of balanced masculine and feminine energy. Beneath is The Priestess' scroll, a reminder of the intuition inherent in this card.

THOTH TAROT

Eight arrows are crossed in a hashed saltire arrangement; their points and feathers are made of crescent moons. A larger, ninth wand lays over top the other eight. Its tail is the Sun and its point is the Moon, recalling Art's (Sagittarius') path on the Tree of Life between Tiphareth (Sun) and Yesod (Moon).

READING THIS CARD

When this card appears in a reading, the time has come to own your strength, use flexibility as a tool or weapon, or stand up for yourself. Flexibility is your best offense and defense. This card represents mastery over both the active and passive polarities; draw on either or both as needed.

If ill-dignified, it's time to consider how your rigidity may be digging you deeper into the hole you find yourself in—whether it's insisting on doing things your way or over-relying on your peace-making skills.

CHAPTER 42
10 OF WANDS: "PUSHIT," TOOL

Thoth Title: Oppression
Planet/Sign: Saturn in Sagittarius
Planetary Ruler: Jupiter
Date Range: December 13 -21
Qabalistic Correspondences: Malkuth of Atziluth
Key Words: suffocation, taking on too much, repression, heaviness, abuse

"Pushit"
Tool
Ænima, 1996

Atu Line

The 10 of Wands, Oppression, is Saturn (planet of limitations, lessons, time, discipline) in Sagittarius (sign of higher thought, philosophy, travel, spontaneity) in Malkuth. To say this is not a happy card is an understatement. The pressure of taskmaster Saturn is bearing down on spontaneous and open-minded Sagittarius, creating a clash of the giants Saturn and Jupiter (ruler of Sagittarius).

This is not the only time we see this combination of influences in a card—we'll encounter the positive face of this pair in 2 of Disks (Jupiter in Capricorn, ruled by Saturn), and their sorrowful cousin in 8 of Cups (Saturn in Pisces, ruled by Jupiter).

But for now, this card represents a burden on the spirit, and the question that arises is, *who or what is playing the role of Saturn here?* The 10 of Wands is a card of biting off more than one can chew, over-commitment followed by martyrdom, or being forced to carry more than is rightly bearable. The only escape is to let go of the burden, to throw off the weight that is binding the spirit.

THE SONG

Tool's "Pushit" is about the fight to throw off one's oppressor, whether that is another person or an aspect of the self. The relationship between the self and the oppressor is so strong because it's based in connection—something shared. Like any abusive relationship, the oppressor feigns love and care for the abused, all the while continuing the abuse. The victim, in order to become the survivor, must learn to distinguish the oppressor's lies from reality. Remaining in the relationship requires extinguishing personal desires and aspirations in order to fit into the tiny, confined space enforced by the Other—and that is precisely where we find ourselves in the 10 of Wands.

This is the final card in the suit of Fire. Issues explored in this suit have made their way from the beginnings of an idea in Kether, to existing in tangible reality by the time it works its way down here into Malkuth. The situation at hand has run its course; the issue has played out to its fullest extent. The best course of action now is to release or kill this situation, issue, idea, impulse, etc. and move on.

At the end of one suit, it's interesting to consider its relationship to the beginning of the next. We could say that the Malkuth of the Wands Tree is the Kether of the Cups Tree, making the Ace of Cups the flipside (twin? mirror? complement? remedy?) of the 10 of Wands. It's an interesting thing to contemplate in light of the final three verses of this track, which I'll leave you to ponder on your own.

TABULA MUNDI TAROT

The leaden anvil of Saturn sits atop a cosmic alchemical flask, smothering the Jupiterian fire within. The fire has consumed two of the ten wands, as evidenced by twin plumes of smoke, but is now dying out for lack of air and space. The constrictive nature of time, limitation, and boundaries snuffs out passion, drive, and industry.

THOTH TAROT

Eight blue, double-ended Jupiterian wands (Sagittarius), capped in flames on both ends, are crossed diagonally on a field of fiery orange. Two larger, leaden (Saturnian) wands bar the entire formation, effectively trapping or blocking the rest.

READING THIS CARD

When the 10 of Wands appears in a spread, it's pointing out something that has grown too heavy, too much, to keep holding onto. The querent has taken on more than their fair share, or the situation is somehow being balanced on someone's back unfairly. It's a card that frequently comes up in situations of inequity, abuse, imprisonment, and control, and the only antidote is to let go and move on, or else separate and escape, in order to embrace compassion and healing for self and others. Ill-dignity mitigates/improves this card, purely because its base dignity is so negative.

CHAPTER 43

ACE OF CUPS: "MONSOONS," PUSCIFER

Traditional Title: Root of the Powers of Water
Element: Water
Qabalistic Correspondences: Kether of Briah
Key Words: emotion, connection, intuition, compassion, love

"Monsoons"
Puscifer
Conditions of My Parole, 2011

Atu Line

As mentioned before, Aces are the seeds of their element, and they aren't yet manifest as anything we can see or recognize. Instead, they contain the *possibility* of the things we associate with that element. The Ace of Cups contains the *possibility* of water, emotion, intuition, connection, and the unconscious. The conditions are right, the seed is there, but we won't see it manifest into anything recognizable until the 2 of Cups. Again, don't be fooled into thinking the Aces are weak. They are the purest, most potent form of their element, emanating straight from the godhead of Kether, and like any great power, it's all about how they're wielded.

Cups are the second elemental emanation, and they are a counterbalance to the Wands. The Ace of Cups contains not only all the possible expressions of water (ice, oceans, rivers, steam, etc.), but it also contains all of the Cups cards, which illustrate everything that water can do (spill, flush, connect, cleanse, purify, heal, etc.). This Ace represents the Magus' consecrated chalice, which in turn represents the magickal power *To Dare* (the courage and love that are necessary to act on one's Will).

THE SONG

It is in the waiting for materialization, in the understanding of the necessity of the element, that one can truly experience the power of the Aces' potentiality—and that is true of this Ace especially. In the final aftermath of the fire of Wands, all is parched and dry, lifeless. In Puscifer's "Monsoons," the narrator describes conditions for rain that are ripening over thirsty land, people, and crops. The precious, resurrective element of water is life-giving and fundamental to the survival of all living things, but even beyond its biological roles, water also represents mercy, compassion, benevolence, psychic connection, and love—the seeds of which reside in the Ace of Cups.

The narrator in "Monsoons" presumably addresses an unnamed deity, pleading for the gift of rain that will bring not only survival but growth, and it's one of the most positive depictions of faith in any of Keenan's songs. Though I don't presume this to be a statement of his own faith, I do believe his experiences growing grapes for wine in the desert have given him an immediate sense of the need for water for the survival of his craft and his family's way of life. "Monsoons" is a tender, hopeful, and reverent track, and one that matches the spirit of this Ace simply and perfectly.

TABULA MUNDI TAROT

A full moon rises over a sacred sea, where a bejeweled shell rests atop a hollow tree trunk, overflowing with the Water of Life. The holy fluid appears to descend from above, dripping down the moon's face and into this depiction of the Holy Graal. Lotus flowers blossom on the surface of the water below, where drips from the shell plunge into the surface.

THOTH TAROT

A large, dual-handled chalice appears to bloom from the center of a lotus flower in a sea of darkness. Light pours into the already brimming cup of holy water, exploding into scalloped ripples of energy that emanate from the cup and are reflected in the fluid below.

READING THIS CARD

When this card appears in a reading, it refers to a source of emotion, particularly agape, compassion, love, forgiveness, and mercy. This could be the beginnings of a new relationship of any kind, the first inklings of romantic love, the first measures of devotion, or the first hint of a vision or prophecy. The Cup is an instrument (and therefore a symbol) of one's emotional and intuitive capacity.

CHAPTER 44

KNIGHT OF CUPS: "OCEANS," PUSCIFER

Traditional Title: King of Cups, Lord of the Waves and the Waters, King of the Hosts of the Sea, King of the Nymphs or Undines
Element/Sign: Fire of Water, last decan of Aquarius and first two decans of Pisces
Planetary Ruler: Neptune in modern astrology and Jupiter in classical astrology
Date Range: February 9 – March 10
Qabalistic Correspondences: Chokmah of Briah
Key Words: supportive, romantic, emotional, reflective, beneficent, tumultuous

"Oceans"
Puscifer
Conditions of My Parole, 2011

Atu Line

K night of Cups represents the fiery part of water. Water is the second of the four elements, the formative counterpart to fire's energy. Whereas fire is the father element, water is the mother element. Water is connective, emotional, and psychic—traits that are common to all the Cups court cards. As you'll recall, Knights are the highest-ranking court cards, the father in the royal family. Taken together, the Knight of Cups represents the Father letter of Yod in YHVH, in the Mother element of Water. The Knight of Cups mostly represents the sign of Pisces, whose key phrase is "I BELIEVE."

This Knight is expectedly more sensitive and compassionate than the Knight of Wands, but he's no pushover. He loves passionately, and when stirred to action he can be every bit as destructive as a tsunami. A romantic at heart, this Knight is a patron in his community, supporting the things that bind us together—love, art, relationships, and compassion.

THE SONG

The weary traveler in Puscifer's "Oceans" is the perfect characterization of the Knight of Cups. The depth of expression in the travelers' eyes, the sorrows and trials they've endured, the moving stories they have to tell—all are common traits of people who fit the Knight of Cups' archetype. The Knight of this suit is passionate about sensitivity, connection, arts, and community. He is fierce in matters of emotion and love—which, depending on his dignity, can be both a blessing and a curse. He tends toward melancholy, and can be prone to depression, pining, and rumination—elements that are all evoked by "Oceans." Deeply sensitive and psychic to a strong degree, yet strong enough to withstand and even direct the rocking waves, this Knight is the romantic, sensitive soul who would not be entirely out of place playing the lead in a romance novel.

TABULA MUNDI TAROT

The Knight rides his white steed out of the waves of the ocean. He holds a golden chalice aloft, and the claw of a crab emerges. The Knight's wings, dress, and armor are in the striking color and style of peacock feathers. His shield bears symbols of the decans over which he has dominion: 7 of Swords (Futility), 8 of Cups (Indolence), and 9 of Cups (Happiness).

THOTH TAROT

This Knight appears to be leaping waves on his white steed, holding a chalice aloft; a crab appears above its rim. The Knight, steed, and the Knight's sizeable blue wings, made of watery waves, take up a great deal of the image. A peacock adorns the lower corner of the card.

READING THIS CARD

Cups court cards are wielders of divine cunts, because Cups are the feminine counterpart of the masculine Wands. Cups are warm, inviting, nurturing receptacles of form and connectivity, sacred wombs that receive the divine seminal influences of the cosmos and weave them into new life, new forms. The fact that every member of this family has a cosmic cunt (literal or figurative) comes through in their personalities. They are nurturing, sensitive, romantic, and indulgent —eager to connect, explore, and receive.

As we've discussed earlier with the Wands court, court cards are some of the most difficult cards for tarot students to learn, because they can mean so many different things: people, places, time periods, themes, and attitudes can all be represented by a court card. The Knight of Cups' appearance in a reading can suggest a person born between February 9 and March 10, or one whose personality is very similar to the description of this card. It can also represent a part of the querent's personality or a role they are playing. This card can also indicate the timing of an event between February 9 and March 10, or the romantic, emotional, or artistic part of the querent's life.

CHAPTER 45
QUEEN OF CUPS: "JIMMY," TOOL

Traditional Title: Queen of Cups, Queen of the Thrones of Water, Queen of the Nymphs or Undines
Element/Sign: Water of Water, first two decans Cancer (last decan Gemini)
Planetary Ruler/Exaltation: Moon rules, Jupiter exalted
Date Range: June 11 – July 11
Qabalistic Correspondences: Binah of Briah
Key Words: nurturing, compassionate, insightful, connected, protective

"Jimmy"
Tool
Ænima, 1996

Atu Line

Queen of Cups represents the watery part of water. Water is the second element, the formative counterpart to fire's energy; fire is the father element, and water is the mother. Water is connective, emotional, and psychic—traits that are commensurate with all the Cups cards. Queens are the second highest-ranking court cards, the mother in the royal family of the court. Taken together, the Queen of Cups represents the Mother letter of Heh Primal in YHVH, in the Mother element of Water.

This Queen is the kind, sensitive, compassionate, and competent female figure of the Cups court. She is the picture of the astrological sign of Cancer, the sign she mostly represents. Cancer's key phrase is "I FEEL," and this Queen definitely *feels*. She differs from the Princess in that the passage of time has allowed her to develop a practicality that allows her to choose how to use her psychic sensitivity and compassion. The Queen of Cups has better boundaries and takes less bullshit than her daughter, who is much more permeable and impressionable.

The Queen of Cups is also the court card correspondent to Keenan's natal Moon and North Node. The Moon in natal charts represents the emotional and physical self and one's self-care, and the North Node location represents the characteristics a person is working to develop in this life.

THE SONG

As the mother of this suit, the Queen of Cups is well-represented in "Jimmy" in two different manners. The mother figure in the song is described as the source of the narrator's stability, and yet she is separated from her child when the narrator is eleven years old. Secondly, the adult narrator is speaking to the narrator's own inner child, reclaiming and reconnecting to it in order to mother it to the best of the adult child's ability in the absence of the narrator's mother.

In "Jimmy," the narrator is describing a process of reclaiming and nurturing one's child-self, to provide to him or her what was missing in childhood. This practical and yet deeply psychic exercise is how adults make themselves whole from childhood trauma—the combination of this exercise and the maternal archetype represented by the mother in the lyrics is completely apt for the function of the Queen of Cups.

TABULA MUNDI TAROT

The Queen leans over a body of water to see her reflection on a cloudy full moon night. Her reflection is faint. Two bees represent her royalty and fecundity, and two lotus flowers represent her intuition and the element of water.

THOTH TAROT

This Queen's throne is at the edge of a body of water. She holds a shell chalice containing a crawfish in one hand, and a lotus blossom in the other. An ibis stands nearby, and the entire scene is reflected in the water below, punctuated by twin lotus blossoms.

READING THIS CARD

True to the maddening nature of the court cards, the Queen of Cups can represent several different types of information. This Queen's appearance in a reading can signify a person born between February 9 and March 10, a person who has a similar personality to the Queen's, the part of a person's personality that matches this Queen's attitude or their personality in a specific role they play, an event that occurs between February 9 and March 10, or a maternal or parenting situation.

CHAPTER 46

PRINCE OF CUPS: "THE HOLLOW," A PERFECT CIRCLE

Traditional Title: Knight of Cups, Prince of the Chariot of the Waters, Prince and Emperor of the Nymphs or Undines
Element/Sign: Air of Water, first two decans of Scorpio (last decan of Libra)
Planetary Ruler: Mars
Date Range: October 13 – November 12
Qabalistic Correspondences: Tiphareth of Briah
Key Words: secrecy, shadow, desire, taboo, obsession

"The Hollow"
A Perfect Circle
Mer de Noms, 2000

Atu Line

P rince of Cups is the airy part of water. Princes are the son of the elemental family, said to combine the active, inspired properties of the Knight and the stable, wise aspects of the Queen into an intelligent, rational element of air. The Prince of Cups represents the Son letter of Vau in YHVH in the mother element of Water. His strong association with the astrological sign of Scorpio, key phrase "I DESIRE," makes him deeply connected with his sexuality and drives, but his airy nature makes that manifest in a way that is intellectualized, even somewhat detached. As a Scorpio, this Prince is ruled by Mars, with all His attendant aggression, dominance, and possessiveness.

THE SONG

"The Hollow" is a fitting song to describe this Prince, who is exceedingly focused and intent on his desires, especially those that feed the shadow side of the self. He may be promiscuous, even prone to sex addiction, or perhaps extremely driven in work or business. "The Hollow" describes this need to fulfill desires, in this instance sexual drives and desires. The need is all-consuming, and, like any addiction, it blunts the narrator's ability to distinguish right from wrong. This theme lines up so satisfyingly with the Scorpionic nature of this Prince—Scorpio is a water sign ruled by Mars, a planet of fire, and this person is wracked by the simultaneous desire for emotional fulfillment (water) combined with fire's destructive and aggressive nature. Like a sexy vampire novel, the theme is at once intensely erotic, dangerous, and pitiful.

And yet, the final verse describes how, somewhere deep in the psyche, the Prince knows he cannot continue this reckless behavior because he will never find deep, lasting connection in this dilettante manner, and he must fill the emptiness in a way that permanently satiates his hunger.

As we've seen so often in this exercise, Keenan's works cast people and situations in sinister and broken shadows, regularly examining the dark or negative aspects of these subjects. "The Hollow" is another example of this spin on a card. The Prince of Cups is not *all* bad. He can also represent other Scorpio attributes, such as deep emotional intelligence, intuition, or a comfort with death, secrets, and money. He is not easily frightened, and he is slow to judge others because he is intensely aware of his own shadows.

TABULA MUNDI TAROT

The Prince drives a chariot decorated with scorpions and pulled by an eagle (both are associated with the transformational forms of Scorpio), over a river at sunset. Overhead, an eagle flies carrying the skeletal remains of a fish, a reference to Hebrew letter *Nun*, and thus the Death card and Scorpio.

THOTH TAROT

This Prince drives a shell-shaped chariot pulled by an eagle. He holds a chalice containing a snake, and in his other hand a lotus blossom. His wings are diaphanously delicate, emphasizing his airy nature.

READING THIS CARD

When the Prince of Cups appears in a reading, his personality is somehow present in the situation at hand. The querent or another person involved could have been born between October 13 and November 12, could have a similar personality to the Prince, or could be acting from a perspective that is similar to this Prince's attitude. The querent could be inhabiting a role that calls on them to draw from the Prince of Cups' strengths or wisdom or perhaps causes them to suffer from his weaknesses. The card can also indicate the timing of an event between October 13 and November 12.

CHAPTER 47

PRINCESS OF CUPS: "BREÑA," A PERFECT CIRCLE

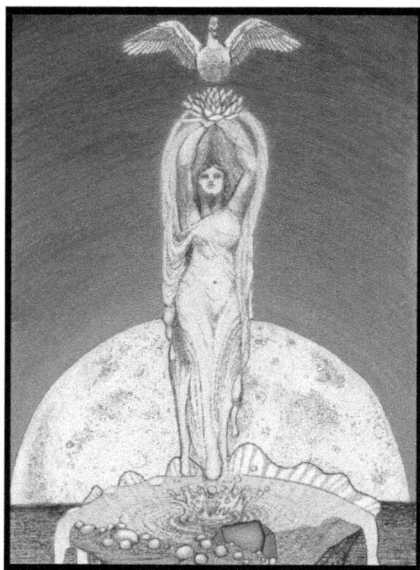

Traditional Title: Page of Cups, Princess of the Waters, Lotus of the
Palace of the Floods, Princess and Empress of the Nymphs or
Undines, Throne of the Ace of Cups
Planet/Element/Sign: Earth of Water, rules quadrant of earth under
the constellations of Libra-Scorpio-Sagittarius
Qabalistic Correspondences: Malkuth of Briah
Key Words: healer, compassionate, sensitive, impressionable

"Breña"
A Perfect Circle
Mer de Noms, 2000

Atu Line

T he Princesses are the daughters of the royal families, and they are the "thrones" or homes of their Aces. They represent the earthy aspects of their suits, so naturally they reside in Malkuth. While the Knights are active, the Queens are practical, and the Princes are intelligent, the Princesses are pure potential; they are the second Heh in YHVH formula. And unlike Knights, Queens, and Princes, who represent slices of time, Princesses represent space and geographic locations.

In this case, the Princess of Cups is the earthy part of water, and the throne of the Ace of Cups. In her is borne all the possibilities of water. As she is composed of the two feminine elements—earth and water—she is deeply feminine and receptive. This Princess lives in the Malkuth of the Briah tree, and she embodies all the possibilities of water here on earth. The Princess of Cups corresponds to the Libra-Scorpio-Sagittarius quadrant of space above Earth, over the Pacific Ocean. This Princess is a force for healing and nurturing. She is highly sensitive, perhaps too much so, but no other court card can match her compassion and innocence.

THE SONG

A Perfect Circle's "Breña" models all this Princess's attributes: opening, receptivity, vulnerability, healing, hope, and a reflective surface. The lyrics are short and simple, but their simplicity perfectly conveys the sweetness and power of this court member's demeanor, her ability to heal even the worst emotional wounds, her kindness and care. She may at times be cloying and suffocating in lavishing attention on others, but it's hard to stay mad at her for long—she means so well.

"Breña" also hints at the sexual comfort of falling into this Princess's embrace. The sex implied here is not "dirty," but rather the sweet refilling of one's emotional cup. To enter this Princess's temple is to be in the presence of the healing, cleansing, compassionate Divine.

TABULA MUNDI TAROT

She appears to float above the Ace of Cups, holding a lotus blossom above her head, from which water cascades down her body, becoming her dress. A full moon rises in the background and a swan flies overhead.

THOTH TAROT

The Princess dances on the water's edge, her dress hem whirling into scalloped waves, holding a chalice containing a tortoise. She is flanked by a dolphin and a lotus blossom, symbols of intuition and water, and crowned by a swan.

READING THIS CARD

When the Princess of Cups appears in a reading, there is the suggestion of an event that occurs in autumn (Libra through Sagittarius), or a person whose personality is similar to the description of the Princess of Cups. It can represent a part of the querent's personality, or how he or she is feeling or acting in the role at question in the reading. The Princess of Cups can also indicate a situation in which dedicated compassion yields healing and change.

CHAPTER 48

2 OF CUPS: "THE HUMBLING RIVER," PUSCIFER

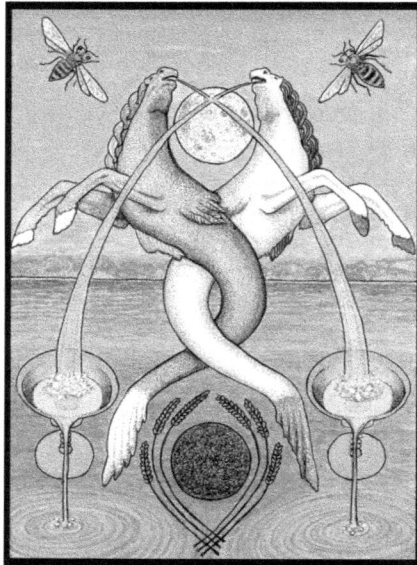

Thoth Title: Love
Traditional Title: Lord of Love
Planet/Sign: Venus in Cancer
Planetary Ruler/Exaltation: Moon rules, Jupiter exalted
Date Range: June 21 – July 1
Qabalistic Correspondences: Chokmah of Briah
Key Words: affection, harmony, love, romance, pleasure

"The Humbling River"
Puscifer
C Is for (Please Insert Sophomoric Genitalia Reference Here), 2009

Atu Line

T
he beautiful 2 of Cups, Lord of Love, represents the first decan of Cancer (sign of nurturing, protection, honor, duty; ruled by the Moon), which is ruled by Venus (planet of beauty, fertility, love, abundance, the maternal). The influence of the loving mother Venus, the caring sign of Cancer, and the wisdom of the second sephira Chokmah creates a truly positive card that is all about the tenderness of true connection with another. Though this card is not purely about romantic love,[1] it does often indicate it.

Of note, the 2 of Cups is the small card correspondent to Keenan's estimated natal Moon and North Node in Cancer. The Moon in natal charts represents the emotional and physical self and one's self-care, and the North Node location represents the characteristics a person is working to develop in this life.

THE SONG

Puscifer's "The Humbling River" has come to be Keenan's signature song on tours and documentaries in the teens, perhaps indicating the importance of this song's philosophy to his outlook. The lyrics speak of having conquered all the elements (the quakes of earth, the wind of air, and fires), but the inability to conquer the river of water. The way of water is surrender, vulnerability, emotional connection, and presence. Water cannot be forced into submission, as it will simply go around an obstacle. We must come together and dissolve into the unity of One in order to finally master this element. It requires a radical shift in our values, toward unity.

Adversity and conflict will never solve themselves—not even the most destructive weapons nor any amount of money are enough to get humanity past this barrier to peace and bliss. This is the realization that not all things can be accomplished by the ego alone. In short, the lesson of Water is to be vulnerable, to surrender, and go under. By being one with our emotions, we conquer them.

One might challenge this match on the grounds that the track is not romantic in the usual sense. This was admittedly a difficult card to match—Keenan is not known for crooning love songs of any kind, after all. My rebuttal is simply this: although it is true that 2 of Cups is usually associated with romantic love, all affection springs from the One Love, what Christians call Agape, and "The Humbling River" is above all else a love song of surrender to the power of loving unity.

TABULA MUNDI TAROT

A pair of hippocampi are entwined fountains emptying into two golden cups below, which overflow into calm, crystalline waters beneath. Bees and wheat stalks represent Venus and fertility, while the full and new moons refer to Cancer.

THOTH TAROT

A lotus pours water into two golden cups, which are full to overflowing, draining into clear waters below. A pair of dolphins entwined about the lotus stem represents the mated pair. Crowley remarked that the card should be renamed Lord of Love under Will, due to harmony of masculine and feminine the card represents.

READING THIS CARD

There aren't many cards in the deck that are wholly good or evil, but this is one of them. It's hard to find a downside to the 2 of Cups— how can you say anything negative about Love? When this card appears, love, joy, harmony, and affection are on the horizon. It can be any kind of genuine, loving connection, but most often it's romantic in nature. Enjoy this gift, and do not take it for granted or abuse its tenderness, but protect and invest in it so that you may enjoy each other for as long as it's meant to last. One final thought: our ability to truly experience love is in direct proportion to our tolerance for vulnerability.

CHAPTER 49

3 OF CUPS: "INDIGO CHILDREN," PUSCIFER

Thoth Title: Abundance
Planet/Sign: Mercury in Cancer
Planetary Ruler/Exaltation: Moon rules, Jupiter exalted
Date Range: July 2 – 11
Qabalistic Correspondences: Binah of Briah
Key Words: celebration, fun, joy, friendship, the Three Graces

"Indigo Children"
Puscifer
V Is for Vagina, 2007

Atu Line

The 3 of Cups is Mercury (planet of communication, commerce, speed, knowledge) in Cancer (sign of hearth and home, nurturance, loyalty, protection; ruled by the Moon) in the third sephira of Binah. This card is known as Abundance, and it's a lovely celebratory card, one of kinship, fellowship, friendship, and frivolity. The card represents the good things in life, and can also indicate mother, father, and child or the possibility of pregnancy resulting from the festivities. Most 3 of Cups cards depict three people enjoying dance, drink, love, and fun; the card is a welcome sight in any reading. It is the Binah of the water Tree, where loving kindness takes form as relationships between beings.

THE SONG

Puscifer's "Indigo Children" is primarily based on the fact that electromagnetic pulses from the Sun, in the form of electrostatic charges from solar magnetic flares, can interfere with and even destroy electronic networks on earth if they are strong enough. Auroras are examples of the mild impact solar magnetic flares have on earth, but when flares are larger, they can cause such damage as rolling blackouts.

The song posits that, should a particularly strong electromagnetic pulse reach the earth, humanity could be plunged back into an age that predates electronic technology, triggering humans to evolve in new ways for survival. Perhaps an event like this could be a catalyst for humans to evolve to have 48 chromosomes rather than the 46 we currently have (looking at you, "46 & Two"), as per esotericist Drunvalo Melchizadek. Humans of the next evolutionary stage are commonly referred to as Indigo Children in New Age and esoteric circles.

This track celebrates and welcomes that scenario of destruction and regression, that humans might through necessity recover both their humanity and divinity, return to the original human social configuration of groups of families in tribes, and remember how to live in harmony with nature. Keenan mentions telling time and calendaring by the stars and planets, and also invokes Sirius, Venus, and the Moon—celestial bodies that have all been attached to the Sumerian/Babylonian Queen of Heaven, Inanna/Ishtar, the goddess of love and sex, who has come to be known as Babalon.[1] Gone are the days of modern human colonialism, technology worship, social isolation, the rat race, consumerism, and all the attendant trappings; instead we have the natural pleasures of love, music, dance, and wine.

In the 3 of Cups description of *The Book of Thoth*, Crowley writes, "the good things of life, although enjoyed, should be distrusted."[2] In the case of this track, Keenan could perhaps be signaling that he recognizes that technology does wonderful things for us, and should be used as tools, but we should not blindly trust or become dependent on it; instead, we should celebrate and focus on the wonders of being human—our capacity to love, to experience joy, to intuit, and enjoy the pleasures of our physical existence—a common theme throughout his song writing.

TABULA MUNDI TAROT

Three chalices stand beneath the lunar phases, and hands issue from each cup: one holding a pomegranate, one holding a golden apple, and the other stalks of wheat—all symbols of feminine beauty and fertility. Between them a lotus blooms on the black sea.

THOTH TAROT

Three pomegranate chalices are filled by lotus blossoms pouring clear water. The chalices fill and overflow into the deep blue sea below.

READING THIS CARD

When the 3 of Cups turns up, good times follow. Vacations, nights out, parties, bonfires, dances, and other celebratory occasions are often indicated by this card. Friend groups can be indicated by this card, as can promotions and other things we celebrate. The card can also indicate pregnancy, as the two cups in the Love card (2 of Cups) become three—that's certainly one kind of abundance!

When this card is ill-dignified, in can represent such emotional betrayals as infidelity, mind-game manipulation, having fun at someone else's expense.

CHAPTER 50

4 OF CUPS: "STINKFIST," TOOL

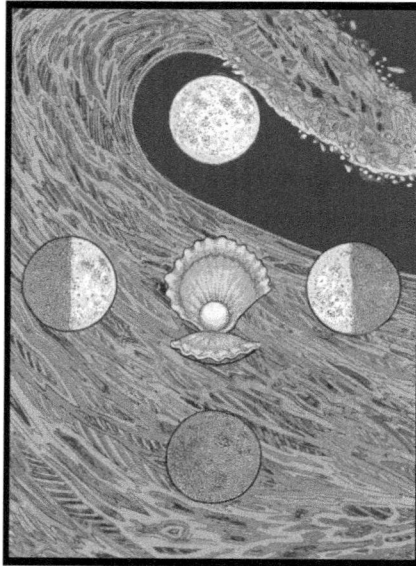

Thoth Title: Luxury
Planet/Sign: Moon in Cancer
Planetary Ruler/Exaltation: Moon rules, Jupiter exalted
Date Range: July 12 - 21
Qabalistic Correspondences: Chesed of Briah
Key Words: over-indulgence, fullness, excess, plenty, boredom

"Stinkfist"
Tool
Ænima, 1996

Atu Line

The 4 of Cups—Moon (planet of mysteries, cycles, the psychic, the dark) in Cancer (sign of hearth and home, nurturance, loyalty, protection; ruled by the Moon) in the fourth sephira of Chesed—is titled Luxury, and it is a card that drips with excess. Here we have the moony-est, most feminine small card —Moon in a Moon-ruled sign in the sephira of indulgent Jupiter's rule—and it's all about bigger, better, faster, more.

If the 3 of Cups is good, then more of a good thing should be even better, right? Not so much. There comes a point when we experience too much of the good things. Too much food, too much drink, too much sex, too much comfort. After a while, we can't even feel the good anymore. Luxury can turn into a sense of entitlement, boredom, numbness, and taking all resources for granted. The 4 of Cups is just that—it's the "spoiled rich kid" card.

THE SONG

"Stinkfist" is the sonic match for this card because it describes the same phenomenon of over-stimulation and numbing of sensation.

In this case, the analogy is sexual: the lyrics describe progressive anal penetration, from finger to fist to arm. Everyone knows what it feels like when sexual pleasure becomes too much; it overwhelms our pleasure centers and becomes painful. If we don't stop, our pleasure centers become numb and all sexual sensation is lost. This is also true in everyday life when any stimulus is overused, whether that is television, advertising, sex, food, money, or drugs. Constant exposure deadens our ability to detect subtlety and nuance, and thus, pleasure is lost. Ultimately, "Stinkfist" asks listeners, "how much, how deeply must you take it in to feel alive?"

This match is particularly thought-provoking in light of Tool's newest tradition of banning cell phones from being used during their shows, much to the chagrin of many fans. At the end of each night's set, the band reluctantly relaxes the cell phone restriction for their final song, which for a long stretch was invariably "Stinkfist." Before launching into the song, Keenan regularly chides the audience for their obsession with, dependence on, and self-referential greediness regarding these handheld devices. Chiding notwithstanding and barely escaped from his lips, the venue is immediately bathed in the cool glow of thousands and thousands of illuminated cellphone screens, upheld by audience members eagerly intent on getting their just deserts by recording the finale. It's their reward for exercising discipline for a couple of hours.

As the tour rolls on, social media spaces are flooded with shitty cell phone recordings of "Stinkfist," without even a hint of irony. It's at once amusing and sad that audiences consistently fail to consider how cell phones and social media have collectively numbed us from experiencing life in the moment, made us into greedy and stupid audiences, turned us into spoiled children who can only think about the toy they cannot play with right this minute, and essentially sent us to live inside the 4 of Cups. Ah, Luxury!

TABULA MUNDI TAROT

In one of the most compelling illustrations of the deck, four phases of the moon surround an oyster containing a perfect pearl. Behind the arrangement is the window of a pipe wave, through which the full moon is visible, while the new moon appears in the depths of the ocean.

THOTH TAROT

A crescent moon crowns the lotus flower that fills four chalices with perfect water. The top cups overflow, but the bottom cups are collecting everything that falls, denying the supply to the shallow waters below.

READING THIS CARD

When this card appears in a reading, we are being urged to back down on the intake and to practice a little austerity, so we can better appreciate luxury when it does come our way. Hangovers, tummy aches, and temper tantrums are often heralded by the 4 of Cups. When it's particularly well-dignified, this card can represent an instance of pampering and indulgence or a restorative experience of some kind, or perhaps may make a reference to a woman's reproductive system, due to the heavy Moon influence on the card.

CHAPTER 51

5 OF CUPS: "MOMMA SED," PUSCIFER

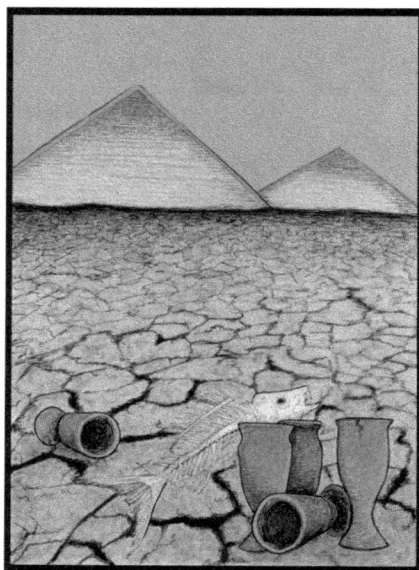

Thoth Title: Disappointment
Traditional Title: Lord of Loss in Pleasure
Planet/Sign: Mars in Scorpio
Planetary Ruler: Mars
Date Range: October 23 – November 1
Qabalistic Correspondences: Geburah of Briah
Key Words: heartbreak, loss, glass half empty, not all is lost

"Momma Sed" (Alive @ Club Nokia)
Puscifer
C Is for (Please Insert Sophomoric Genitalia Reference Here), 2009

Atu Line

The 5 of Cups—Mars (planet of aggression, war, masculinity, dominance) in Scorpio (sign of secrets, taboos, sex, death) in the sephira of war Geburah—is called Disappointment, which may actually be an understatement for the suffering this card often brings. Here, Mars rules the first decan of Scorpio, Mars rules Scorpio, and Mars rules Geburah, the realm of the fives. As He is the war-bringer, this is altogether too much Mars for one poor Cups card.

The 5 of Cups is about loss, particularly the kind that involves losing something precious to you. As Fortune's Wheelhouse podcast hosts Susie Chang and Mel Meleen discuss in their "Five of Cups" episode,[1] this card takes away something precious—something you were not ready to lose—and forces you to come to terms with letting go.

As mentioned earlier, the fours in tarot are stability, like the legs of a table, but the addition of a fifth always upsets the cart. The fives destabilize the structure and comfort we once knew. As the tarot has already taught us, changes come; nothing lasts forever.

THE SONG

Puscifer's "Momma Sed" is quite fitting for 5 of Cups. The images of storms and thunder particularly fit the influence of Mars on the crisis of loss, as does Keenan's use of martial and masculine words and phrases (son, pride, suck it up, take it like a man), graphic sexual euphemisms about life using and abusing us, and the comparison of heartbreak to the typically male ailment of kidney stones. The word choices deliberately cast a masculine pall on heartbreak—an emotional experience that is usually likened to the feminine— portraying grief as the relentless, domineering, and cruel lover it is.

Incidentally, Lon Milo DuQuette compares Mars in this card to an aggressive male in a relationship, noting that Mars is "blowing a fiery blast upon the relationship"[2] with His consort in this card, Scorpio. Mars' blast destroys what would've been the slow burn of their passion, and that also fits with the metaphor of life as a rapist.

Beyond the original, the Alive @ Club Nokia version of this track, with its slowed tempo and ethereal sound, does an astounding job of getting at the grief and heartbreak of this card and the depth of suffering it represents. It's a challenging card, and at the same time, this version of the song also encourages the gentle 'chin-up' attitude the card calls for, even if that chin is soaked in tears.

TABULA MUNDI

The lake we first saw in the Death card has completely dried up. In the foreground on the cracked earth, we see the remains of the fish we saw in Death and five wine chalices, two of which are overturned and empty. In the background at some distance stand two pyramids against a red sky.

THOTH TAROT

Five cups are arranged in a reverse pentagram formation, signaling the triumph of matter over spirit. The lotus blossoms that once poured pure, clean water into the cups have completely dried up, their roots a tangled and knotted mass. The body of water below has turned brackish and stagnant, and the sky above is orange.

READING THIS CARD

When the 5 of Cups comes up in a reading, I often tell the sitter to expect a half-empty glass scenario, in that they won't get everything —or possibly anything—they hoped for. But they will gain something from it, even if it's strength of character or perspective, so they could choose to see the glass as half-full if they desire. After all, we learn more from loss than gain, and without disappointment, it's all "Stinkfist" (4 of Cups, Luxury), all the time. Regardless, this too will eventually pass, because changes inevitably come.

CHAPTER 52

6 OF CUPS: "THIRD EYE," TOOL

Thoth Title: Pleasure
Planet/Sign: Sun in Scorpio
Planetary Ruler: Mars
Date Range: November 2 - 12
Qabalistic Correspondences: Tiphareth of Briah
Key Words: indulgence, emotional fulfillment, desire fulfilled, comfort, gratification

"Third Eye"
Tool
Ænima, 1996

Atu Line

The 6 of Cups, Sun (planet of freedom, innocence, life, growth) in Scorpio (sign of secrets, taboos, sex, death, money; ruled by Mars), is aptly named Pleasure. This is emotionally fulfilling, wonderful, cozy goodness—there's the innocence and positivity of the Sun, but also the emotional depth and darkness of Scorpio, the fixed water (feminine) sign. Scorpio's motto is "I DESIRE," and this card it a perfect expression of that. Who doesn't desire feeling good?

Furthermore, sixes reside in Tiphareth (which means this card has a double solar influence), and are the number of the Christ Consciousness, the heart center, the seat of the Buddha. So again, we see a six small card demonstrating the balance between the masculine and feminine, this time in the realm of emotions and the heart. Traditionally, 6 of Cups speaks to pleasant memories from the past, as well as pleasant memory making.

THE SONG

The final track on Tool's *Ænima*, "Third Eye," hits on those themes of childhood's innocent, intuitive universal connection lost and found again, plus a bonus of reveling in the shadow, the unknown, and the higher self via an eye-opening hallucinogenic "trip" that takes us to new places and shows us the wonders of the universe. "Buy the ticket, take the ride," as Hunter S. Thompson so famously wrote in *Fear and Loathing in Las Vegas*.

The entirety of this track's celebratory outlook on shadow and intuition integration are summed up by embedded clips of Bill Hicks' standup comedy during the opening interlude. "Third Eye" opens with Hicks' bit about the influence drugs have had on art, particularly music. He invites audience members who don't believe that mind-altering substances have positive impacts on the human experience to promptly divorce themselves from music, which has been so often enhanced by the effects of chemical technology.

Seconds later, a second Hicks bit materializes in the opening drum cadence, describing a young man's realization of the truly awe-inspiring nature of matter, energy, and consciousness as facilitated by the hallucinogen LSD, commonly known as acid. This is quickly followed by a third clip in which our friend Bill calmly reminds us that the government's so-called War on Drugs is nothing less than a long-term battle to restrict freewill, hamper personal freedom, and control the perceptions of the masses.

Today's theoretical and experimental sciences are beginning to reveal how much Hicks' observations are true: not only is the universe an astonishing arrangement of energy, matter, and consciousness, but using chemical technology to alter our consciousness allows us to "play" in the psychic stew we're swimming in. Through the intentional use of mind-altering substances, we can permanently alter our perceptions of reality, reveal depression and anxiety for the mind tricks they are, explode myths of separateness, and release the life-strangling grip of dogma, logic, and reason— impacts which last long after the trip has ended.

Keenan's accompanying lyrics describe one such trip and the realizations gained from leaving waking assumptions behind to explore the dream of human experience, untethered to so-called "reality." The awakening of psychic perception, often referred to in new age and occult circles as "the third eye opening," is the result of this fantastic odyssey of the mind, and at once the narrator's understanding of the world around him is completely exploded and forever changed. Heart and mind opened, the narrator rejoices in the momentary complete integration of light and dark, conscious and subconscious, magickal and mundane—the feeling of complete wholeness last experienced in the exploratory stage of childhood.

TABULA MUNDI TAROT

High above a lake, an eagle soars, framed by a twelve-pointed star (references the 12 astrological signs and therefore is a solar symbol) and the sun. Beneath, a downward pointing pyramidal arrangement of 6 cups appears. The liquid in the cups ripples, creating eye-like patterns on their surfaces.

THOTH TAROT

Six shining, golden cups are generously fed by six lotus blossoms under a pristine sky and above crystalline waters. Each cup contains a nascent serpent, symbolic of Scorpio and the beginnings of life.

READING THIS CARD

The 6 of Cups is the well of consciousness, creation, and connection— it's the realization that the universe is infinite and made of energy we commonly call love, and that we are all connected to it at all times.

When this card appears in a reading, pleasurable circumstances are at hand, whether via reverie or direct experience. The 6 of Cups is a reminder to tap into the perceptions of your intuition and truly remember that we are all one in a boundless ocean of love, for when are we more connected than when wrapped in the blissful arms of pleasure?

If this card is ill-dignified, it can represent the misuse or abuse of plant medicines or substances, or continuously pursuing the pleasures of inebriation. In situations unrelated to psychic journeying, an ill-dignified 6 of Cups can indicate romanticizing or living in the past, emotional selfishness, or being fooled in love.

CHAPTER 53

7 OF CUPS:
"UNDERTOW," TOOL

Thoth Title: Debauch
Planet/Sign: Venus in Scorpio
Planetary Ruler: Mars
Date Range: November 13 - 22
Qabalistic Correspondences: Netzach of Briah
Key Words: inebriation, illusions, embarrassment, shame, trauma

"Undertow"
Tool
Undertow, 1993

Atu Line

And now the blissed-out comfort of the last card, the 6 of Cups, has terrifyingly morphed into the addicted debauchery of the 7, because nothing can stay the same forever. Everything changes. The 7 of Cups, Venus in Scorpio, is called Debauch. In this card, Venus (planet of feminine beauty, fertility, and voluptuousness) is comfort, and Scorpio (sign of secrets, taboos, sex, death, money; ruled by Mars) is the darkness. They come together in Venus' home turf of Netzach, and this is where we learn that when we take comfort in the dark, sometimes things can get out of hand. The double-Venus influence, when combined with the powder keg of Mars-fueled Scorpio, is a recipe for feminine desecration and violation, bad trips, and things that started out as a little harmless fun that suddenly took a turn for the nightmarish.

The 7 of Cups' other major manifestation is self-deceit. This card is often nicknamed The Seven of Illusions; many decks' illustrations include seven chalices filled with symbols that represent each of the Seven Deadly Sins (or Seven Virtues if you tilt your head and shift your gaze just so). It's the card of believing that you have more options, more control, more runway, than you actually do, and it's frequently associated with addiction, as is Tool's "Undertow."

THE SONG

"Undertow," Tool's magnum opus on addiction, describes the risks one takes each time we use a substance to attain an alternate state of being. If it feels too good, it can become hard to resist, and if we do it too much, we lose our ability to reason, to think clearly, to feel, and to truly engage with the world around us. Once we're caught in the undertow of inebriation, of wanting to always feel numb and sated, of being willing to abdicate our self-control to the substance, that undertow can drag us down into the Abyss, the Shadow, and literally kill us.

Further, the specter of death that hangs over addiction brings so much more than just the risk of ending life. With it also comes shame and guilt and suffering of a magnitude that can scarcely be put into words. Running away from the pain only seems to drive us deeper into the arms of the very force that put us here, carrying us one step closer to the maws of the Reaper.

In this way, the black death of addiction to numbness follows not just the drug fiend, but also the war-scarred soldier, the raped woman, the abused child, and every other human who has stared deeply into the Abyss and been driven to the edge of madness and self-loathing. If we spend too long inside the horror of trauma, if we don't fight to surface, we may lose ourselves in the deep, gaping hole that the 7 of Cups represents.

TABULA MUNDI TAROT

A scattered formation of seven chalices appears in the night, their stems made of twisting green serpents. Much of the lake below the twin crescent moons has dried up and the water is stagnating.

Bubbles rising from the chalices contain nascent serpents, symbolic of Scorpio, new life, and the underside of the psyche.

THOTH TAROT

This card is the picture of putrefaction. Wilting lotus blossoms drip fetid, slimy fluid into seven waiting chalices. The cups are over-flowing with the repulsive stuff, which falls into the stagnant water below in glowing green glops. Shades of green completely dominate the sky, water, and cup formation in this darkly organic card.

READING THIS CARD

When this card appears in a reading, the querent is potentially in a dangerous place and the reading could very well take a serious turn. The dark indulgences represented by the 7 of Cups may seem like risqué, but hardly life-threatening, larks. Regardless of whether it's a substance, sex, gambling, staying in a toxic relationship, or other indulgence that easily aligns with addiction, eventually all dysfunction spirals down into nonfunction absent intervention. This card usually indicates sexual or patriarchal trauma that has not yet been dealt with or healed, and its shadow is at the root of the dysfunctional behavior and a destructive force in the querent's life. Honesty with one's self is of the utmost importance at this time.

When the 7 of Cups comes up in a reading, it is important for the reader to encourage the querent to get the help they need from a trusted therapist, substance abuse counselor, or other trained professional. If, in a moment of sobriety and clarity, the querent can see the pattern for what it is, they can intervene in the cycle—an action we see clearly in the next card, the 8 of Cups.

CHAPTER 54

8 OF CUPS: "POTIONS," PUSCIFER

Thoth Title: Indolence
Traditional Title: Lord of Abandoned Success
Planet/Sign: Saturn in Pisces
Planetary Ruler/Exaltation: Neptune (modern)/Jupiter (classical)
rules, Venus exalted
Date Range: February 19 – 29
Qabalistic Correspondences: Hod of Briah
Key Words: abandonment, walking away, cutting ties, giving up,
leaving sorrows behind

"Potions"
Puscifer
C Is for (Please Insert Sophomoric Genitalia Reference Here), 2009

Atu Line

T he 8 of Cups, Saturn (planet of lessons, limitations, discipline, time) in Pisces (sign of intuition, connection, sensitivity; ruled by Neptune) in Mercury's sephira Hod, is the card of walking away, particularly when walking away is difficult or contrary to what is prudent.[1] The combination of Saturn and Pisces here yields the deep melancholy of understanding tinged with grief; this is a card of acknowledging the truth of the matter and cutting one's losses.

The meaning of this card is made abundantly clear when juxtaposed with its foil, the 6 of Swords. While the 6 of Swords is about reaching for your full potential by moving in the direction of your calling and what you want, the 8 of Cups represents the difficult feat of leaving behind what hurts you and holds you back, or perhaps less nobly, simply giving up and walking away.

THE SONG

Puscifer's cover of Tapeworm's "Potions" is a great track to illustrate the 8 of Cups' journey away from the unwanted. This card heralds a long and difficult walk, one that we'd gladly numb any way we could —and song's the image of potions of forgetfulness filling all manner of vessels is too perfect a reference to the suit of Cups to pass up.

The traditional Hermetic title of this card is Success Unfulfilled or Abandoned Success, which may sound like if one had simply stayed and kept working, success would've come. My experience has been that's not necessarily true. Instead, the situation is one that has not achieved success...there is no "yet" stated or implied. This card often gets a bad reputation as the card that symbolizes abandonment or "bailing."

However, I return your attention to the card's basic interpretation: leaving behind an emotional (the card is a Cup, after all) situation. Whenever emotions are involved—whether that emotion is love, anger, fear, or sadness—there is attachment. Leaving something behind that you're attached to requires enormous strength, and continuing strength to keep putting one foot in front of the other to keep carrying you further away from the situation or person.

The "Potions"/8 of Cups journey can describe getting over the heartbreak of the loss of a lover, overcoming the fear of leaving an abusive situation of any kind, the resignation of walking away from a fight when you know you're in the right, the self-love required to sever ties to a toxic friend or relative, or the grief of cutting losses on something you've worked long and hard on. In every case, leaving is difficult, but there is a reason why you must, for your or others' sake.

TABULA MUNDI TAROT

The remains of the ship that appears in The Moon card are now a shipwreck deteriorating on the shore of some unknown land under a moonless night. Eight skeletal shells that were once coiled drinking horns float in formation above the lonely scene; no life is evident in the card.

THOTH TAROT

Eight cracked and chipped cups stand in formation above a dark sea on a moonless night. Five of the cups are matched with lotus blossoms, but only two blossoms are able to pour even sickly trickles of water into their cups, which eventually received enough to overflow and fill two more below. The other half of the cups are empty.

READING THIS CARD

When 8 of Cups appears in a reading, the querent is being asked to truly examine the possibility of leaving something behind, and to be brutally honest about the motivations for doing so. Are you running away from difficulty, responsibility, or duty? Or are you doing what is best for yourself, others, or the situation in the long-term? There is no inherent judgement in the card either way—the point is to get clear on motivations for leaving or staying—but the card's presence indicates the possibility of leaving is certainly on the table.

Whether the card is well- or ill-dignified gives great insight as to whether the querent is running away from something they need to face—in which case they are destined to continue being haunted by this issue—or if they are truly doing what needs to be done in walking away, putting an end to the suffering once and for all.

CHAPTER 55

9 OF CUPS: "DEAR BROTHER," PUSCIFER

Thoth Title: Happiness
Planet/Sign: Jupiter in Pisces
Planetary Ruler/Exaltation: Neptune (modern)/Jupiter (classical)
rules, Venus exalted
Date Range: March 1 - 10
Qabalistic Correspondences: Yesod of Briah
Key Words: contentment, all is well, emotional and material
comforts, joy

"Dear Brother"
Puscifer
Donkey Punch the Night, 2013

Atu Line

The 9 of Cups' title is Happiness, and it is truly one of the most joyful cards in the pack—a welcome sight after the sorrows and trials of several of the preceding Cups cards. The 9 of Cups represents the height of water's power, thanks to Jupiter (planet of gifts, abundance, expansion, growth) in Pisces (sign of intuition, sensitivity, receptivity; ruled by Neptune) nestled together in dreamy, Moon-ruled Yesod. This is the contented sigh of emotional fulfillment, long-held wishes granted, the blissful family, the satiated heart.

THE SONG

Anyone who is a fan of Keenan's work will be unsurprised that the 9 of Cups, Happiness, was without exaggeration the most difficult card in the deck to match. Keenan is far too much the realist to speak of happiness without its twin of grief. And while the nines of the tarot represent the suit's energy at peak fullness, the implied point about peaks is that they precede valleys. The 9 of Cups, influenced by Jupiter in Pisces, is no different. For while the card is about emotional fulfillment and joy at their fantastic best, we should know by now that nothing lasts forever, and this, too, shall pass.

"Dear Brother," Puscifer's ode to a fallen brother, may seem like a backwards selection to represent supreme happiness at first blush, it does describe a time of intense enjoyment and pleasure, even if it is succeeded by utter loss and despair. Such is life. Crowley writes about this card in *The Book of Thoth*, "Jupiter in Pisces is good fortune, but only in the sense of complete satiety... [there is] no such thing as absolute rest."[1]

Indeed, Keenan here describes times of fantastic excess and fortune's favor, both ideas squarely in the purview of the greater benefic, Jupiter. Who else could bestow the good luck of close calls and the expansiveness of never-ending parties? And what other sign could be more down for an intense emotional ride than the dreamy, intuitive ocean of Pisces, whose fishes are content to endlessly swim without concern for direction or order? Jupiter and Pisces have no concept of "when to say when" by themselves, let alone together.

TABULA MUNDI TAROT

A lively formation of seven bowls, each filled with pure water and a koi fish, forms a fountain of happiness. The fish stream water from bowl to bowl, leaping, playing, and filling two spiral drinking horns below. The three gunas of the Fortune card, the lemur, owl, and serpentine hand of Typhon, also play in and partake of the abundant waters.

THOTH TAROT

A formation of nine large, golden chalices fills the entire frame of the card. Nine lotus blooms hang above the chalices, each filling their cup below. Water, as liquid gold, streams from all of the cups, and the cups overflow with joy. The placid water below reflects the golden light of bliss.

READING THIS CARD

So, when the 9 of Cups comes your way, the message is *yes, this happiness is the real deal, and you better enjoy it to its absolute fullest while it's here.* This card should cause a leap of the heart and a re-kindling of the spirit when it's pulled, because joy is here or else is quickly on its way. Watch for opportunities to embrace the pleasures you've always wished for. If asking about the likely outcome of a particular course of action, seeing this card is an indicator that things will go marvelously according to plan. Go forth and enjoy the fruits of your labor!

This is a card that is difficult to dampen, even with ill-dignifying cards around. At worst, an ill-dignified 9 of Cups can indicate a missed opportunity for happiness, self-sabotage, or perhaps failing to recognize happiness right in front of you.

CHAPTER 56
10 OF CUPS: "SOBER," TOOL

Thoth Title: Satiety
Planet/Sign: Mars in Pisces
Planetary Ruler/Exaltation: Neptune (modern)/Jupiter (classical)
rules, Venus exalted
Date Range: March 11 - 20
Qabalistic Correspondences: Malkuth of Briah
Key Words: saturation, fullness, emotional situation reaches conclu-
sion, over-ripeness

"Sober"
Tool
Undertow, 1993

Atu Line

———————————————————————

The 10 of Cups, Mars (planet of aggression, dominance, war, masculinity) in Pisces (sign of receptivity, sensitivity, intuition; ruled by Neptune) in earthly Malkuth, is the last card of the emotional suit of Cups, and it signals the culmination point of water's energy. Tens in the minor suits are often described as the fruit on the vine that has gone past the point of ripe; it is over-ripe, sickly-sweet, and on the verge of rotting. At this stage, the juices turn to alcohol: an apt symbol for 10 of Cups.

The title of the card is Satiety, the state of being satiated, and although many people interpret this as being satisfied, that's really spinning it a little too positively. In this delicate state, there is altogether too much emotion; one drop more and there will be spillage of some kind! What was ecstasy in the 9 has now become drunkenness—an excess of pleasure. And anyone who has been drunk before knows there is a very, very fine line between the pleasure and misery of drunkenness.

THE SONG

Tool's 1993 breakout single "Sober" is the track for this card, because the lyrics are, in effect, arguing for abandoning sobriety, wishing for the oblivion of drunkenness. The double-negative famously tends to throw listeners off, but the line "Why can't we not be sober" can be restated as *why can't we be drunk?* There are other layers of metamorphosis in this song that could be explored, but wishing for drunkenness is the surface aim of the narrator in this song, and the reason for the match in this case.

The self-loathing and bitterness of this track are also appropriate sentiments for the 10 of Cups. When a night of drinking has gone south, one loathes themselves for getting into this state, and is bitter toward the substance, too. We often set out to drink in the first place to escape something we don't want to feel or think about—pain or perhaps loneliness—which is just another face of self-hatred and regret.

It would be easy to call this an addiction card, but I interpret the 10 of Cups as the temporary (literal or figurative) state of being drunk. If this state of oblivious numbness is achieved too often,[1] that is of course a problem, but the act of getting drunk alone does not an addict make. More often than not, it's just a need for escape from reality, and the same is true in the card.

TABULA MUNDI TAROT

Ten opium poppy pod-shaped cups in an unstable pyramidal formation overflow with the water of oblivion that resembles opium milk, which streams down their bulbous shapes to a puddle below. Below, a body of water exhibits wave patterns that resemble brain waves during sleep. Above, perched on the uppermost level of a ten-level pyramid, is the gryphon from The Tower card holding a poppy pod from The Moon card in its beak. The sky is martial red.

THOTH TAROT

An angry red and orange background visually fights with the rest of the cards from this suit of water. Ten golden chalices arranged in a Tree of Life formation forcefully spray streams of water between them. Water falls in transparent sheets, but somehow does not collect below. Despite being a card in the water suit, the influence of fire is keenly felt here.

READING THIS CARD

When the 10 of Cups comes up in a reading, there is some emotional situation or issue that has run its course, and it's time to let it go. Holding onto the pain, wallowing in it like drink after drink, will only further your misery and regret. It's time to sober up and move on emotionally. Usually when this card appears in a reading, the querent already knows exactly what they're wallowing in but just hasn't found the strength to deal with it. The reader is in a unique position to encourage the sitter to stop beating the dead horse and to move on with their life, and the surrounding cards will provide indication of the querent's current ability and likelihood to do so.

CHAPTER 57
ACE OF SWORDS: "UPGRADE," PUSCIFER

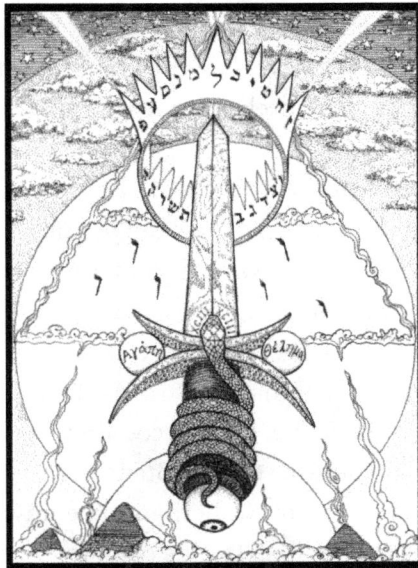

Traditional Title: Root of the Powers of Air
Element: Air
Qabalistic Correspondences: Kether of Yetzirah
Key Words: intelligence, ideas, thought, identity, mental power

"UPGrade"
Puscifer
Existential Reckoning, 2021

Atu Line

S words correspond to the element of air, and the magickal power To Know. They are the third elemental emanation. To Know is the exercise of intelligence to learn the information and wisdom needed to ascend higher, and it's no surprise that Swords are tied to the intellect, ideas, philosophy, skills, and knowledge.

Aces are the seeds of their element. They are not yet manifest in any form we recognize. In them exist the *possibility* of the things we associate with them. Ace of Swords contains the *possibility* of air, intelligence, ideas, wisdom, and consciousness. The conditions are right for air, the seed is there, but we don't see it manifest into anything recognizable until the 2 of Swords. This may sound like the Aces are weak or ineffective, which couldn't be further from the truth. They are the purest, most potent form of their element, straight from the godhead of Kether, and like any great power, the test is in how they are wielded. In this case, the Ace of Swords is the Magus's sword, and also Excalibur, the magickal Sword of King Arthur's Camelot tale.

THE SONG

"UPGrade" from Puscifer's *Existential Reckoning* treats the mind as the organic computer that it is. The lyrics describe updating one's mental operating system to rectify errors in thinking and outlook, and to recover from despair. This is such a great metaphor for the Ace of Swords (a.k.a., the mind), because it affirms that the mind is indeed malleable, and that the Ace of Swords can be wielded both destructively and constructively, depending on the perspective and intention of the wielder.

There are several phrases and words here that also specifically lend strength to this match. The first couplet of the lyrics mentions alleviating the emotion of despair—certainly an apt description of the previous card, the 10 of Cups. Naturally, the Ace of Swords represents slapping a cosmic reset button after the traumatic end of the emotional heart-wringing of the last suit.

What could relieve of us of the angst that developed while living all up in our hearts?

Clear thinking, divorced from emotional attachment.

The Ace of Swords is that clarity of the blade, slicing through and eliminating attachments to that which is unnecessary or unwanted. It's interesting to note the word "choose" figures prominently in the first line; recall The Lovers card is associated with the Hebrew letter *Zain*, which means sword, and deals with making a choice between options.

The lyrics also mention using certain magickal words, incantations, psalms, mantras...all tools of the intellect. Words are among the primary tools of the Magus; words communicate first and foremost, and they are symbolically represented as the airy Sword—the invoked force. Thus, this song also activates the archetype of the Magus, or Mercury, Himself a deity of Air, the element of the Swords suit.

Finally, the track repeatedly muses, *I don't know*, which also reminds us of the magickal power that the Swords correspond with: To Know.

On the whole, this track is such a delightful expression of the Ace, which contains all of the Swords suit within it. This match neatly ties together many of the typical Swords-related issues and topics: ideas, magick, invoked force, communication, conflict, technology, and thinking in general. We will revisit all of these over the course of the next thirteen cards.

TABULA MUNDI TAROT

The Ace of Swords is pointed upward in a forced perspective illustration, the hilt closest to the viewer and the tip pointed heavenward through the opening of a crown with 22 points (symbolic of the 22 Hebrew letters and the major arcana). The crown coincides with the top of the glyph for air, the element associated. The sword is engraved with the Greek words *thelema* (will) and *agape* (love), the two most important concepts in Thelema. The sky, smoke, and starry space feature prominently in this card, as expressions of air in the natural world.

THOTH TAROT

The Ace of Swords appears in the clouds, its tip pointed through a crown. The sword's guard and hilt are made up of the Moon's phases (full, new, and crescents), and the snake of enlightenment twines around the handle. The Greek word *thelema* appears on the blade, due to the Swords representing invoked force; *agape* is presumably engraved on the other side.

READING THIS CARD

When the Ace of Swords appears in a reading, it refers to a source of wisdom. This could be the seed of a new idea, the inspiration for an invention, the first bits of a new philosophy, or skills, facts, ideas, and identities belonging to the querent or a person involved in the situation at hand. The makings are present for any of these, the "sword" just needs to be taken up and used. The Sword is an instrument (and therefore a symbol) of one's mental faculties.

CHAPTER 58

KNIGHT OF SWORDS: "JERK-OFF," TOOL

Traditional Title: King of Swords, Lord of the Winds and Breezes,
King of the Spirits of the Air, King of the Sylphs and Sylphides
Planet/Element/Sign: Fire of Air, first two decans of Gemini (last
decan of Taurus)
Planetary Ruler: Mercury
Date Range: May 11 – June 10
Qabalistic Correspondences: Chokmah of Yetzirah
Key Words: judgmental, intelligent, argumentative, ideological, on
the offense

"Jerk-Off"
Tool
Opiate, 1992

Atu Line

K night of Swords represents the fiery part of air. Air is the
third element, the combination of the fire of the inspired
father element and the practical, formative mother
element of water—yielding the intellectually detached, philosophical element of air. Knights are the highest-ranking court cards, the
father in the royal family of the court cards. Taken together, the
Knight of Swords represents the Father letter of Yod in YHVH, in the
Son element of Air.

The Knight of Swords mainly represents the sign of Gemini,
whose key phrase is "I THINK." It's such a fitting pairing, because if
there is one thing Knights of Swords and Geminis love to do, it's
think. They are constantly turning ideas over in their minds, considering every situation from multiple perspectives, trying on new identities, and picking others' brains.

THE SONG

As the dangerously explosive combination of fire and air, the Knight of Swords represents fierce, deadly attack. Swords are the suit of conflict, battle, and the mind. In Tool's "Jerk-Off," the narrator is that Knight of Swords, the self-proclaimed arbiter of karmic justice. This Knight has determined the cause of the injustice, and is contemplating why he shouldn't solve this problem himself instead of waiting for the Universe to catch on to the atrocities being committed by the jerk-off at hand (sorry for the pun...not really). It is a card of swift retribution and correction.

TABULA MUNDI TAROT

This Knight appears to be charging, his steed leaping upward into the air. He is armed with swords in both hands, his wings are made of sparse individual feathers, and his helmet is winged—all symbols of the air element and of the influence of airy Mercury. The speed with which the Knight is moving makes the clouds appear as streaks across the sky.

THOTH TAROT

The Knight and his steed dive downward from some great height, flying down to attack some target. His armor is green, his wings resemble a propeller made of dragonfly wings, and his golden horse is without reigns—as though this Knight can steer his mount purely with his thoughts. He bears two swords, one for creation and the other for destruction.

READING THIS CARD

Sword court cards are a blend of Wands' force and Cups' form, making them both determined and insightful. Because Swords are the masculine offspring of Wands and Cups, they are cool, detached, analyzing, calculating decision-makers. They are adept at planning and developing ideas and philosophies, making arguments, and organizing and communicating information. They are full of brainy swagger and never shy away from a debate. They eat conflict and competition for breakfast!

As with the other court cards, there is much information packed into the Knight of Swords card. The Knight of Swords' appearance in a reading can indicate a person born between May 11 and June 10, or a person with a similar personality to this Knight. Sometimes this card represents a part of the querent's personality or a role they are currently being called to play. This card can also indicate the timing of an event occurring between May 11 and June 10, or a judgmental or vengeful situation.

CHAPTER 59
QUEEN OF SWORDS: "THE WEAVER," PUSCIFER

Traditional Title: Queen of Swords, Queen of the Thrones of Air, Queen of the Sylphs or Sylphides
Planet/Element/Sign: Water of Air, first two decans Libra (last decan Virgo)
Planetary Ruler/Exaltation: Venus rules, Saturn exalted
Date Range: September 12 – October 12
Qabalistic Correspondences: Binah of Yetzirah
Key Words: discerning, advisor, level-headed, no-nonsense, wise

"The Weaver"
Puscifer
Conditions of My Parole, 2011

Atu Line

Queen of Swords represents the watery part of air. Air is the third element, the combination of the inspired father element of fire and the practical, formative mother element of water—yielding the intellectually detached, principled, and philosophical element of air. Queens are the second highest-ranking court cards, the mother in the royal family of the court cards. Taken together, the Queen of Swords represents the Mother letter of Heh Primal in YHVH, in the Son element of Air.

The Queen of Swords is an intuitive intellectual, frequently an expert in her field of practice. She is associated mostly with the sign of Libra, key phrase "I BALANCE." This Queen is informed, principled, professional, and more than competent to do battle. She fights fiercely and practices compassion toward others—she is a consummate advocate, such as an attorney or social worker. While she may have a kindness at her core, she also suffers no foolishness—her no-

nonsense personality is illustrated by the severed head she is typically shown holding aloft.

THE SONG

Puscifer's "The Weaver" is an apt depiction of this Queen, whose experience and knowledge allow her to see beyond what is immediately observable. Her willingness to be curious and a perpetual learner has yielded an advanced development of intuitive sight and an unshakeable security in her world view. She is intimate with the sorrows of this world, and yet is faithful to the notion that it could be made right, whole, better. As a "mini-Adjustment card," this Queen treats her pursuit of justice with religious fervor and is not afraid to take aggressive steps to course correct. Her actions may come across as rash, but that is only because her intuition has correctly identified what will yet come to pass.

TABULA MUNDI TAROT

Perched upon a throne supported by sword blades high among the clouds, this Queen is the fulcrum of a giant scale that holds two balanced ouroboroses in the shape of lemniscates. In one hand, she holds a downward-pointed sword, symbol of justice brought to the microcosm; in the other, the hair of a severed head.

THOTH TAROT

The Queen is seated on a throne of clouds. Behind her is the pinwheel shape which Harris uses to represent air throughout the suit; in her right (active) hand is a sword held somewhat awkwardly out and downward, representing force applied to earthly things, and in her left hand she grasps the severed head of a bearded man.

READING THIS CARD

Court cards can represent people, time periods, places, attitudes, and themes—the sheer diversity of information included in them can be overwhelming at first. The Queen of Swords' appearance in a reading can suggest a person who is born between September 12 and October 12, or a person whose personality is similar to the description of the Queen of Swords. It can represent a part of the querent's personality, or how he or she is feeling or acting in the situation at hand. The Queen of Swords can also indicate the timing of an event between September 12 and October 12, or a balanced or just situation.

CHAPTER 60

PRINCE OF SWORDS: "VANISHING," A PERFECT CIRCLE

Traditional Title: Knight of Swords, Prince of the Chariot of the Winds, Prince and Emperor of the Sylphs and Sylphides
Planet/Element/Sign: Air of Air, first two decans of Aquarius (last decan of Capricorn)
Planetary Ruler/Exaltation: Saturn rules
Date Range: January 10 – February 8
Qabalistic Correspondences: Tiphareth of Yetzirah
Key Words: visionary, ideologue, rebel, able to argue either side, uncommitted

"Vanishing"
A Perfect Circle
Thirteenth Step, 2003

Atu Line

P rince of Swords is the airy part of air. Princes are the son of the royal family, said to combine the active, inspired properties of the Knight and the stable, wise aspects of the Queen. The Prince of Swords is a double-shot, as he represents the son letter of Vau in YHVH in the son element of Air.

This is a personality that makes up for what it lacks in emotion with intellectualization. His extremely airy nature makes him difficult to pin down—one rarely knows how he really feels or what his true opinions are, because he can argue any side of any case. This Prince is mainly associated with Aquarius, whose key phrase is "I KNOW," and isn't that the truth? The Prince of Swords has a mind that can win any argument, heart, or prize it decides on—his rationale is unperturbable, and his wit and charm are devastatingly attractive, but when confronted with situations that require vulnerability, force, or patience, he's left with little in the way of resources.

THE SONG

A Perfect Circle's "Vanishing" is the perfect demonstration of the Prince of Swords, this airy part of air. What better way to describe this often completely detached personality than with lyrics that invoke the ungraspable element of air? "Vanishing" is pure expression of someone ruled by the air element, indeed. The track speaks to the untethered, detached nature of Aquarians, who are so intellectually driven, living in their own headspace, that they sometimes seem like they aren't truly manifest on this plane of existence. This Prince is unconcerned with physical reality or emotions, and trying to reach him can sometimes feel like trying to grab handfuls of wind. Ideas, thoughts, skills, facts, knowledge—these are the realms of this uber-rational Prince.

TABULA MUNDI TAROT

The sylphide creatures pulling this Prince's chariot are pulled in opposite directions, although he seems not to notice; he seems to be distracted and is looking off to the distance. His wings are insect wings, and his helmet is winged, as well. He is armed with a sword in one hand, and a sickle in the other, symbolic of his ability to both construct and destroy.

THOTH TAROT

This green Knight is doubly armed with sword and sickle, and he appears to be charging into battle, but his chariot is pulled by child-like figures that are heading in different directions, willy-nilly. The image is broken into shards, referencing the conflict that this Prince finds himself at home in, and on the whole, the image evokes sensations of movement and action.

READING THIS CARD

Court cards are some of the most diverse cards in the pack in terms of their possible interpretations—they can represent people, time periods, places, attitudes, and themes. The Prince of Swords' appearance in a reading can suggest a person who is born between January 10 and February 8, or a person whose personality is similar to that of the Prince of Swords. The card can represent a part of the querent's personality, or how he or she is feeling or acting in the role at question in the reading. The Prince of Swords can also indicate the timing of an event between January 10 and February 8, or a detached or emotionally cool situation.

CHAPTER 61

PRINCESS OF SWORDS:
"COLD AND UGLY," TOOL

Traditional Title: Page of Swords, Princess of the Rushing Winds, Lotus of the Palace of Air, Princess and Empress of the Sylphs and Sylphides, Throne of the Ace of Swords
Element/Sign: Earth of Air, rules quadrant of earth under the constellations of Capricorn-Aquarius-Pisces
Qabalistic Correspondences: Malkuth of Yetzirah
Key Words: calculating, detached, fierce, cool, warrior, responsiveness

"Cold & Ugly"
Tool
Opiate, 1992

Atu Line

P rincesses are the daughter in the royal family, and they are the "thrones" or homes of their Aces. They represent the earthy aspects of their suits, so naturally they reside in Malkuth. While the Knights are active, the Queens are practical, and the Princes are intelligent, the Princesses are pure potential; they are the second Heh in YHVH formula. And unlike Knights, Queens, and Princes, who represent slices of time, Princesses represent space and geographic locations.

The Princess of Swords is the earthy part of air, and the throne of the Ace of Swords. This Princess lives in the Malkuth of the Yetzirah tree, so she contains all the potential of air on earth—from wind to breath and everything in between. The Princess of Swords corresponds to the Capricorn-Aquarius-Pisces quadrant of space above Earth, over the Americas. As the Swords represent the intellect, ideas, imagination, intuition, daydreams, science, philosophy, knowledge, skills, and psychosis, they are fast moving and often in conflict. The Princess, being the earthy member of this family, is grounded and steely.

THE SONG

The Princess of Swords has been compared to the Greek goddess Athena, daughter of Zeus and truly her father's daughter. She is agile, whip-smart, and a stunningly effective warrior on the battle-field and in debate. Alas, neither Athena nor this Princess have much use for watery emotions or connection, preferring thought over feel-ing. In fact, those touchy-feely things make her wary and even—just a little—scared. She is not spiritual, but places her "faith" in the trustworthy concreteness of science. M.M. Meleen describes this Princess as a "warrior of the mind" who "battles to liberate herself from delusion."[1]

"Cold & Ugly" from Tool's debut *Opiate* exemplifies the Princess's cold, hard edge and resistance to the messy, emotional parts of life. And in a kind of sad irony, her resistance to any kind of vulnerability makes her somewhat driven by fear. So, although she is fierce and strong, she is by no means perfect.

TABULA MUNDI TAROT

The Princess dances with her sword in perfect balance. Air swirls around her, playing with her hair and clothing, and rising in smoky tendrils in the background. Above her head is the crown that appears on the Ace of Swords card (for which this Princess serves as the throne).

THOTH TAROT

This Princess defends her altar against forces unseen attacking from above. Her wings are the pinwheel shape of the Swords suit in this deck, and her garments are all feminine, save for the soldier's helmet she wears. She wields her sword downward in what appears to be a defensive posture.

READING THIS CARD

Court cards are some of the most diverse cards in the pack in terms of their possible interpretations—they can represent people, time periods, places, attitudes, and themes. The Princess of Swords' appearance in a reading can suggest an event that occurs in winter (Capricorn through Pisces), or a person whose personality is similar to the description of the Princess of Swords. It can represent a part of the querent's personality, or how he or she is feeling or acting in the role at question in the reading. The Princess of Swords can also indicate a situation in which ideological or intellectual power is used to achieve real-world impact.

CHAPTER 62

2 OF SWORDS: "FEAR INOCULUM," TOOL

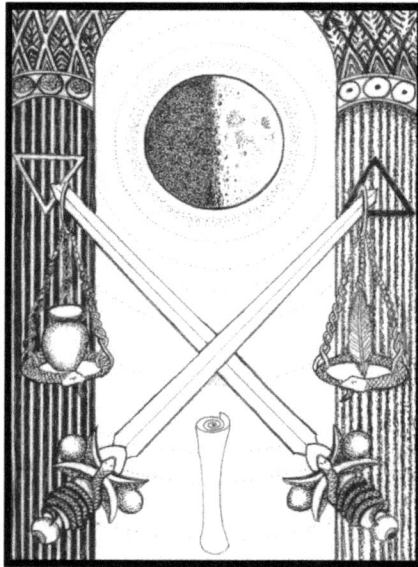

Thoth Title: Peace
Traditional Title: Lord of Peace Restored
Planet/Sign: Moon in Libra
Planetary Ruler/Exaltation: Venus rules, Saturn exalted
Date Range: September 23 – October 2
Qabalistic Correspondences: Chokmah of Yetzirah
Key Words: balance, setting to rights, meditation, quiet, reprieve

"Fear Inoculum"
Tool
Fear Inoculum, 2019

Atu Line

The 2 of Swords, entitled Peace, is a card of karmic balance. Its astrological associations are Moon (planet of cycles, mystery, intuition) in Libra (sign of balance, symmetry, fairness; ruled by Venus)—a blend of The Priestess and Adjustment energies—and its location in the wise sephira of Chokmah lends it a meditative and clear-minded quality that befits its title. The 2 of Swords speaks to returning to level-headed balance and fairness after the emotional strains of the Cups, especially the emotional saturation of the 10. This is not to insinuate that peace is always restored in a peaceful manner; don't forget swords are weapons made for dealing with conflict, and the suit is one that is primarily concerned with conflict and discord.

The original title of the card, Lord of Peace Restored, references this idea; however, Crowley shortened the title to "Lord of Peace," reasoning that all the twos reside in Chokmah, still in the supernal triad and just outside the godhead of Kether, and therefore peace hasn't been lost yet.

289

THE SONG

The first track of and first release from Tool's *Fear Inoculum* reflects the original title of Peace Restored, and it also represents a total break from the old outlook of Tool, which historically suffered in the notion of separateness and loneliness in this life. "Fear Inoculum" is a spell, a magickal working that brings unity to the masses, rather than extolling the early-Tool virtues of extreme independence and pure self-reliance. As the lyrics note, it is intended to recast a narrative—one that was previously anything but peaceful.

Again, we see the element of air represented by the concept of breath and breathing, something we also saw in "Pneuma." In "Pneuma," the breath is the unifying Breath/Word of the All, that which animates every living thing in our universe with the energy of the All. By contrast, in the early verses of "Fear Inoculum," breath and breathing have been twisted into something that carries contamination and infection—something to be feared—so that a negative power can continue to control us by convincing us that we're each on our own and must survive all by ourselves. This poisonous outlook controls us, makes us fearful of our brethren, and pushes us further away from unity with each other and the All.

Banishment is the crux of the magickal working here, severing the ties that the manmade reality of modernity has over the narrator and the rest of us. This track is quite literally a ritual is expelling the negative influence of the sickness of separateness, distrust, and inequity. The lyrics command the spirit of separateness/disparity to leave and purges all of humanity of its venom, which keeps us from reaching enlightenment and holds us collectively back from reuniting with the All. This is an excellent illustration of the 2 of Swords, a restoration of sanity and peace, and an immunity against a previously deeply disturbed situation.

TABULA MUNDI TAROT

Two crossed swords create the fulcrum of a scale weighing a canopic jar against a feather. The swords closely resemble the Ace, and between their hilts is a scroll representing the wisdom of The Priestess. In the background, a quarter moon appears between the pillars of Jachin and Boaz (which represent male and female, light and dark, force and form, etc.).

THOTH TAROT

A pair of elaborately hilted swords are crossed in saltire fashion, united by a blue rose representing the Holy Mother. Pinwheels of air issue in all four directions from the rose. Two smaller daggers uphold the symbols of the astrological influences, Moon and Libra, on their points.

READING THIS CARD

When the 2 of Swords is drawn, there is a need to restore or create balance and fairness in the situation at hand. The querent would do well to seek out a state of quiet through meditation, yoga, tai chi, journaling, exercise—whatever practice brings them peace. There is also an element of intuition in this card, such that the querent could benefit from some mental distance and detachment from the topic. This is a decision that needs to be made from a place of equity and balance in order to avoid the destruction of vengeance, keeping in mind that there will still be tension after all is said and done, but there will at least be justice.

If ill-dignified, some action needs to be taken in order to re-establish balance—something more decisive than merely clearing the mind with meditation or going for a jog. A decision must be made and enacted in order to set the situation to rights again.

CHAPTER 63

3 OF SWORDS: "FEATHERS," A PERFECT CIRCLE

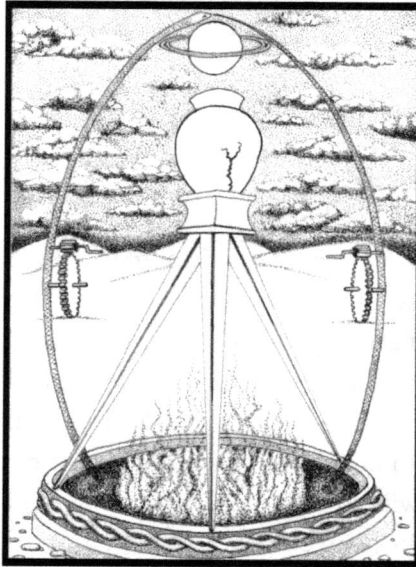

Thoth Title: Sorrow
Traditional Title: Lord of Sorrow
Planet/Sign: Saturn in Libra
Planetary Ruler/Exaltation: Venus rules, Saturn exalted
Date Range: October 3 - 12
Qabalistic Correspondences: Binah of Yetzirah
Key Words: heartbreak, sorrow of enlightenment, collective suffering, old patterns and wounds

"Feathers"
A Perfect Circle
Eat the Elephant, 2018

Atu Line

The 3 of Swords, Sorrow, is associated with Saturn (planet of lessons, limitations, discipline, time) in Libra (sign of balance, symmetry, fairness; ruled by Venus), as well as the third sephira of Binah, Understanding. This card is typically interpreted as heartbreak, but it is actually more profound than that.

As Lon Milo DuQuette notes, the 3 of Swords is the sorrow of enlightenment, not the mere "death of a loved one or the loss of a lover."[1] This is the sorrow of the Buddha, the enlightened understanding that existence is suffering and bliss, and that these extremes are part of the same wonder of breathing. It's all shit, and it's all ecstasy, because they are one and the same. The human experience is entirely about reaching toward that understanding, of getting through the pain and suffering and realizing that in the grand scheme of things, our ability to feel even the most painful loss is an absolutely exquisite gift, a miracle.

THE SONG

A Perfect Circle's "Feathers" is such a beautiful representation of this card. To begin with, feathers are traditionally a symbol of the air element, and of course Swords are the suit of air. So that's a nice little nod. Beyond that, the track is about sharing our pain, suffering, and trauma with others in order to transform them to lightness, relief, and compassion. The universality of suffering is what binds us to our brethren, what teaches us to love and be loved: it's the cornerstone of humanity.

In both the 3 of Swords and "Feathers," we effectively journey from the heaviness of Saturn's suffocating oppression and harsh lessons to the delicate lightness of Libra's airy scales, which reference the Egyptian goddess Ma'at and the scales she uses to weigh the souls of the dead against her feather. The souls as light as her feather can pass to heaven; the souls that are heavier are doomed to the underworld. It is not the souls who've never known suffering that pass the test; we all endure the suffering of sadness's pendulum swing. What makes the difference is what we have done with that pain. Did we use it as a bludgeon against others? Or did we let it make us softer, more compassionate, more merciful toward our brothers and sisters? We become feather-light by releasing the weight of our most grievous suffering and injuries of the past.

TABULA MUNDI TAROT

Meleen's interpretation of this card is visually arresting. A cracked canopic jar rests on the blades of three swords above a blue-hot fire. Around this arrangement and completely containing it is an ouroboros that begins and ends at Saturn. Gears on either side rotate the ouroboros as a symbol of time's continuous passage. The sky above is overcast and threatening rain.

THOTH TAROT

Among the darkest cards of the *Thoth* pack, this 3 of Swords is set off by a cloudy background of black and grey (references Binah) with tinges of blue, green, and yellow, which are symbolic of the suit, sign, and ruling planet. In the center, three swords pierce a lotus blossom, and the force of the pressure at their meeting bends two of the blades and sheds many flower petals.

READING THIS CARD

When the 3 of Swords appears in a reading, there is anguish, pain, and heartbreak, most often rising from an old trauma, habit, or role that the querent is compulsively activating. The sorrow has been relived so many times that the path is a rut, a pattern of thought the querent finds themselves treading over and over again. At this time, the querent has been granted an opportunity to choose between letting the sorrow dominate their life, or learning to see it as merely an event in the past in order to embrace healing and move forward. With some time and distance, the querent can look back and remember not only what happened and how it hurt, but also see how the experience has helped them grow and metamorphosize into their current state.

This is a card of coming to broader terms with all that is hard in life—the disappointments, the tragedies, and the senseless pain that accompanies our experiences on this plane—and learning to understand those things from the perspective of faith, balance, and peace instead of perceiving them as personal attacks. If we allow it, this card can help us to learn to recognize and heal over-identification with the victim.

CHAPTER 64

4 OF SWORDS: "BREAD AND CIRCUS," PUSCIFER

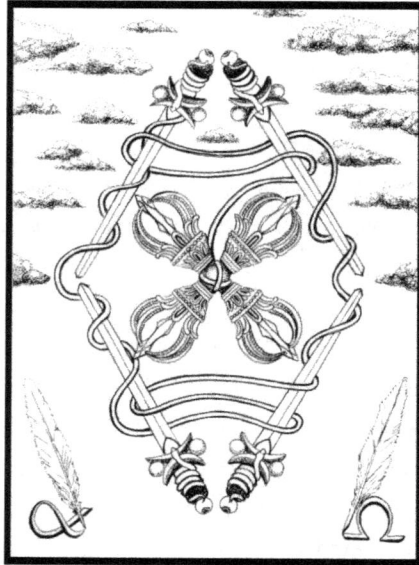

Thoth Title: Truce
Planet/Sign: Jupiter in Libra
Planetary Ruler/Exaltation: Venus rules, Saturn exalted
Date Range: October 13 - 22
Qabalistic Correspondences: Chesed of Yetzirah
Key Words: rest from conflict or stress, temporary respite, order, balance, justice

"Bread and Circus"
Puscifer
Existential Reckoning, 2021

Atu Line

T he 4 of Swords is entitled Truce, and is associated with Jupiter (planet of gifts, abundance, expansion) in Libra (sign of balance, symmetry, fairness; ruled by Venus) in the first sephira below the Abyss, Chesed. While the magnanimity of Jupiter combined with the balance of Libra seems like it would be a really positive combination, especially in Chesed, alas, it's a somewhat tepid card even when well-dignified.

Despite common interpretations of this card as simply the need for respite or rest, Crowley particularly did not have an especially positive perspective on this card. In various passages of *The Book of Thoth*, he describes the 4 of Swords as:

- "refuge from mental chaos, chosen in an arbitrary manner,"[1]
- "it argues for convention,"[2]
- "minds too indolent or too cowardly to think about their own problems hail joyfully [a] policy of appeasement,"[3]

- "on the lines of the strong man armed, keeping his house in peace,"[4] and
- "the picture of the formation of the military clan system of society."[5]

THE SONG

Puscifer's "Bread and Circus" perfectly syncs with Crowley's disappointed and disgusted outlook on this card. Keenan's lyrics clearly call out the increasing anti-intellectualization and stupefaction of modern American culture and daily life, and the public's seeming willingness to be lulled into a dazed and entertained, if not entirely unpleasant, acquiescence in exchange for a false sense of security and superficial distractions from misery and exhaustion. "Bread and Circus" describes a culture that has traded its self-determination, creativity, and power in order to have only the most basic needs (bread) met with a little titillation on the side (and circus). The society described herein is on a permanent respite based in numbness, distraction, blind patriotism, propaganda, manipulation, and a lack of self-determination.

Keenan seems to be firmly in Ben Franklin's camp when it comes to the responsibilities of an active and engaged citizenry, as expressed in a letter Franklin penned on behalf of the Pennsylvania General Assembly: "those who would give up essential liberty to purchase a little temporary safety deserve neither liberty nor safety."

TABULA MUNDI TAROT

Four swords are arranged in a diamond shape on a lightly cloudy, brilliant sky-blue background. Within the diamond is the vajra weaving shuttle of the Fortune card (reference to Jupiter, the planet associated with this card). In the bottom corners, feather quills draw the alpha and omega symbols as a reference to Libra's scales.

THOTH TAROT

Four sword tips meet over a many-petaled lotus on a cross of green
—a reference to Venus, ruling planet of this card's Libra correspondence. In the background are myriad yellow (air) pinwheels of air on
a sky blue (Jupiter) background.

READING THIS CARD

When this card appears in a reading, there is a need for rest and
respite (sorry, Uncle Al), but the real question is: how engaged is the
querent in the situation at hand? The 4 of Swords points to poor
boundaries—either being too detached or too enmeshed. If too
detached, what measure of self-determination are you giving up in
exchange for not having to think about it? If too enmeshed, how
much do you really think you're able to accomplish when you're
burned out? A temporary break from the situation can afford you the
opportunity to regain your strength and sort your thoughts, but this
is not a permanent reprieve. Eventually you'll have to return and face
the situation head-on, or be forever controlled by it.

CHAPTER 65

5 OF SWORDS: "RIGHT IN TWO," TOOL

Thoth Title: Defeat
Planet/Sign: Venus in Aquarius
Planetary Ruler: Saturn
Date Range: January 20 - 29
Qabalistic Correspondences: Geburah of Yetzirah
Key Words: aggression, conflict, unfair fighting, passivity brings defeat

"Right in Two"
Tool
10,000 Days, 2006

Atu Line

The 5 of Swords, Defeat, is associated with Venus (planet of beauty, fertility, love, nurturance) in Aquarius (sign of intellect, visions, humanitarianism, possibility; ruled by Saturn). Here, nourishing Venus is getting shut out by coldly analytical Aquarius, in Mars' sephira of war, Geburah. It is a decidedly bleak card that indicates naked aggression, cold war, and rationalized violence—it is the quintessential conflict card.

Because of its suit, the 5 of Swords is a card of intellectual and communicative conflict (air element traits), and it often indicates arguments in which cruel things are said and/or done, which can never be taken back. The card instructs those on the offense to fight fairly, and those on the defense to be strategic and proactive as opposed to passive when attacked.

THE SONG

Tool's "Right in Two" is an apt illustration of the 5 of Swords at work: the lyrics describe humans' seemingly insatiable need to fight, dominate, own, and rule others, which manifests in the forms of warfare, colonialism, and environmental prostitution. The frustrating inability of mankind to simply share, take only what they need, and live in peace is at the heart of both the card and the song, and the unfortunate result is the destruction of what was once beautiful and plentiful.

Sometimes, trouble appears up on our doorstep, seemingly unprovoked. Conflict is the way of this world, for better or worse, and it is how all meaningful progress is made. What matters is being clear about what direction we're pursuing with that progress. In other words, if in the end a fight is necessary, let it be because it came looking for you, rather than you spoiling for it.

TABULA MUNDI TAROT

On a pale blue field, an eagle attacks a dove, completely destroying the rose of love that the dove carries. Beneath, four broken swords are no match for the large, red sword of war, which breaks open their formation to access the cosmic egg, symbol of life and all possibility.

THOTH TAROT

Five swords meet at their tips, creating an inverted pentagram shape and obliterating the peaceful rose that was once there. The petals of the dead flower now trace the pentagram shape around the swords. The background is chaotic shapes and disintegrating pinwheels on an uneasy background of green and purple.

READING THIS CARD

When the 5 of Swords appears in a reading, consider what role you're playing in the conflict at hand. Are you the aggressor, greedily stomping your opponent for every inch you can gain at all cost? Or are you the victim with your hatches battened down, just trying to survive the onslaught? Summarily, are you fighting fairly? A fair fight is between two similarly positioned opponents, so either pick on someone your own size, or else summon your righteous fury and strategically rise to your own defense.

This card is difficult to aspect positively. Even if "ill-dignified" by positive cards all around, 5 of Swords still indicates a difficult situation, uncomfortable at the very least. Fives tend to represent struggle, and this card is the struggle of the mind. Mental abuse, psychological manipulation, and cruel words are regular associations here.

CHAPTER 66

6 OF SWORDS: "POSTULOUS," PUSCIFER

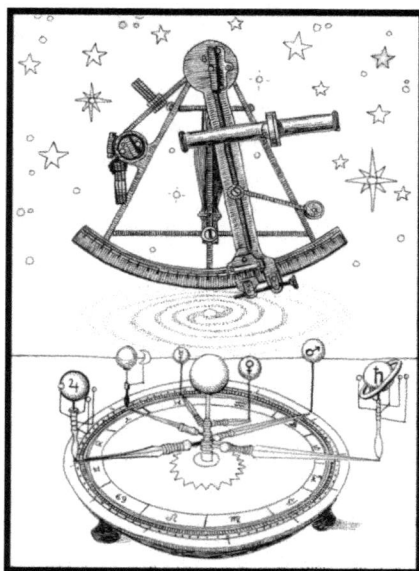

Thoth Title: Science
Planet/Sign: Mercury in Aquarius
Planetary Ruler: Saturn
Date Range: January 30 – February 8
Qabalistic Correspondences: Tiphareth of Yetzirah
Key Words: perfection of the human mind, life purpose, crystalliza-
tion of knowledge and skill

"Postulous"
Puscifer
Existential Reckoning, 2020

Atu Line

T he 6 of Swords, Mercury (planet of communication, commerce, speed, knowledge) in Aquarius (sign of intellect, visions, humanitarianism, possibility; ruled by Saturn), is called Science, and according to Crowley, it represents "the full establishment and balance of the idea" of Swords.[1]

Sixes are the cards of Tiphareth, the heart chakra, and also the intellect, via their relationship to the Prince-Sons (air) of the tarot. The intellectual influence on this card is absolute, as the planet, sign, sephira, and suit are all correspondent to airy intellect, ideas, knowledge, etc. Crowley also wrote that the 6 of Swords is "the perfect balance of all mental and moral faculties, hardly won, and almost impossible to hold in an ever-changing world, declares the idea of Science in its fullest interpretation."[2]

Earlier, in the 8 of Cups entry, we contrasted that card with this one, noting that the 8 of Cups is moving away from what is no longer desired, while the 6 of Swords is moving toward what is wanted. In fact, this card is heavily associated with one's "calling" in life.

THE SONG

Puscifer's 2021 release, *Existential Reckoning*, is overall an extremely well-suited album to represent the swords suit and the element of air, and "Postulous" (a play on the word "postulate," which means to assume or posit as truth) in particular is a great representation of 6 of Swords, with its focus on finding balance and moderation in service to one's purpose.

Although it shares an important chunk of its lyrical content with another track on this album, "Theorem" (including the actual word "science"), "Postulous" includes language that is specific to pursuing a mission and vision, much like one would do in pursuit of their calling. It mentions the stages of creation, from idea to understanding to practice to implementation—all of which are activities endemic to Swords' focus on the intellect and its capacities.

Additionally, this track also includes words related to integration and synthesis, which are concepts that belong to Mercury, the planetary ruler; Mercury is the third alchemical element—neither male nor female—and it is the animating force that applies to, combines, and actualizes the other two. This process is fundamental to reaching self-actualization, the state that truly frees us to follow our will.

TABULA MUNDI TAROT

One of *Tabula Mundi's* most brilliant cards, 6 of Swords blends symbolism from The Magus (Mercury) and Star (Aquarius) cards. In the starry night sky, a sextant hangs over a galaxy, measuring cosmic distances. Beneath, six sword blades are the arms of an orrery, or model of the solar system. The two scenes illustrate "as above, so below" as an expression of science.

THOTH TAROT

Six sword tips meet over what Lon Milo DuQuette terms "a Rose Cross of Being," the symbol of the manifest microcosm (the five-petaled flower) nailed to the macrocosm (six squares arranged as a cross). The arrangement is enclosed in a circle within a square, also symbolic of the micro and macrocosms. The grey (Mercury) background is filled with well-formed pinwheels in balanced geometric patterns, revealing the perfected beauty of the cosmos.

READING THIS CARD

This card is frequently an indicator of the querent's life purpose and its discovery. When the 6 of Swords is drawn in a reading, pay close attention to what puts you in a state of "flow" and provides you with a deep sense of purpose, then have the courage of your convictions and pursue them. This card can also indicate a situation that has finally achieved clarity of direction and purpose, or one in which the querent is uniquely suited to lead.

Even when ill-dignified, this card still hints at possible wondrous advances in the situation in question, albeit the realizations may come slowly, or the querent may experience resistance to change or may be thwarted by outside forces.

CHAPTER 67

7 OF SWORDS: "7EMPEST," TOOL

Thoth Title: Futility
Traditional Title: Lord of Unstable Effort
Planet/Sign: Moon in Aquarius
Planetary Ruler: Saturn
Date Range: February 9 - 18
Qabalistic Correspondences: Netzach of Yetzirah
Key Words: dishonesty, communication breakdown, cruel words,
outnumbered, attack

"7empest"
Tool
Fear Inoculum, 2019

Atu Line

T he 7 of Swords, Moon (planet of cycles, mysteries, ancestry, and divine feminine) in Aquarius (sign of intellect, visions, humanitarianism, possibility; ruled by Saturn), is entitled Futility. It is the element of air/intellect in Venus's sephira of Netzach, Victory, which sounds lovely. However, the double influence of Saturn in Venus's garden is a real mind-fuck. Saturn is so restrictive, and Aquarius is so rational, that they stamp all the beauty, fertility, and maternal strength out of poor Venus. She has no choice but to acquiesce.

Crowley describes the card in *The Book of Thoth* thusly: "there is vacillation, a wish to compromise, a certain toleration. But in certain circumstances, the results may be more disastrous than ever. This naturally depends upon the success of the policy. This is always in doubt as long as there exist violent, uncompromising forces which take it as a natural prey."[1]

All of the sevens in the minor arcana of the tarot are associated with varying types of honesty and integrity; the 7 of Swords particularly deals with dishonesty concerning information, including lying to oneself or others, or being lied to.

THE SONG

Now, indulge me for a moment while I spin off a tangent regarding 7 of Swords' match, Tool's "7empest"—I promise it will all tie together in the end.

Tool members noted in multiple interviews that much of the music on the *Fear Inoculum* album just happened to come out in time signatures of seven, and that thematically, the number seven has many correspondences and tie-ins to spiritual concepts that various members have studied. A handful of spiritual concepts worth considering in reference to sevens, and therefore also "7empest," include:

- As mentioned above, in the minor arcana of the tarot, sevens deal with honesty and integrity
- Atu VII or Key 7 of the major arcana of the tarot is The Chariot, symbolic of honor, duty, missions, progress, success
- The seven classical planets of Sun, Moon, Mars, Mercury, Jupiter, Venus, and Saturn as representations of the seven major forces in the universe.
- The seventh sephira on the Tree of Life, Netzach, which is unbalanced on the pillar of Mercy/Force, low on the tree, and ruled by Venus
- The seven spheres of human consciousness, or the lower sephiroth on the Tree of Life beneath the Supernal Triad: Chesed, Geburah, Tiphareth, Netzach, Hod, Yesod, and Malkuth
- Numerologically, seven is associated with wisdom
- The Seven Deadly Sins: pride, greed, lust, envy, gluttony, wrath, and sloth

- The Seven Heavenly Virtues: prudence, justice, temperance, courage/fortitude, faith, hope, and charity
- The seven chakras, or energy centers of the body, in Eastern spiritual teachings: root, sacral, solar plexus, heart, throat, third eye, and crown
- The seven operations of the alchemical process: calcination, dissolution, separation, conjunction, fermentation, distillation, and coagulation, which culminate in the transformation of lead to gold, the common man to the enlightened one.
- The heptagram, or seven-pointed star, is associated with the Mother of Abominations, the goddess Babalon, as well as with the act of creation: "Participation and will are required to draw the heptagram...Seven: the holiest of holy numbers signifying the completion of God's creative act. When a man applies conscious thought and draws a seven-pointed star, he becomes with God a cocreator of the universe."[2]

As you can see, the number seven is an important integer in the occult, one that carries a high concentration of information and symbolism. The fact that "7empest" is spelled with the Arabic numeral in place of a capital T cannot be ignored. But what about the word *tempest* itself? Are there any occult references to the word tempest?

Interestingly enough, Brian Brown's 1923 book, *The Wisdom of the Egyptians* contains a remarkably relevant chapter entitled "The Vision of Hermes"[3], which describes a conversation between the gods Osiris and Hermes that includes several symbols appearing in this track. After discussing the journey of souls incarnating downward through the *seven* lower sephiroth of the Tree of Life into the physical reality of Malkuth, Hermes has a vision of the suffering of those souls who have forgotten their origins in Kether and are trapped on this earthly plane of Malkuth. That is, they are stuck in material reality and unable to ascend back to Godhead. The force that holds them here in Malkuth (on earth) is described as *a tempest*. Many earth-bound souls fight and eventually free themselves from the tempest's winds to begin the return journey to Kether; others simply lose all consciousness and perish here.

From the text:

> "The words of the wise are like the seven notes of the lyre which contains all music, along with the numbers and the laws of the universe. The vision of Hermes resembles the starry heaven, whose unfathomable depths are strewn with constellations. For the child this is nothing more than a gold-studded vault, for the sage it is boundless space in which worlds revolve, with their wonderful rhythms and cadences. The vision contains the eternal numbers, evoking signs and magic keys. The more thou learnest to contemplate and understand it, the farther thou shalt see its limits extend, for the same organic law governs all worlds."[4]

The *Oxford Dictionary* definition of tempest is a violent, windy storm. And in the context of the discussion above, this storm is the force of materialism that blinds us to our true nature, that obscures our intuitive connection to both the Divine and as well as our collective memory of where we as conscious beings came from and whence we are supposed to return—the Source, the All, the Light, Kether. In other words, the tempest is the lie that humans in physical reality buy into: that nothing exists beyond what we can perceive using our five physical senses and logic. The lyrics in "7empest" intend to call out the aspects of life in this this plane that do us spiritual harm and keep us from ascending to enlightenment.

Furthermore, I also think I would be remiss if I didn't point out that there is room for a theory that Keenan was thinking of a particular avatar for this force in the U.S. at the time of writing these lyrics. Regardless of our personal opinions, Keenan has made his negative opinion of the 45th president clear (see Puscifer's video for "The Arsonist" if you need proof).

"Tempest in a teapot," the most well-known phrase using this word, is a euphemism for someone who exhibits large anger or excitement about a trivial matter—something constantly demonstrated by the Twitter feed of this particular president.[5] A tempest, as noted above, is a violently windy storm. Calling someone a tempest is comparable to calling them a "gas bag" or "full of hot air." The word "trump" is also slang for fart in Britain—a different kind of hot air. Incidentally (and admittedly at the risk of straying too far into conspiratorial territory), there are seven members in the First Family, including Donald Sr., Melania, and Trump's five children. When considering the meaning of 7 of Swords as dishonesty and destruction via compromise with a deceitful party, along with the descriptions of the 7empest's behaviors, it's a pretty clear match between the card and track.

Storms don't last forever, though, and violent storms are especially prone to run out of steam quickly. Regardless of the interpretation of "7empest"—whether as a generic force of materialism in this plane, or as a particular person who exhibits the characteristics of this force—the meaning of the song is clear: tempests gunna tempest.

It is what it is, and we should not expect any force to do aught but act in accord with its true nature. In a way, Keenan is putting forth the idea that there is no point in seeing universal forces as having a good or bad value, but it is best to simply acknowledge things as they are and move forward in a constructive direction without feeling the need to judge or decry it. Don't stand around and bitch about it—do something to get yourself beyond it.

TABULA MUNDI TAROT

A dust storm in the desert traps a lone camel, stranding it without water. In the sky beneath the full moon, a large, seven-pointed star contains seven smaller seven-pointed stars, a central dagger, and six swords surrounding it. The dagger is clearly trapped and held at sword point by the six others.

THOTH TAROT

Six small swords attack a seventh, larger, central sword, shattering it. The hilts of all seven swords are decorated with planetary glyphs, and the air "pinwheels" are beautifully formed but scattered on a pale blue background.

READING THIS CARD

When the 7 of Swords appears in a reading, it's time for some honesty. Someone in the situation at hand is not being straight with others or themselves, or some important information is being withheld. There may be machinery of deception at work, or an illusion that has been constructed to divert attention away from the situation's true nature. This card can also indicate a literal break-down in communication, whether a missed message, a language barrier, or some other kind of communication that misses its mark.

CHAPTER 68

8 OF SWORDS: "ROSETTA STONED," TOOL

Thoth Title: Interference
Planet/Sign: Jupiter in Gemini
Planetary Ruler: Mercury
Date Range: May 21 - 31
Qabalistic Correspondences: Hod of Yetzirah
Key Words: getting hung up on details, feeling trapped, no good options

"Rosetta Stoned"
Tool
10,000 Days, 2006

Atu Line

The 8 of Swords, entitled Interference, is associated with Jupiter (planet of expansion, gifts, abundance, material wealth) in Gemini (sign of ideas, debate, learning, duality; ruled by Mercury), in Mercury's sephira of Hod. Since Mercury rules both the sephira and Gemini, there's a double dose of The Trickster's energy here. The 8 of Swords is the card of believing you are trapped when you're not—of being convinced that the bars you perceive around you make up your prison cell, when really, they're in no way containing you. Like the long-time prisoner who stays obediently inside the cell even after the door is flung open, the 8 of Swords is being your own ruthless prison guard in a detainment of your own making.

Crowley calls this card "the error of being good-natured when good-nature is disastrous."[1] Jovial, expansive Jupiter is met with the cold intellect of the Swords, and that is further confounded by a double dose of Mercurial detours, resulting in "sheer unforeseen bad luck."[2] Crowley further remarks, "trivial incidents have often altered

316

the destiny of empires, brought to naught 'the best-laid plans of mice and men.'"[3]

THE SONG

In this comedy of errors, I give you Exhibit A, Tool's "Rosetta Stoned."

The narrator, a first-rate fuck-up and all-around unfortunate idiot, spins a tale of being abducted by extraterrestrials and given a great, secret message for all humanity. But it 'just so happens' that he's just dropped a bunch of acid and is presently tripping his face off, so he can't remember what they say...and he of course forgot to bring a pen to write it all down. Of all the humans on earth who could be tapped to be a messenger, the aliens naturally choose someone in no shape to do anything of consequence. Of course they did!

Rosetta Stoned is a perfect track to represent the 8 of Swords and the way we humans get in our own way with our big, dumb brains. We let small details and our fixations on them destroy our focus. We fail to see the big picture because we think we're smarter than we are. Rather than receive the message from his 'visitor,' and letting the beauty of this cosmic contact wash over him—even if he can't remember the exact words he received after all is said and done—he instead spends the entire trip worrying about a goddamned ink pen. Typical.

TABULA MUNDI TAROT

The vajra weaving shuttle from the Fortune card is shown, its thread tangled and wound around the hilts of eight swords arranged pommel to pommel in an eight-pointed star of chaos. A red lion (solar) and a white eagle griffin (lunar) fight for control of the thread even as it winds around their paws and claws, trapping them.

THOTH TAROT

An angry purple bruise background is shot through with pinwheels that have devolved into red streaks and lines. In the center, a stack of six unique small swords is barred by a pair of larger, matching swords, trapping the six beneath.

READING THIS CARD

The 8 of Swords reminds us to question everything we think is holding us back. When this card appears in a reading, the immediate response should be to re-examine the situation at hand for potential tricks the querent may be playing on themselves. How are they convinced that they're confined when they aren't? Usually when this card comes up, the querent fervently believes they only have a few options, and they all suck. However, there are always more options available to us than what we see at first glance—if horizons are broadened even slightly, a better path forward may become visible.

This card can be ameliorated by positive surrounding cards. In this case, the Jupiter/Gemini influence produces a racing mind. The querent may be overwhelmed by information, options, or ideas. This paralysis can only be conquered by making a choice—the very act that is likely to be most intimidating at this moment, but is the only remedy.

CHAPTER 69
9 OF SWORDS: "VICARIOUS," TOOL

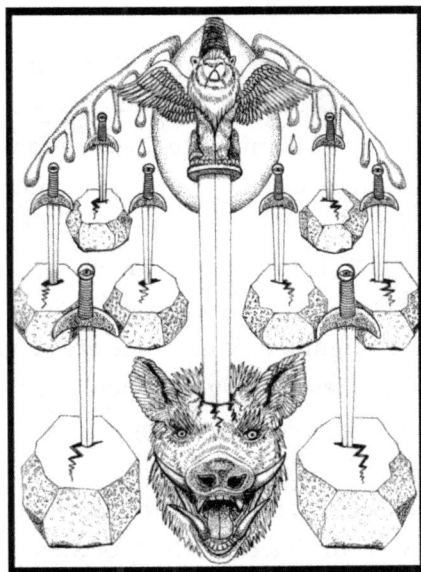

Thoth Title: Cruelty
Traditional Title: Lord of Despair and Cruelty
Planet/Sign: Mars in Gemini
Planetary Ruler: Mercury
Date Range: June 1 to 10
Qabalistic Correspondences: Yesod of Yetzirah
Key Words: nightmares, anxiety, depression, stress

"Vicarious"
Tool
10,000 Days, 2006

Atu Line

The dreaded 9 of Swords, arguably the harshest card in the deck, is called Cruelty. It's associated with Mars (planet of war, aggression, dominance, destruction) in Gemini (sign of ideas, debate, learning, duality; ruled by Mercury) in the Moon's otherworldly sephira of Yesod, making clear its meaning of mental torment and anguish. This card is often associated with nightmares, anxiety, and depression.

If especially well-dignified, it can indicate writer's block or the anxiety that accompanies making a difficult decision, but anyone who has experienced these knows they are no walk in the park, either.

As previously discussed, nines in the minor arcana represent the suit at its peak power. In this case, the 9 of Swords is the height of Swords' conflict, disruption, and the mental power used therein. Crowley calls it "agony of the mind"[1], and that is exactly how depression, overthinking, and over-analysis produce paralysis, fear, and misery. The 9 of Swords is the realm of "the unconscious primitive instincts, of the psychopath, of the fanatic."[2]

THE SONG

Tool's "Vicarious" is the track matched with this card, for its callousness toward suffering, for its gratuitous violence, and for the way it revels in death and grief—specifically the tragedies that befall others. The track describes the human tendency toward fascination with death—a perversion that arises from our inherent fear of it. In wrestling with this age-old terror, fascinated aversion gives way to pure entertainment, which then leads on to desensitization and cruelty.

While it's tempting to call this a phenomenon of modern-day society, that would be inaccurate. Let's not forget the ancient Romans and their coliseum pastimes of setting wild animals loose to tear convicts limb from limb for the amusement of the masses. Although violence is not new to the human condition, electronic communications such as film, television, social media, and news coverage have all made it effortless and physically safe to indulge our need to partake of death anytime we desire.

"Vicarious" also includes a passage that refers to the Universe's callousness and voracious nature, a theme that Tool first visited on *Undertow* in "Disgustipated," when Keenan explores the notion of life feeding on itself. "Vicarious" carries the idea further to implore the listener to abandon the "Love and Light" ethos in recognition of this simple truth about the way the Universe works: all things that live, die. Of that we can be sure, and there should be no value assigned to that fact. It's neither good nor bad, it only is. This is the meaning of the Universe being callous toward us and voracious about devouring our lives—not that it's menacing, but that it is simply indifferent.

And while the song's narrator tries to normalize our cruelest forms of entertainment by trying to convince the listener that they and the rest of humanity are in on it, too, it is apparent in the construction of the lyrics that the narrator is not reliable, nor meant to be relatable, as evidenced by his assertions that no one cares about a story until someone bleeds and that he prefers to watch others suffer instead of suffering himself. The misery that the subjects of television violence are suffering is commensurate with the pain that is being inflicted and endured in this, the cruelest card of the pack.

Keenan's body language during live performances seems to further support these ideas, as he casually sits down on the edge of his platform to sing the song, flippantly swinging his feet, acting bored, lounging around the stage, etc. His physical presentation of "Vicarious" is so contrary to his typical posture during performance that it can't be ignored. In sum, the track is constructed to hold a mirror up to the listener, as if to say, *if you agree with this song, ask yourself why? And is that a good thing?*

TABULA MUNDI TAROT

On a field of angry, bright red, eight swords dripping blood pierce eight boulders, while a ninth bloody sword pierces the third eye of the screaming boar from The Tower (Mars) card. Above, the hilt of the ninth sword is a winged lion perched on the cross-guard. Behind the lion is a winged orphic egg, its wings made of green, dripping mucus.

THOTH TAROT

A dull, brown background is filled with nine broken and chipped swords dripping blood. The airy "pinwheels" in the background are malformed and disintegrating into messy piles of lines along the bottom of the card.

READING THIS CARD

When the 9 of Swords appears, it can point out pain the querent is experiencing or inflicting on others. It is not uncommon for this card to appear in especially stressful periods of life, such as when work or primary relationships are difficult. When surrounded by other difficult cards, it can indicate serious mental health issues, such as suicidality, severe depression, or panic attacks. If surrounded by more positive cards, it can indicate being faced with an important decision or struggling with blockages that impede progress—both are stress-inducing and fit the 9 of Swords' energy, as well.

CHAPTER 70

10 OF SWORDS: "DESCENDING," TOOL

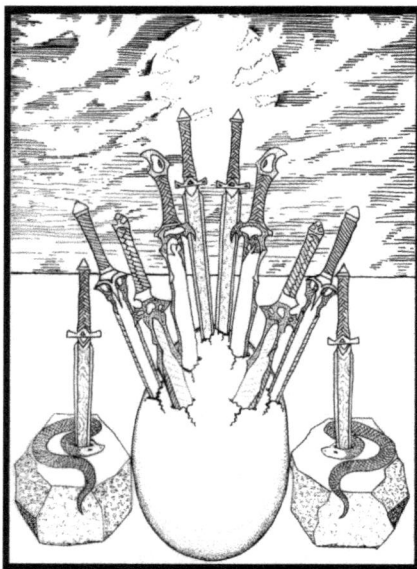

Thoth Title: Ruin
Planet/Sign: Sun in Gemini
Planetary Ruler: Mercury
Date Range: June 11 - 20
Qabalistic Correspondences: Malkuth of Yetzirah
Key Words: the worst is over, the morning after, self-defeating thoughts

"Descending"
Tool
Fear Inoculum, 2019

Atu Line

The 10 of Swords is the 'morning after' the horror of the 9 of Swords. The decision has been made, the fever broken, death/transformation has finally come, and now the task of picking up the pieces and healing lies ahead. The worst is over, but the cold grey light of dawn is anything but comforting—this is the second worst card in the deck, right after the 9 of Swords itself.

The 10 of Swords is entitled Ruin, and ironically, its astrological associations are Sun (planet of innocence, freedom, growth, life) in Gemini (sign of ideas, debate, learning, duality; ruled by Mercury) in the earthly sephira of Malkuth. One would think that these elements would bring some optimism, and in truth they are mitigating forces, but in Malkuth, the airy, intellectual energy that began so strong in Kether is now spent and has reached its final destination. Tens in the minor arcana represent the suit's energy at the point of over-ripeness. The fruit is rotting on the vine, and it's time to move on—in Ruin, there is nothing more to harvest here but stagnation and suffering.

THE SONG

Tool's "Descending" is such an amazing match for the 10 of Swords for several reasons. First of all, the title is reminiscent of the progress of the soul from Kether to Malkuth, down through each iteration of the tree, Wands to Cups to Swords to Disks. As we travel this path downward from pure energy (Ace of Wands) to ultimate physical existence (10 of Disks), energy is slowing and condensing, and is therefore becoming less divine and more earth-bound. On one side of the coin at hand is the 10 of Swords, the Malkuth of the Air Tree, and on the other is the Kether of the Earth Tree, the Ace of Disks; the next step down is into the Chokmah of the Earth Tree, the 2 of Disks, heralding the progression from the mind's ideas to physical reality.

The subject matter of "Descending" is the coming environmental catastrophe—one that will bring sweeping change to life on this planet as we know it, and at this point is no longer avoidable. All we can do is mobilize our efforts to the maximum degree and hope that it is enough to at least survive as a species. It should not go without notice that *mitigate* means "to make less severe, serious, or painful" —it does not mean prevent or reverse. No, the track acknowledges that we are thoroughly committed to the path of Ruin before us. We're fucked. All we can do is brace ourselves for impact and then pick up the pieces that are left after the ultimate disaster.

Bleak as this outlook may be, there is something of a meta-silver lining here, if I may be so bold. We are collectively soon to be reborn. What kind of experience we have next is wholly dependent on our actions now. It is also interesting to consider how several aspects of the song work together to conjure the imagery of birth:

- the sounds of the ocean are symbolic of the salt water of the womb,
- "floating nescient" evokes the image of a fetus floating in the amniotic sac,

- "quickened" is a word that is used to describe the moment when a fetus moves for the first time in utero or to describe the fetus's development in the womb towards viability,
- the "drive to stay alive" is also descriptive of the heightened state of arousal and even panic that infants experience during birth—such a radical change in existence can feel like dying, but is it really?

Again, we see the parallels between death and birth, that they are never truly separate. The Malkuth of one Tree is the Kether of the next.

TABULA MUNDI TAROT

Eight swords pierce an egg, killing all possibility of life springing from it. On either side of the egg are boulders, upon each a snake is impaled by a ninth and tenth sword. In the background is a hazy sky; clouds obscure the sun.

THOTH TAROT

A mix of whole and broken swords are arranged in a Tree of Life pattern, their blade tips meeting in the middle of the design. A heart-hilted, broken sword glows in the position of Tiphareth. The background is shades of red, orange, and yellow; the pinwheels of the swords suit appear to be paired and battling to disintegration.

READING THIS CARD

When the 10 of Swords appears in a reading, it is signaling that the end of an idea, identity, system, or framework is nigh. The mental construct in question no longer fits the needs of the situation, and if progress is to be made, it must be abandoned. This card can also be a heads-up that the querent or someone involved in the situation has outgrown an identity, and is ready to be someone else. Finally, this card indicates that the worst is over, even if it in no way guarantees that what's ahead will be easy.

CHAPTER 71

ACE OF DISKS: "LIGHTEN UP, FRANCIS," PUSCIFER

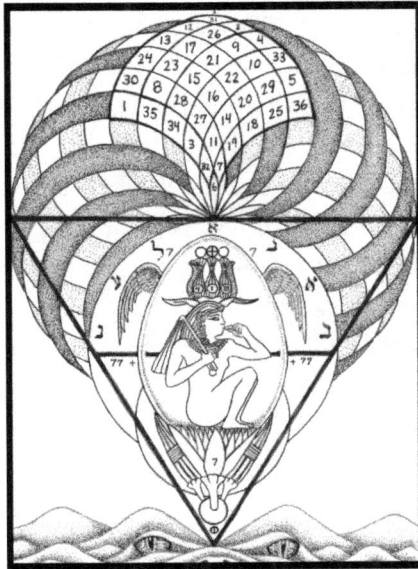

Traditional Title: Root of the Powers of Earth
Element: Earth
Qabalistic Correspondences: Kether of Assiah
Key Words: material reality, resources, money, health, harvest, abundance

"Lighten Up, Francis"
Puscifer
V Is for Vagina, 2007

Atu Line

Disks correspond to the element of earth, and the power To Keep Silent. They are the fourth elemental emanation, and they balance the suit of Swords. To Keep Silent is the practice of discipline to internalize and act upon what has been learned. It is a time for doing, for practice, and for reverence. Now is not the time for running the mouth. This element is deeply associated with the body and physical resources.

Aces are the seeds of their element. They are not yet manifest in any form we recognize. In them exist the *possibility* of the things we associate with them. Ace of Disks contains the *possibility* of earth, stability, abundance, growth, and security. The conditions are right for earth, the seed is there, but we don't see it manifest into anything recognizable until the 2 of Disks. This Ace represents the Magus' pantacle, the representation of all of tangible reality.

As we've discussed before, it's best not to be fooled into thinking the Aces are weak. They are the purest, most potent form of their element, straight from the godhead of Kether, and like any great power, the test is in how they are wielded.

THE SONG

The title "Lighten Up, Francis" is a reference to the comedy film *Stripes*, which starred Bill Murray and was released around the time Keenan joined the U.S. Army. In the film, a group of young slackers are in for rude awakenings when they join the military as a quick and easy way to change their lives. The character Francis acts menacing and psychotic as a means of self-protection and coping—a defense mechanism promptly destroyed by the drill sergeant's dry call-out to "lighten up, Francis."

As the card that follows the difficult ending of the mental suit of Swords, the Ace of Disks presents with a radical shift into the body, the material, and the earth. After the brainy Swords have left us broken in the cold, gray light of the morning after (10 of Swords), the Ace of Disks beckons us to get out of our heads, and get back in the solid, secure truth of our bodies. And Puscifer's "Lighten Up, Francis" does just that. The beat and the groove just beg to be danced to, and in dancing, we are reminded of the simple joys of possessing a body. This is a far cry from the Keenan of Tool, whose persona might never have allowed for the earthy pleasure of a good ass-shaking.

The lyrics include several references that make this track an awesome representation of the Ace of Disks. There are several references to escaping the drudgery of the menial life of employment, rules, laws, and boredom. Rickson Gracie, a 9th-degree Brazilian Jiu-Jitsu red belt, is certainly a representative of the power of earth, and famed dancing movie-star pair Fred Astaire and Grace Kelly are the picture of graceful earth. And my personal favorite, the very first line, contains a subtle reference to Heh as the Mother (water), and Heh as the Daughter (earth). The Princess of Disks (who is by extension the daughter named here) is earth, here on earth—today, now—and all the modernity and humanity that implies. It's a humorous and unexpectedly breathtakingly perfect representation of the Ace of Disks, and one of the songs that convinced me that this system of pairing Keenan's music with the entire tarot was possible.

331

TABULA MUNDI TAROT

Meleen's rendition of the Ace of Disks is a beautifully complex mala design that references Babalon and Beast conjoined to create the sum of material reality. A whirling solar disk contains the cosmic egg and Harpocrates, the passive, silent twin of Horus. The disk floats above the rolling, green hills of the earth, which also is the body of Sebek, the Egyptian crocodile god of creation and destruction. As is traditional, Meleen's personal mark is incorporated into this card via the image of the child in egg, which is the Sabian symbol for the degree of her Ascendent.

THOTH TAROT

Crowley's personal sigil is prominently displayed in the center of the Ace of Disks, surrounded by peacock feathered wings in tones of yellow, gold, and green. The entire image recalls the overall design and embellishments commonly seen on paper currency—the quintessential symbol of material manifestation and valuation.

READING THIS CARD

When this card appears in a reading, it refers to material resources, such as health and wealth, and all of the tangible things that contribute to those—workplaces, body parts, bank accounts, etc. The Ace of Disks is also the maker's card, the card where the deck maker traditionally places his or her sigil, stamp, or signature. The Ace of Disks often indicates that the time is right to bring an idea into reality—particularly one that the querent is uniquely positioned to create or bring forth. Alternatively, it can also reference one's overall health or ability to produce or earn resources. The Disk is an instrument (and therefore a symbol) of one's material reality.

CHAPTER 72
KNIGHT OF DISKS: "SWEAT," TOOL

Traditional Title: King of Disks or Pentacles, Lord of the Wide and Fertile Land, King of the Spirits of the Earth, King of the Gnomes
Planet/Element/Sign: Fire of Earth, first two decans of Virgo (last decan of Leo)
Planetary Ruler: Mercury
Date Range: August 12 – September 11
Qabalistic Correspondences: Chokmah of Assiah
Key Words: steady, methodical, provider, organized, systematic

"Sweat"
Tool
Opiate, 1992

Atu Line

K night of Disks represents the fiery part of earth. Earth is the final element, the combination of the inspired father element of fire; the practical, formative mother element of water; and the intellectual and wise son element of air—yielding the stable, abundant daughter element of earth. Knights are the highest-ranking court cards, the father in the royal family of the court cards. Taken together, the Knight of Disks represents the Father letter of Yod in YHVH, in the Daughter element of Earth. This Knight represents mostly the sign of Virgo, whose key phrase is "I ANALYZE."

Crowley remarks in *The Book of Thoth* that this Knight is mainly concerned with food production.[1] The Knight of Disks is courageously steadfast, and his dominion over the bounties of the earth make him a natural provider, whether in business, farming, sales, or wealth management. Where the other Knights are shown with their horses charging, this Knight's steed has all four hooves planted firmly on the ground. He is unmoved, committed to his plans and strategies, and married to the land of his abundance.

334

THE SONG

Tool's "Sweat" describes a character who is at turns a hunter and a thinker, and always the fisherman. Vacillating between the heat of day and the cool of night, this song references the dream state and alternate states of consciousness. The hunter is aggressive, the thinker passive, and the fisherman always searching and patient. The track illustrates the struggle for survival and advancement, cycling between awareness and the fugue state. The Knight makes philosophical progress toward enlightenment at night when all is quiet, but loses it all each day in the heat and fight for survival, sweating both ways.

The song references altered states in both the day and night, one devolving into violence and mayhem, the other evolving into elevated consciousness. Which is reality? Which is the dream? "Sweat" explores the survival mechanism in humans, the border between that which makes us human, and that which makes us animalistic. This fits well with the Knight of Disks, fire of earth, the combination of the highest and the lowest elements. He keeps doing both, as he knows no other way. The song's title is a reference to achievement through toil and sweat, something also second nature to this Knight, whose prudence, endurance, and dedication are among his most shining and admirable characteristics.

TABULA MUNDI TAROT

As the only Knight whose steed is not actively charging, the Knight of Disks is shown in a moment of deep thought as his horse quietly grazes. He holds a flail as his weapon—a tool used to separate wheat from chaff, and his shield displays symbols from the small cards that he rules: 7 of Wands and 8 and 9 of Disks. Above him appears his sigil, a winged stag with a solar disk.

THOTH TAROT

Harris' Knight of Disks is shown atop his shire horse, who seems to be interested in anything but battle. The Knight's weapon is a flail, further evidence that he is much more concerned with the provision of sustenance than the conquering of far-off lands. His shield, a form of Disk, radiates solar energy out to the productive fields surrounding him, symbolic of this Knight's fertility and prolificacy.

READING THIS CARD

Disk court cards are a blend of Wands' power and Cups' tangibility, making them both abundant and practical. Because Disks are the feminine offspring of Wands and Cups, they are driven, cautious, generous, productive providers. They are adept at bringing ideas and plans to fruition, managing practical affairs, and multiplying resources. They are slow moving, predictable, stubborn, and can be literalists, but they are also ethical, hardworking, and earnest.

Court cards are notoriously hard to read, because they can represent so much! They can be people, time periods, places, attitudes, and themes. The Knight of Disks' appearance in a reading can suggest a person who is born between August 12 and September 11, or a person whose personality is similar to the description of the Knight of Disks. It can represent a part of the querent's personality, or how he or she is feeling or acting in the situation at hand. The Knight of Disks can also indicate the timing of an event between August 12 and September 11, or a methodical, stable, predictable situation.

CHAPTER 73

QUEEN OF DISKS: "JUDITH," A PERFECT CIRCLE

Traditional Title: Queen of Disks or Pentacles, Queen of the Thrones of Earth, Queen of the Gnomes

Planet/Element/Sign: Water of Earth, first two decans Capricorn (last decan Sagittarius)

Planetary Ruler/Exaltation: Saturn rules, Mars exalted

Date Range: December 13 – January 9

Qabalistic Correspondences: Binah of Assiah

Key Words: stubborn, determined, effective, practical (as opposed to philosophical)

"Judith"
A Perfect Circle
Mer de Noms, 2000

Atu Line

Q ueen of Disks represents the watery part of earth. Earth is the final element, and Queens are the second highest-ranking court cards, the mother in the royal family of the court cards. Taken together, the Queen of Disks represents the Mother letter of Heh Primal in YHVH, in the Daughter (Heh Final) element of Earth.

This Queen corresponds mostly to the sign of Capricorn, with the key phrase "I USE." The Queen of Disks is the ultimate boss lady, standing squarely in her power and unafraid of seeming mannish or losing men's interest. However, while she may be abundant and sturdy (thanks to her earth suit), she is not known for questioning things or thinking too deeply about the philosophical implications of her actions (which would be more in the purview of the Queen of Swords).

THE SONG

This Queen can be faithful beyond what is deserved, naïve, and a blind follower. And yet, she's also known to be industrious, severe, conservative, fruitful, and ambitious. What emerges is the picture of a woman unconcerned with the abstract, but intensely focused on material facts, physical abundance, and steadfast dedication to her values. "Judith" is aptly suited to this card, as the song famously addresses issues of religion, faith, and naïveté vis a vis Keenan's mother, Judith, her long-term illness, and her continued Christian faith despite the blows life dealt her. The narrator in the track speaks bitterly about all the suffering the subject has endured, and yet, she still carries out the work and the duty of the faithful servant-follower with strength and grace. The narrator is clearly frustrated with the cognitive dissonance of continuing to follow a deity that allowed such harm to come to her, and that narrative deftly frames the positive and negative aspects of this Queen.

TABULA MUNDI TAROT

Meleen's Queen of Disks is set upon her throne in the deepest night. She holds a Disk that contains symbols of the alchemical elements (Salt, Sulphur, and Mercury) in primary colors—symbolic of their relationship to one another as the basic building blocks of material reality. Behind the Queen is an hour-glass, a reference to Saturn, the ruling planet of Capricorn. The Queen's sigil overhead is the winged goat and the crossed tools of industry.

THOTH TAROT

A sumptuously dressed Queen sits on her throne, covered in all manner of furs and finery, looking out over her vast lands. She seems to be contemplating all that will be planted and grown in her fields come spring. Her crown is a large, spiral-twisted set of mountain goat horns, and she holds a disk and scepter. She is accompanied by the mountain goat of Capricorn.

READING THIS CARD

Court cards can represent people, time periods, places, attitudes, and themes—the sheer diversity of information included in them can be overwhelming, especially for those who are just learning tarot. The Queen of Disks' appearance in a reading can suggest a person who is born between December 13 and January 9, or a person whose personality is similar to the description of the Queen of Disks. It can represent a part of the querent's personality, or how he or she is feeling or acting in the situation at hand. The Queen of Disks can also indicate the timing of an event between December 13 and January 9, or a situation that calls for productivity, ownership, or stewardship. And as "Judith" illustrates, this card can also indicate blind followership or naivete.

CHAPTER 74

PRINCE OF DISKS: "EAT THE ELEPHANT," A PERFECT CIRCLE

Traditional Title: Knight of Disks or Pentacles, Prince of the Chariot of the Earth, Prince and Emperor of the Gnomes
Planet/Element/Sign: Air of Earth, first two decans of Taurus (last decan of Aries)
Planetary Ruler/Exaltation: Venus rules, Moon exalted
Date Range: April 11 – May 10
Qabalistic Correspondences: Tiphareth of Assiah
Key Words: slow movement, focused on the material, salt of the earth, competence, caution

"Eat the Elephant"
A Perfect Circle
Eat the Elephant, 2018

Atu Line

P rince of Disks is the airy part of earth. Princes are the son of the royal family, said to combine the active, inspired properties of the Knight and the stable, wise aspects of the Queen into an intelligent, rational element of air. The Prince of Swords represents the Son letter of Vau in YHVH in the daughter (Heh Final) element of earth.

This Prince's combined mental and physical strength make him an industrious, dependable, and capable entrepreneur. Along with the last decan of Aries, he represents the first two thirds of Taurus, a sign whose key phrase is "I HAVE." The Prince of Disks is fertile and diligent, willing to work for the luxuries he owns and desires, and is always coming up with new ways to obtain them. He's also generous, steady, and has the best work ethic of any of the court cards. He is driven to succeed on the material plane, and has the makings to become an incomparable provider like his father, the Knight of Disks, later in life.

Of special note, this card is the court card correspondent to Keenan's natal Sun in the final decan of Aries. In fact, the Prince of Disks' personality and characteristics are fairly important in Keenan's natal chart, as this Prince also oversees Keenan's natal (retrograde) Mercury and Jupiter, too. As you may have guessed based on planetary descriptions throughout this book, the natal Sun placement sheds light on a person's general outlook on life, Mercury rules over a person's communication and thinking style, and Jupiter gives an indication of a person's gifts and talents. Having these placements likely contributes mightily to Keenan's endless work ethic, lengthy list of projects, and diverse entrepreneurial endeavors.

Also, no doubt you've heard folks blame all kinds of snafus on Mercury retrograde, but the trend of making a big deal out of this common phenomenon of a planet appearing to move away from earth during its normal orbit is overblown. The author also "suffers" from a retrograde natal Mercury, and if her experience has rendered any insight, it would be that Mercury's retrograde status at Keenan's birth most likely manifests as introversion and heightened intuition.

THE SONG

A Perfect Circle's "Eat the Elephant" embodies this Prince's discipline and determination to act, to do something—anything—to make tangible, real world progress. This Prince is tied to the astrological sign of Taurus, which corresponds to The Hierophant in the major arcana and speaks to learning and teaching as well as the possession of a broad system of resources. The process of learning, teaching, or obtaining anything precious requires this Prince's steadfast nature and willingness to try.

"Eat the Elephant" emphasizes that progress is made one step at a time, particularly in its slow and steady tempo and straightforward lyrics. The insistence of putting one foot in front of the other is the simple creed of this Prince. He knows that if he just begins, he'll find his momentum and his planned path will inevitably lead him directly to his goal. This wisdom is something I returned to repeatedly in the process of producing the book you're reading now.

In the face of intimidation and overwhelm, just begin.

TABULA MUNDI TAROT

This fertile Prince is shown in a chariot drawn by a bull; flowers adorn the wheels, and symbols of this Prince's masculine and earthy influences decorate the body of the chariot and his shield. Rolling, green hills populate the background. Above, the Prince's sigil features a winged bull's head with the letter Vau (Hebrew letter meaning *nail*, correspondent to The Hierophant and Taurus, this Prince's main sign) over the third eye.

THOTH TAROT

Harris' iteration of this Prince shows him driving a steel chariot composed of a multitude of disks, pulled by a bull, symbolic of Taurus, the Prince's main astrological association. He holds a scepter topped with globe and equal-armed cross, symbolic of his dominion over the earth element. In the other hand, he holds the disk of his suit. The background is filled with an abundance of harvested crops.

READING THIS CARD

Court cards are some of the most diverse cards in the pack in terms of their possible interpretations—they can represent people, time periods, places, attitudes, and themes. The Prince of Disks' appearance can suggest a person who is born between April 11 and May 10, or a personality similar to the description of the Prince of Disks. It can represent how a querent is feeling or acting in the role at question in the reading. The Prince of Disks can also indicate the timing of an event between April 11 and May 10, or a situation which demands steady effort, planning, or an entrepreneurial spirit.

CHAPTER 75

PRINCESS OF DISKS: "MAGDALENA," A PERFECT CIRCLE

Traditional Title: Page of Disks or Pentacles, Princess of the Echoing Hills, The Rose of the Palace of Earth, Princess and Empress of the Gnomes, Throne of the Ace of Disks or Pentacles
Planet/Element/Sign: Earth of Earth, rules quadrant of earth under the constellations of Aries-Taurus-Gemini
Qabalistic Correspondences: Malkuth of Assiah
Key Words: potential, pregnancy, kindness, generosity, fertility

"Magdalena"
A Perfect Circle
Mer de Noms, 2000

Atu Line

P rincesses are the daughter of the royal family, and they are the "thrones" or homes of their Aces. They represent the earthy aspects of their suits, so naturally they reside in Malkuth. While the Knights are active, the Queens are practical, and the Princes are intelligent, the Princesses are pure potential; they are the second Heh in YHVH formula. And unlike Knights, Queens, and Princes, who represent slices of time, Princesses represent space and geographic locations.

The Princess of Disks is the earthy part of earth, and the throne of the Ace of Disks. As this Princess lives in the Malkuth of the Assiah tree, she embodies all the possibilities of earth here on earth—in all its pleasure and glory, messiness and pain. The Princess of Disks corresponds to the Aries-Taurus-Gemini quadrant of space above Earth, over Europe and Africa.

She is the final card in the court and the throne of the Ace of Disks, which means she contains a little of everything that came before her, and therefore—perhaps this may come as some surprise —she is the most powerful card in the deck. In the Thoth deck she is visibly pregnant, and we know that she is literally pregnant with possibility. Because she is earth of earth, Malkuth of Malkuth, she contains all the energy that has worked its way down the Path of the Flaming Sword from Source (Kether), all the way down to the material plane. She is every idea, every possibility, every potentiality, in manifest form.

THE SONG

"Magdalena" is most certainly an apt depiction of this Princess. Understood to be an exotic dancer, the titular character is referred to as a temple, a goddess, and a black Madonna. All of these recall not just the sensuality and purity of Princess energies, but specifically describe this Princess's energy as earthy—touchable, holdable, in the flesh before our eyes and hands.

She is the feminine principle of earth in manifest form, and since Disks represent our bodies, all the attendant lust of the flesh is included here. The aspects of the feminine form that are often cited as the most attractive and beautiful are those that contribute to reproduction and support of children—hips, belly, breasts, etc., further reinforcing her capacity to incubate, birth, and raise new realities. The narrator's desperation to touch and be touched by her holiness is another indication of this card and all its sanctity. It is the desire to experience the miracle of human existence, and the price that is willingly paid to see it through.

TABULA MUNDI TAROT

The Princess of Earth stands upon the land she rules. As the throne of the Ace of Disks, she represents all of material reality, and the fertility principles that make it possible. She is Babalon, the Great Chalice of the Universe, birthing and reaping us all. She is earth of earth, Heh Final in YHVH, fertility embodied.

THOTH TAROT

A visibly pregnant Princess stands before her altar holding the Ace of Disks and a downward-pointed scepter, symbolic of her rulership over the material world. She is richly adorned in furs and a helmet of goat horns, also symbolic of her fertility and power.

READING THIS CARD

Perhaps by now the court cards are a little less intimidating, since we have made our way completely through all sixteen permutations of the elements in people. You may have guessed that the Princess of Disks' appearance in a reading can suggest an event that occurs in spring (Aries through Gemini), or a person whose personality is similar to the description of the Princess of Disks. It can represent a part of the querent's personality, or how he or she is feeling or acting in the role at question in the reading. The Princess of Disks can also indicate literal or figurative pregnancy, or a situation of potentiality —one in which the only limits are self-imposed.

CHAPTER 76
2 OF DISKS: "H.," TOOL

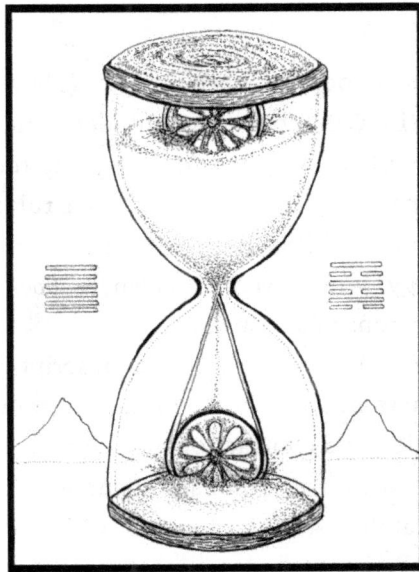

Thoth Title: Change
Planet/Sign: Jupiter in Capricorn
Planetary Ruler/Exaltation: Saturn rules, Mars exalted
Date Range: December 22 - 30
Qabalistic Correspondences: Chokmah of Assiah
Key Words: expansion and contraction, rebalancing of load, juggling, progress

"H."
Tool
Ænima, 1996

ATU LINE

The 2 of Disks is associated with Jupiter (planet of abundance, expansion, gifts) in Capricorn (sign of determination, structure, accomplishment; ruled by Saturn). Here, Jupiter, the planet of growth and expansion, is paired with a sign ruled by Saturn, the planet of limitations and lessons. The result is a push-me-pull-you exchange of energy, which M.M. Meleen in *Book M: Liber Mundi* compares to the pistons of a cosmic engine.[1]

The card's title, Change, is the perfect description for the impact of these two planets in the second (and therefore dual) sphere of Chokmah. Expansion and contraction, give and take, up and down—the nature of the universe is constant change. The constancy of change is itself stability—think of riding a bike or balancing spinning plates—the persistent movement is what allows balance.

As with any two in the deck, this card deals in duality, a universal principle reflected in the symbols of the Self and the Other, the mirror, the scales, the twins, and the lovers. Any time there are two, there is also a question of balance. Depending on the suit, the balance in question is of energy, emotion, ideas, or physical existence. Of course, in the 2 of Disks, it's referencing balance in the material world, and Crowley says this card is "the picture of the complete manifested universe, in respect of its dynamics."[2]

THE SONG

Tool's track "H." is the selection for this card. The narrator in this piece is exploring his relationship with the Other, and how engaging in the relationship changes him. Based on the time period this track was released, this song is likely one of Keenan's early explorations of fatherhood and how quickly it changed his identity and perspective. The entrance into parenthood often triggers a re-examination of one's identity, beliefs, and shadow. By committing to raising another human, one is immediately brought face to face with their own shortcomings and darkness, often inspiring all kinds of change in the parent.

Furthermore, looking into the eyes of one's own child is in some ways like looking into a mirror—another symbol of duality. To see oneself in another person is startling. Parents have to face down their fears of repeating mistakes or passing their flaws on to their children; parenthood requires the willingness to face one's shadow and surrender the ego in order to prioritize another person over oneself.

Perhaps the "trippiest" element of this experience is the knowledge that this tiny human who resembles you will one day replace you—as your body ages toward death, someday that tiny human will be the carrier of your genetic line as you yourself pass into the great beyond. The resulting vulnerability and connection to this new human is beyond our ability to express, more important than life itself, and yet destroying everything the parent thought they knew about themselves—death by consideration, if you will.

TABULA MUNDI TAROT

Two disks are contained in the upper and lower chambers of an hourglass, invoking the Saturnian (Capricorn's ruling planet) concept of time. Between them is a lemniscate belt that rotates the two in opposite directions and drains the sand from top to bottom. On either side of the hourglass appear the first and last I Ching trigrams, a reference to expansion (Jupiter) and contraction (Capricorn/Saturn), the two forces that drive the engine of the universe.

THOTH TAROT

Two disks, drawn in the style of yin-yang, appear one above the other with an ouroboros twisted into an infinity symbol encompassing them. The background is shades of blue, purple, indigo, lavender, black, and white—emphasizing the influence of Jupiter and Saturn, and the principle of duality.

READING THIS CARD

The 2 of Disks captures a magnificent state of flux, which can be experienced in a variety of ways throughout life. When this card appears, change is afoot. The universe revolves in its cyclical ways, and as we are earthly mirrors to the skies (as above, so below), our lives also revolve in cycles. Times of growth are followed by fallow periods. The rise to power is inevitably followed by decline. Birth leads irretrievably to death. This is the way the Universe works, neutrally and infinitely rising and slouching through time and space.

CHAPTER 77

3 OF DISKS: "TALKTALK," A PERFECT CIRCLE

Thoth Title: Works
Planet/Sign: Mars in Capricorn
Planetary Ruler/Exaltation: Saturn rules, Mars exalted
Date Range: December 31 – January 9
Qabalistic Correspondences: Binah of Assiah
Key Words: industriousness, construction, building, dedication to the goal

"TalkTalk"
A Perfect Circle
Eat the Elephant, 2018

Atu Line

T he 3 of Disks, known as Works or Work, is associated with Mars in Capricorn—an incredibly effective and productive duo. Mars, the planet of aggression and dominance, is exalted in Capricorn, the sign of accomplishment, determination, and industry. These two together are the definition of getting shit done, and when you consider the card's number is three and thus the card is located in Binah, the sephira of the mother and of form, the 3 of Disks is a fantastic representation of fertility that produces tangible outcomes on the material plane. This card is an excellent partner in supporting one's motivation and endurance to build structure around an idea or concept.

THE SONG

A Perfect Circle's "TalkTalk" is an ideal match for this card, with both the song and card carrying the same overall message: DO something constructive to move toward the goal. The ostensible meaning of the track is sociopolitical, commenting on political leaders' lack of meaningful action to ameliorate entrenched problems that plague our society, from poverty to violence to climate change. The track is especially taking aim at so-called Christians who claim to follow the example of Jesus, but whose actions speak otherwise.

Sociopolitical tie-ins aside, "TalkTalk" is especially a great match for this card for its middle refrain about the futility of faith and words without the necessary actions to back them up. No matter how strong one's faith (Wands, fire), feelings (Cups, water), or ideas (Swords, air) may be, without actions taken on the material plane (Disks, earth), none of it matters. It's the nature of the practice of magick, too: acts on the astral plane must be backed up on the physical plane if they are to have "real" impact on what we commonly perceive to be "reality."

TABULA MUNDI TAROT

The glyphs of alchemical Sulphur, Salt, and Mercury appear inside the twists of a central DNA strand. A lightning bolt strikes the middle glyph, Salt, activating the material aspect of the element. In the background is a brick masonry wall in the process of being built.

THOTH TAROT

A top-down view of a pyramid-shaped structure reveals disks at the three corners of the base, which appear to be whirling and thus blowing sand across the desert floor, away from the structure. Each disk contains an alchemical glyph, with Mercury appearing on the upper corner of the diagram, and Salt and Sulphur on the lower corners.

READING THIS CARD

When this card shows up in a reading, it's time to get to work. The time has come to move beyond simply contemplating your idea or task, to making tangible progress in the material world toward your goal. True progress requires focusing all thoughts, emotions, and actions on the outcome you desire—the aspirant must be a self-contained and unified front. Above all, quit talking about it and take action. It's time to get serious in your commitment to your plans, to invest yourself in your ideas, and to get off your ass.

Ill-dignity for this card can indicate stalls in the process, barriers to overcome, ideas that are sabotaging the work, or other reasons why the process may be dragging or thwarted.

CHAPTER 78
4 OF DISKS: "THE DOOMED," A PERFECT CIRCLE

Thoth Title: Power
Traditional Title: Lord of Earthly Power
Planet/Sign: Sun in Capricorn
Planetary Ruler/Exaltation: Saturn rules, Mars exalted
Date Range: January 10 - 19
Qabalistic Correspondences: Chesed of Assiah
Key Words: fortified, hoarding, wealth, resources, influence

"The Doomed"
A Perfect Circle
Eat the Elephant, 2018

Atu Line

———————————————

P ower, the 4 of Disks, is associated with Sun (planet of freedom, growth, independence, life) in Capricorn (sign of determination, structure, accomplishment; ruled by Saturn). It is the Chesed of the material world, the civilization that arises from the order imposed by the Emperor's plans and dominance (The Emperor is Atu IV in the major arcana). This is the card of fortresses and banks, guarded by the tightest of security measures. The unfortunate side effect of Power is the need to preserve it. In this card, we see not only the establishment of control, but the maintenance of it. Once you ascend to the seat of power, you must hold onto it through rules, regulations, systems of "Law and Order, maintained by constant authority and vigilance,"[1] enforcement, and might.

THE SONG

A Perfect Circle's "The Doomed" illustrates the 4 of Disks very well. This track is framed in Christian symbolism of the Seven Deadly Sins and the Seven Virtues, as well as references to shifting beatitude (meaning "supreme blessedness") between these two sets of values. The track postulates that power has shifted, perhaps irrevocably, from the righteous to the dishonorable in the world, that the battle between good and evil has reached a new level of desperation and crisis. When the indecent gain the upper hand over the decent, the measures they employ to keep themselves in power are the doom of the innocent.

As mentioned earlier, the 4 of Disks, too, has a dark side. Power wielded in righteousness can be a savior, but when power coalesces around greed and lack of compassion, the results are terrifying. Like the infamous Stanford Prison Experiment, in which subjects were divided into prisoners and prison officers, it's frighteningly easy to surrender our values when the rules of power allow or call for values opposed to our own. It's as if we have an inherent bias in favor of abdicating to regulations, assuming that someone else has already done the moral figuring in the making of the rules.

TABULA MUNDI TAROT

The face of the Green Man from The Devil card appears amid four coins marked with the motto of the Roman Empire "Soli Invicto" (to the unconquered sun), crowns, and the spirit of the heart from The Sun card (the associated major arcana cards for 4 of Disks are The Sun and The Devil). Beneath this arrangement is a fortress to store and protect the riches this card suggests.

THOTH TAROT

Interestingly, this card's illustration includes no disks. A top-down view of a four-sided fortress reveals the security of the facility. It is guarded by four watch-towers, each emblazoned with a glyph of one of the four elements. The structure is surrounded by a moat; a single bridge provides the only way in and out. It is evident that the disks and other riches held within are of much value to the owner.

READING THIS CARD

When this card appears in a reading, it can be read as both stability and greed, depending on the cards surrounding it. This world is what we choose to make it, for we are the literal makers of the reality in which we live. If well-dignified, this card can indicate that the fruits of the querent's labors have enriched them considerably, or else they have a useful level of power or influence in the situation at hand. If ill-dignified, however, the 4 of Disks warns against miserly attitudes and behavior; power maintained at all cost and at the expense of others eventually becomes its own prison.

CHAPTER 79

5 OF DISKS: "TICKS & LEECHES," TOOL

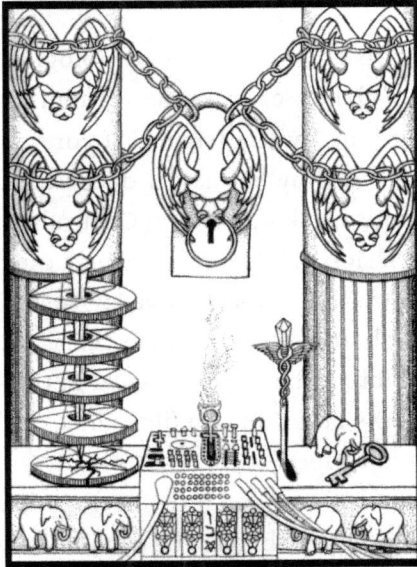

Thoth Title: Worry
Planet/Sign: Mercury in Taurus
Planetary Ruler/Exaltation: Venus rules, Moon exalted
Date Range: April 21 – 30
Qabalistic Correspondences: Geburah of Assiah
Key Words: money or health worries, solution in sight but unacknowledged, slowed thinking and communication, frustration

"Ticks & Leeches"
Tool
Lateralus, 2001

Atu Line

The 5 of Disks, Worry, has astrological associations of Mercury (planet of communication, commerce, speed, knowledge) in Taurus (sign of luxury, material comforts, beauty, abundance; ruled by Venus). It doesn't sound so bad, until one considers that this is taking place in Geburah, the sephira of war, conflict, and aggression. If Mercury brings quicksilver thinking, Taurus brings a slow and steady love of material comfort, and Geburah is constant battle, it's no wonder this is the card of material concerns. All the stability that was achieved in the 4 of Disks is now being disrupted by the addition of a fifth wheel, balance is lost, and volatility is now in full effect.

Crowley notes of this card and its I Ching equivalent: "The idea is of strangling, as dogs worry sheep...The economic system has broken down; there is no more balance between the social orders."[1] He further notes, "The general effect is one of intense strain; yet the symbol implies long-continued inaction."[2]

In *Understanding Aleister Crowley's Thoth Tarot*,[3] Lon Milo DuQuette characterizes the fundamental questions of this card as,

"Am I being pulled into a predicament I can't get out of? Am I in over my head? Will I be crushed by the blind momentum of this system?" With the pentacle created by the Disks on this card being reversed, we see that the material has the upper hand over the spiritual in this arrangement, a cause for worry and distress indeed.

THE SONG

"Ticks & Leeches" is a strange bedfellow on Tool's *Lateralus* album—its explosive anger seems to clash against the rest of the spiritual and evolutionary nature of the track list. Considering the group's long-standing conflict with their record label, as well as their sometimes-jaded view of fans and the music industry, it's possible that this track is a response to demands on the group for new music that satisfies a certain kind of label or sound. Perhaps this was the band's "fuck you" to the boxes that the industry attempts to put them in, or a primal scream of resentment against a machine that gobbles up individual artistic expression and shits out cookie-cutter formulas for revenue.

Regardless of the accuracy of this theory, the track and the card both speak to the resentment of feeling helplessly swept up into the maws of a monster that threatens one's material stability or even existence. Both showcase the dis-ease of being used, the vulnerability of not having control over one's resources, the desperation to regain that control, and the sinking fear that all is lost and will never be regained.

TABULA MUNDI TAROT

Here we see evidence of both the major arcana cards associated with 5 of Disks. The Magus' DJ equipment is in the foreground, obviously having a severe malfunction that is resulting in smoke rising from the control panel and the shattering of the bottom of the five disk "records" in the rack. In the background, the Kerubic bull and pillars from The Hierophant card frame this image, and chains run between them and a central bull-headed lock, blocking the way through. This is the picture of all progress ground to a halt.

THOTH TAROT

Five disks are arranged in an inverted pentagram pattern. Beneath them are larger, corresponding wheels that appear to be damaged and cracked in various ways, and locked against one another such that none of them can rotate. While nothing is moving, force and pressure continues to build against the blockage, promising great damage when the wheels are finally freed.

READING THIS CARD

When this card appears, the querent could be experiencing frustration at best, and dire material circumstances at worst; they could be worried about their physical, financial, familial, or professional health. The difference between survival and going under is the attitude—are you laying down and waiting for your demise, or are you keeping your head up and watching for opportunities to improve your circumstances? Pick those suckers off and keep truckin'. If you need help remembering that abundance is infinite and nothing is impossible in this Universe, spend some time with the priestly Hierophant, Atu V in the major arcana, who will happily remind you that you, too, are a blessed child of the Universe.

CHAPTER 80
6 OF DISKS: "JAMBI," TOOL

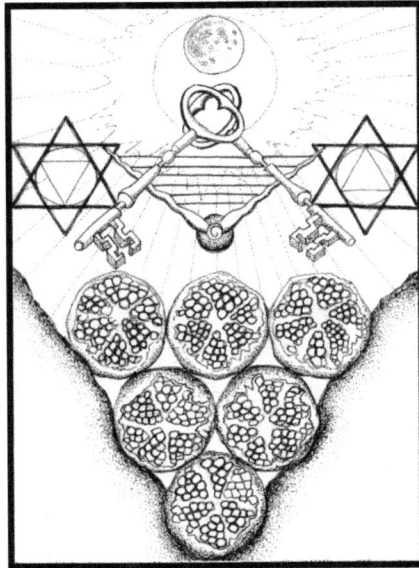

Thoth Title: Success
Planet/Sign: Moon in Taurus
Planetary Ruler/Exaltation: Venus rules, Moon exalted
Date Range: May 1 - 10
Qabalistic Correspondences: Tiphareth of Assiah
Key Words: benevolence, mentorship, generosity, achievement

"Jambi"
Tool
10,000 Days, 2006

Atu Line

_____

T he 6 of Disks, entitled Success, is Moon (planet of cycles, mystery, intuition) in Taurus (sign of luxury, material comforts, beauty, abundance; ruled by Venus) in the sunny sixth sephira of Tiphareth. It's a lovely combination, as the Moon is exalted in Taurus and Tiphareth is the sphere of the sun, the mind, the Christ consciousness, and victory. *The Book of Thoth* describes this card's lunar/solar harmony: "...the Moon, being in Taurus, the sign of her exaltation, the best of the Lunar qualities are inherent. Moreover, being a Six, the solar Energy has fertilized her, creating a balanced system for the time being."[1]

Here is a brief moment in the sun, when we can pause to enjoy our triumph in making our dreams come true. It is the house built and established as a family's home; the promotion that brings abundance, prestige, and protegees to teach; the satisfaction of fruitful labors that bring a vision to material reality. Crowley also fittingly describes this card as "settling down."[2]

THE SONG

The narrator in Tool's "Jambi" describes opulent success while acknowledging that wealth and abundance are merely tools to bring safety and joy to one's most important relationships. It is interesting to note the mentions of the Sun (and thus its homophone, son) throughout "Jambi," for these further illustrate what's at the heart of a parent's drive to succeed.

Crowley even describes Tiphareth and the sixes (again, the sephira of the Sun/son) as the material expression of the ideals of Chokmah (the sephira of the father): "consciousness at its most harmonized and balanced form...the son is an interpretation of the father in terms of the mind."[3] Incidentally, Jambi was released during a period when Keenan was unmarried and had only one child, his son.

Regardless of who the narrator is, "Jambi" makes crystal clear where the narrator's priority lies: using present material success to bolster and feed into the future success of and connection to his beloved, and through that, his own soul's evolution and ascension. Like the 6 of Disks, "Jambi" exhibits this single-minded pursuit of heart-centered growth is the guiding light of the narrator's path. Incidentally, this is the most frequently played song from *10,000 Days*,[4] a regular staple of Tool's live sets since this album was released. I like to think of it as the band members' love song to their families.

TABULA MUNDI TAROT

Six pomegranate "disks" rest in an inverse pyramid arrangement (a reference to the glyph of elemental earth) nestled in the valley between two hills. Above them are the heptagrams of water and fire, the complete divine feminine and masculine, whose harmonious union is represented by the matching silver and gold keys from The

Hierophant card. Further above are the moon superimposed on the sun, another reference to balanced masculine and feminine.

THOTH TAROT

Six disks contain all the planetary glyphs but the Sun's; the solar luminary's disk is the much larger disk upon which these are resting. The arrangement of the smaller disks around the edge of the larger one suggests a round table of mentorship, mutual aid, equality, and perfection. The central disk bears the 49-petaled rose and equal-armed cross as representations of the sun's power and centrality here. The background is comprised of harmoniously repeating iterations of disks interspersed with beams of light.

READING THIS CARD

When this card appears, the querent is invited to celebrate and enjoy their success, then pay it forward by investing in others in some way, such as caregiving, mentoring, benevolence, charitable giving, etc. This is a familial and community leadership card, and the heart leads best when it is open and generous. The 6 of Disks is a sweet, but passing stage—enjoy the success while it's here, and be sure to use it to make the best of the world around you.

An ill-dignified 6 of Disks can signal a lack of gratitude, a lack of recognition of one's own successes, or even using a position of influence or power to harass, harm, or sabotage others.

CHAPTER 81

7 OF DISKS: "BOTTOM,"
TOOL

Thoth Title: Failure
Planet/Sign: Saturn in Taurus
Planetary Ruler/Exaltation: Venus rules, Moon exalted
Date Range: May 11 – 20
Qabalistic Correspondences: Netzach of Assiah
Key Words: loss of will to keep going, giving up with success in sight, laziness, abandonment

"Bottom"
Tool
Undertow, 1993

Atu Line

F ailure, the 7 of Disks, is influenced by Saturn (planet of limitations, lessons, discipline, time) in Taurus (sign of luxury, material comforts, beauty, abundance; ruled by Venus) in Venus's sephira of Netzach. This is quite obviously a poor combination of influences, which the title of the card confirms. The 7 of Disks represents the total loss of all at stake, for lack of endurance and effort. Crowley remarks, "Labor itself is abandoned; everything is sunk in sloth"[1] and he also notes that the card carries the energy of blight and bad money.[2]

Mel Meleen describes this card as the Garden of Eden after The Fall, when the lower seven sephiroth descend into chaos, separated from the Supernal Triad above by the necessary buffer of the Abyss.[3] The 7 of Disks is the failure to continue pursuing ascendance, to the tune of the old adage, "you only fail when you stop trying."

THE SONG

"Bottom" from Tool's *Undertow* is a song filled with abuse, oppression, and radioactive self-loathing, a combination of guilt and shame with nothing left to lose but the charge of rage that fills the narrator's being. The lyrics describe long-term abuse at the hands of a sinister force, and the numbing and enervating impact of surviving within this system of hate and callousness. The battered eventually lose the will to keep trying to rise above the pain, and become willing to settle for whatever scraps of existence they can scrape up from the bottom of life. The song's title is succinct, distilling the essence of the concept and wasting not one letter.

TABULA MUNDI TAROT

Meleen's 7 of Disks is an illustration of the Tree of Life after the fall of man from Tiphareth/Eden. YHVH stands guard above the abyss in the form of the Kerubic angels of the zodiac: Lion (Leo), Eagle (Scorpio), Human (Aquarius), Bull (Taurus). Above them, the supernal triad rests undisturbed. Below, the lower 7 sephiroth "disks" (symbolic of all material reality) have been devoured by a multi-headed dragon of chaos.

THOTH TAROT

The card is awash in grey, lavender, and indigo, as though the scene was entirely made from stone or metal, perhaps lead (Saturn). Seven disks are arranged in what Crowley calls "the geomantic figure Rubeus, the most ugly and menacing of the Sixteen."[4] The coins bear images representing Saturn and Taurus.

READING THIS CARD

The card likewise cuts to the chase: if you choose to stop struggling to rise, you are definitively choosing to sink. In this circumstance, there is no one else to blame, for you have chosen your fate. This is a time to reach out for help and support from others, to embed yourself in a larger system of support, and to dig deep. Keep working to rise above the circumstances holding you down.

CHAPTER 82
8 OF DISKS: "THE PATIENT," TOOL

Thoth Title: Prudence
Planet/Element/Sign: Sun in Virgo
Planetary Ruler/Exaltation: Mercury rules, Mercury exalted
Date Range: August 23 – September 1
Qabalistic Correspondences: Hod of Assiah
Key Words: patience, investment, long-term commitment,
dedication

"The Patient"
Tool
Lateralus, 2001

Atu Line

The 8 of Disks, Sun (planet of growth, freedom, independence, life) in Virgo (sign of systems, details, patience, commitment; ruled by Mercury) in Mercury's sephira of Hod, is called Prudence. This is a great little Mercurial card —there is a tight relationship between the Sun and its 'little buddy' Mercury, who is never more than 28 degrees away in the skies. Virgo and the eighth sephira Hod are both ruled by Mercury, and the addition of the Sun here keeps the energy materially productive and abundant. The card represents the dedication and care needed to plan, plant, grow, and harvest something valuable—there is nothing risk-taking or lackadaisical about this card—hence the title Prudence. Crowley compares this card to the "husband-man,"[1] and "intelligence lovingly applied to material things, especially those of the agriculturalist, the artificer, and the engineer."[2]

THE SONG

Tool's "The Patient" expresses this commitment and dedication perfectly with its willingness to patiently wait out the completion of the process, and the acknowledgement that waiting for the fruits of labors on a difficult path is challenging. At every step along the way, we must recommit to going forward, because as we've seen in the 7 of Disks before, choosing to stop working at any point is choosing to walk away from any chance of success.

A large piece of commitment, and the source of the discipline it so often creates, is the willingness to continue shepherding a process despite monotony, boredom, and infinitesimally small increments of progress. It demands a trust in the process, a comfort with ambiguity and the unknown, and a deep respect for delayed gratification; in other words, it demands patience.

TABULA MUNDI TAROT

The Hermit's lantern, symbolic of The Hermit and Virgo, warms a nest of eight eggs. The flame within the lantern is a six-pointed star symbolic of the Sun. The steady, warm light of the sun makes life possible.

THOTH TAROT

Eight disks bloom in the center of eight flowers growing up a hearty tree; the base of the trunk bears the glyph of Virgo. Each blossom is shaded by a leaf, shielding and protecting the blooms from over-exposure. The background of the card is a brilliant yellow, recalling the sun's light.

READING THIS CARD

When the 8 of Disks appears in a reading, commitment and dedication are called for. This card frequently appears when long-term (but usually finite) commitments are in play: beginning a training or degree program, taking on a large project at work, building a house, starting a business, etc. The road may be demanding, but the results will be worth it. If ill-dignified, this card can indicate such things as making a foolish commitment, failing to honor one's commitments, or completing work shoddily.

CHAPTER 83

9 OF DISKS:
"MONEYSHOT,"
PUSCIFER

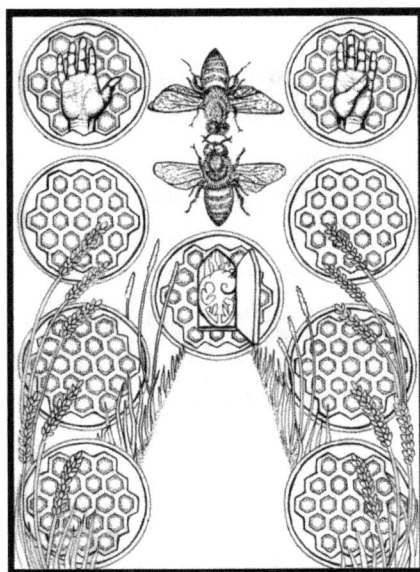

Thoth Title: Gain

Planet/Sign: Venus in Virgo

Planetary Ruler/Exaltation: Mercury rules, Mercury exalted

Date Range: September 2 – 11

Qabalistic Correspondences: Yesod of Assiah

Key Words: increase in income, material gain, flourishing garden, growth

"Moneyshot"

Puscifer

The Money Shot, 2015

Atu Line

The 9 of Disks, Gain or Material Gain, is associated with Venus in Virgo (sign of systems, details, patience, commitment; ruled by Mercury) in Yesod, the ninth sephira of the Moon. It's an incredibly abundant card—all parties are quite fertile in the feminine manner of flourishing gardens: Venus the Mother, the waxing and waning belly of the Moon, and Virgo the Virgin and keeper of the harvest. Crowley observes of this card: "It shows good luck attending material affairs, favour, and popularity... [it] signifies the multiplication of the original established Word—by the mingling of 'good luck and good management'."[1]

THE SONG

Puscifer's "Moneyshot" is the track matched to this card for its abundance that borders on ridiculousness. The lyrics describe someone who has gone from motivated, driven, and powerful to bored, bloated...and still powerful. The extended pornographic metaphor, introduced by the song's title, paints an image of a young, passionate lead porn actor given way to a bored, complacent star whose libidinous acts are purely means to an end. Likewise, in the description of the 9 of Disks, Crowley remarks, "The suit of Disks is much too dull to care; it reckons up its winnings; it doesn't not worry its head about whether anything is won when all is won."[2]

The continuous use of the words grinding, banging, and "here it comes" throughout the track emphasizes the perfunctory nature of porn—a manufactured substitution for the glory of real, hot sex with another horny person, a truly fulfilling orgasm, and the height of fulfillment.

The line "Moneyshot your load" (filming your orgasm) can also be interpreted as "Money shot your load" (currency assassinated your orgasm); the first describes the concept of making sure the male orgasm is filmed as 'proof' that the actors are having 'real' sex, and the second is the suggestion of money assassinating one's drive, one's spunk, one's essence.

TABULA MUNDI TAROT

Eight honeycomb disks are arranged into two columns framing this card. A path up the middle of the card leads to the ninth disk, which also contains a door (Daleth, the letter assigned to The Empress) which opens to reveal the heart from The Empress card (Venus). Two honey bees represent the fertility of both Venus and Virgo.

THOTH TAROT

Nine disks are arranged in clusters of three, with the middle trio representing the basic elements of magick, and the other two sets as coins marked with symbols of the Moon, Mercury, Venus, Mars, Jupiter, and Saturn. The background is full of lush pastels and verdant greens in symmetrical bursts of light.

READING THIS CARD

When this card appears in a reading, it's a sign of great luck in material matters. It's admittedly a very materialistic card, and one that makes no value statements about how that luck comes or is managed. The job of pornography is to get you off, not preach to you about what your favorite flavor of smut means or how orgasming 'should' be accomplished. It is the querent's job to take care of the morals and values. Likewise, the 9 of Disks does not demand much in the way of accountability, it is simply winning.

This card is also the natural progression of the eight, in that after putting in the work, we receive returns. We followed the proper steps in the correct order, and this is the expected and delivered result.

CHAPTER 84

10 OF DISKS: "AUTUMN," PUSCIFER

Thoth Title: Wealth
Traditional Title: Lord of Wealth
Planet/Sign: Mercury in Virgo
Planetary Ruler/Exaltation: Mercury rules, Mercury exalted
Date Range: September 12 – 22
Qabalistic Correspondences: Malkuth of Assiah
Key Words: legacy, inheritance, philanthropy, investment, genetics

"Autumn"
Puscifer
Money $hot, 2015

Atu Line

—————————————

The final minor arcana pip card, the 10 of Disks, is appropriately named Wealth, and its correspondences are Mercury (planet of communication, commerce, speed, knowledge) in Virgo (sign of systems, details, patience, commitment; ruled by Mercury) in the tenth sephira of Malkuth (Kingdom or the Earth). Unlike the other tens of the minor arcana, which uniformly express a state of over-saturation approaching rottenness, this ten is the accumulation of the material in the form of wealth. This is not simply cash money in hand; this is legacy-building wealth—the kind that is passed on to descendants in the form of investments, property, and possessions. It is wealth accumulated to the point of needing to be directed towards some kind of honorable work, lest it stagnate and fester into miserliness and decay.

This generational concept is further driven home by the fact that all of tarot is cyclical—as soon as one cycle ends, we come out at the top of the next cycle—wealth and genetic health transcend generation, passing onward to the next matriarch or patriarch rising to take their parents' place. So, too, it is with the tarot. The 10 of Disks—the totality of the journey and all that has been learned and made manifest—feeds right back into the Ace of Wands, and the journey begins anew. In addition to the meaning of this card as wealth, there is also a strong death flavor here—specifically of a long, full life coming to a close, and the adventure of regeneration that awaits in the great beyond.

THE SONG

Puscifer's "Autumn" closes out our musical journey, representing the sum total of the hard work to build a life worth living, and the all-too-human pleading to stave off death as long as possible so that a lifetime's fruits can be savored and enjoyed for as long as possible. The narrator acknowledges that their autumn years cannot last forever, and that winter, that season of the death and re-birth of the sun, will inevitably come for them, too.

The use of the word prudence in the lyrics is interesting here. "Prudence" is both the state of cautious action and careful stewardship, as well as another name for major arcana card XXI, The Universe (aka Saturn, who as the cosmic teacher and limit-bringer is the definition of prudence). Another little interesting nod to Saturn is Keenan's mention of skin and bones, which are body parts that correspond to Saturn. The relationship between the song and the card is further supported by Crowley, who likewise writes of the 10 of Disks, "This card to the other thirty-five small cards is what the twenty-first trump, The Universe, is to the rest of the trumps."[1]

TABULA MUNDI TAROT

Ten disks in the form of coins are arranged in the figure of the Tree of Life. Each coin bears a symbol of Mercury, Virgo, or the Sun, and the tenth coin bears a four-fold Tree of Life design. The arrangement is suspended in the night sky above the entrance to the underworld, as seen in The Hermit card (Virgo).

THOTH TAROT

On an indigo background of disks in the form of coins, a bright gold set of ten disks are laid out in the pattern of the Tree of Life. The bottom coin, in the position of Malkuth, is much larger than the others, a visual representation of the accumulation of material resources and wealth. All of the coins are stamped with various symbols of Mercury, except for the coin in the position of Hod, which contains a symbol of the Sun, all of which indicate Mercury as the transformative principle that returns energy to Source and begins the cycle anew.

READING THIS CARD

When the 10 of Disks is drawn, consider where there is wealth (whether as money, health, influence, or other physical forms) in the situation at hand, and how well it is being used and directed. The card can also indicate inheritance, both monetary and genetic, as well as the passing of elders, the receipt of a large sum of money or some item of sentimental or monetary value, or ascension into a higher echelon or societal standing. Something has reached the end of its natural life, and the querent should prepare themselves to gracefully surrender it to the passage of time.

CHAPTER 85

FUN WITH MAYNARD TAROT

Now that we have made our way through the entire seventy-eight cards of the deck and developed some understanding of the structure, themes, correspondences, and interpretation of the cards, you may be thinking, *how the hell do I put all this together and actually use it?*

Whether you want to use tarot as a divination tool, as a self-development tool, or both, the best way to get comfortable with the cards is by doing what is easiest and the most fun: fuck around with them. Practice shuffling them. Put them in order, rearrange them by all their various commonalities, arrange them in the Tree of Life formation, examine the images on the cards and how the images relate to and interact with one another. Meditate with them. Sleep with individual cards under your pillow, one per night, noting your dreams each morning. Imagine yourself inside the scenes they depict. The more you interact with the symbolism and correspondences of each card, the more familiar and comfortable you'll become.

Truthfully, this is a large part of how I got to know tarot, and how I got comfortable reading for myself and others. I'm endlessly fascinated by the ways that tarot's symbols and themes interact with each other and the world around me. I still conduct these explorations often, just for fun, and I'm always learning and noticing more —even after twenty years of reading professionally! So, in that spirit, I'd like to share just a few of the ways you can use Keenan's music and this book to help you on your tarot odyssey.

The first thing I did when I completed the outline of this book was create a full playlist of the songs that correspond to all of the cards (the second thing I did was make an incredibly nerdy spreadsheet of the cards and song data so I could analyze it all for patterns). The playlist was my constant companion for the duration of the writing, and I highly recommend you have access to a playlist of these tracks for convenience. You can find and follow mine on Spotify,[1] or if you prefer, build your own playlist of the songs used here. It will come in handy not only as you read through the book, but also for these interesting and eye-opening exercises:

- **Musical divination** – develop and write down an open-ended (not yes/no) question, ask it, then hit random play on the playlist. The track(s) that play next correspond to your card(s). I recommend using as few as possible, but no more than three. Before you look each song up in the book, listen. Completely setting aside whether you like the song or not, write about how the music and lyrics makes you feel (angry, determined, sad, euphoric, etc.). What memories do you associate with this song? How does this information relate to your question? Now, look up the song, pull the corresponding card, and proceed to interpret the reading as normal, taking into account the information you first gleaned while listening to the music, and using that to augment what is in the book.
- **Tarot reading as playlist** – develop and write down an open-ended (not yes/no) question, lay out cards using the card layout or spread of your choice, and then

translate your reading into a playlist by listening to the cards' corresponding songs in order of the reading. This works with any spread you like—past-present-future, Celtic Cross, etc. There are thousands of spread ideas online, but between you and me, the most effective spreads are those you create yourself. As in the point above, listen to the songs first before reading their entries, and note your own personal reactions to and associations with that song.

- **Translate songs into cards** – I'm sure you've noticed that not every Keenan song is included here. How did I determine which to use and which to pass on? Though there were many cards that had more than one possible song match and I had to make some difficult choices, many songs simply couldn't be adequately represented by just one card alone. Some songs need two or three cards to describe them. For this exercise, choose a song that isn't included here; read the lyrics and listen to the track. What cards comprise the overall message? Try to pare it down to the fewest cards for the most laser-focused interpretation. Once you've chosen your cards based on the song, read them. What additional information can you glean about the song from the cards, and vice versa?

- **Create a "you" playlist** – one of the most enlightening activities you can do when learning tarot and how to apply it to your life is to examine the cards that correspond to your birthdate. There are major arcana cards representing your sun sign and its ruling planet, a court card that includes your birthdate in its range, and a minor arcana card that corresponds to the decan of your sun sign in which you were born.[2] Each of these cards can be revealing for you in terms of your personality, traits, issues, and more. For each of these cards, listen to the song associated. Again, notice how you feel about the song and what it reminds you of before reading the card entry in the book; take note of all patterns you notice, connections you make, and synchronicities.

- **Create a "that time" playlist** – think of an important period in your life, a time for which you have vivid memories. What songs are associated with your memories of that period? If they are songs from our playlist, what do their associated cards tell you? If they are songs not included here or made by other artists, what cards would you match them to, and what do those cards tell you about that important period of your life?

- **Create your life's soundtrack** – similar to above, if you had to describe your life in a dozen songs—Keenan's or otherwise—what would you include? If they are songs from our playlist, what do their associated cards tell you? If they are songs not included here or made by other artists, what cards would you match them to, and what do those cards tell you about yourself and your life?

- **Find the card/song for your lifetime and this year** – to find your lifetime card, add the digits of your birthdate together using your birth year, then reduce the resulting number by adding its digits together until you have a number 21 or less. To get this year's card, add the digits of your month and date of birth with this year and reduce as above. The number of the card is your major arcana card and song for this lifetime/year.

- **What song/card matches of mine would you change? Why?** As I mentioned in the introduction, my intention here is not to be the "final word" on the intersection of these two topics. Instead, my hope is that I've illustrated my project in such a way as to inspire you to create or make it your own.

INTERESTING OBSERVATIONS MADE DURING THE WRITING OF THIS BOOK

For those interested, and purely for my own delight, here are some of the observations and analytical findings sparked by this project. I leave it to you to speculate on their significance, if any.

It will probably come as no surprise to longtime fans, but the hardest cards to match were often the happier, more pleasant cards. The 9 of Cups was without exaggeration the hardest card to match.

Most likely owing to its sheer size, Tool's catalogue supplied the majority of the matches (35), followed by Puscifer (25), and A Perfect Circle (17), and Deftones/Keenan (1).

In terms of albums, Tool's *Ænima* supplied the most tracks (9) as card matches, followed by their *Lateralus* and A Perfect Circle's debut, *Mer de Noms* (7 each). Incidentally, these three are consecutive albums released between 1996 and 2001.

Of the matched songs in Keenan's catalogue, the most (19) were written between Keenan's ages of 36 and 40 years old (Tool's *Lateralus*, and A Perfect Circle's *Thirteenth Step* and *eMOTIVe*). This was also the time period in which he wrote the most major arcana card matches (8).

The fewest matched songs (13) were written between his ages of 47 and 51 (Puscifer's *Conditions of My Parole*, *Donkey Punch the Night*, and *Money$hot*), and the majority of those were matched to major arcana cards (6).

The majority of the Air element cards are matched to songs from Keenan's three most recent consecutive albums: A Perfect Circle's *Eat the Elephant*, Tool's *Fear Inoculum*, and Puscifer's *Existential Reckoning*. Incidentally, all of these albums share common themes of modernity, technology, and popular culture—topics deeply concerned with ideas, intellect, conflict, commerce, and general mercurial themes.

AFTERWORD

I hope that in reaching the end of this journey, you've had some joy, some moments of revelation, a few clues into where to go next, and some quality time with your favorite music. More than anything, this project was designed to help you connect more deeply with art, yourself, and the Divine. Writing this book has revealed and opened doors I never knew existed, and it's my sincere hope that you've enjoyed reading it as much as I've enjoyed creating this labor of love and fandom.

I would like to leave you with some parting observations and values that have helped me in my tarot practice along the way. Whether you choose to study to become a professional, read just for friends for fun, or read exclusively as a personal meditation and spiritual practice, these morsels will help you keep the faith, keep on the path, and keep going...

WORDS ON DIVINATION: A TAROTIST'S CREED

1. If you remember anything, let it be this: connect with and thank deity every time you practice tarot. *Every time.* Remember this always, because your beliefs will change. Your practice will change. Your understanding of God will change. But no matter what, always acknowledge and thank Source as you currently understand IT.

2. With time, you'll be tempted to believe that what comes through in readings is All You, that you are just That Good. This temptation will be with you always. Never fail to tell others *they can do this, too.*

3. Never miss an opportunity to teach what you know to eager students. This is how we guarantee the survival of our lineage in any way that matters. The art and science of tarot must survive. *This human wisdom must survive.*

4. Tarot is no parlor trick; it is magickal technology. It must be handled with the veneration one would accord a wise mage. To truly practice tarot, one must come to *understand it* as magickal technology. Respect the wisdom you hold in your hand.

5. All things are cyclical. Through a daily practice of tarot, you are attuned to this universal wisdom. A lifetime tarot practice committed to continuous growth produces a capable witch/magickian.

6. Tarot teaches you how to tell Universal Time. A lifetime practice produces a time mage.

7. Tarot teaches you to read patterns. A lifetime of practice produces a seer of visions, a visionary.

8. A lifetime practice of tarot is a religion of self-examination and self-development. We who choose to walk this path necessarily commit to ever-onward growth.

9. Let us see this as our sacred vow: that we will pass the wisdom of tarot on with purpose and integrity. We place our faith in the collective truth of the practice of tarot.

To Thoth, Creator of the Secret Wisdom of Tarot, I commit my hands, voice, and cards. I serve in His Magnificent Name, and my service is blessed. As I will, so mote it be.

BIBLIOGRAPHY

Aiwaz, and Aleister Crowley. *Thelēma: The Holy Books of Thelema*. Berkeley, CA: S. Conjoined Creation, 2015

Brown, Brian. *The Wisdom of the Egyptians*, 1923. Included in *The Fragrance of the Mystical Rose: The Revelation of the Out-of-body Travel Celestial Mysteries from the Enclosed Garden of God* by Marilynn Hughes, 2014; accessed via Google Books October 25, 2019, p356-57.

Chang, T. Susan. *Tarot Correspondences: Ancient Secrets for Everyday Readers*. Woodbury, MN: Llewellyn Publications, 2018

Chang, T. Susan and M.M. Meleen. *Fortune's Wheelhouse*. Podcast Season 2, Episode 19, "Five of Cups". Released May 9, 2018

Crowley, Aleister. *777 and Other Qabalistic Writings of Aleister Crowley*. First published as *The Qabalah of Aleister Crowley*. San Francisco: Red Wheel/Weiser, LLC, 1973. Reprint, San Francisco: Red Wheel/Weiser, LLC, 1986

Crowley, Aleister. *The Book of Thoth by Master Therion* (Aleister Crowley): *A Short Essay on the Tarot of the Egyptians*. London, O.T.O., 1944. Reprint, Newburyport, MA: Weiser Books, 2017

DuQuette, Lon Milo. *Understanding Aleister Crowley's Thoth Tarot*. Newburyport, MA: Weiser Books, 2017

Grey, Peter. *The Red Goddess*. London: Scarlet Imprint, 2007

Hauck, Dennis William. *The Emerald Tablet: Alchemy for Personal Transformation*. New York: Penguin Compass, 1999

Keenan, Maynard James and Sarah Jensen. *A Perfect Union of Contrary Things*. Milwaukee, WI: Backbeat Books, 2016

"Maynard James Keenan." *Wikipedia*, Wikimedia Foundation, 2 May 2020, https://en.wikipedia.org/wiki/Maynard_James_Keenan

McIver, Joel. *Unleashed: The Story of Tool*. New York: Omnibus Press, 2009

Meleen, M.M. *Book M: Liber Mundi*. Barre, MA: Atu House, 2015

Tate, Karen. *Sacred Places of Goddess: 108 Destinations*. San Francisco: CCC Publishing, 2006

DISCOGRAPHY

A Perfect Circle. *Eat the Elephant*. New York: BMG Rights Management (US) LLC, 4050538374315, 2018

A Perfect Circle. *eMOTIVe*. Hollywood, CA: Virgin Records America, 7243 8 75270 2 7, 2004

BIBLIOGRAPHY

A Perfect Circle. *Thirteenth Step*. Hollywood, CA: Virgin Records America, 7243 5 80918 1 6, 2003

A Perfect Circle. *Mer de Noms*. Hollywood, CA: Virgin Records America, 7243 8 49321 2 1, 2000

Deftones and Maynard James Keenan. "Passenger." *White Pony*. Beverly Hills, CA: Maverick Records, 9 47667-2, 2000

Puscifer. *Money $hot*. Jerome, AZ: Puscifer Entertainment, 670541704431, 2015

Puscifer. *Donkey Punch the Night*. Jerome, AZ: Puscifer Entertainment, no catalog number, 2013

Puscifer. *Conditions of My Parole*. Jerome, AZ: Puscifer Entertainment, no catalog number, 2011

Puscifer. *C Is for (Please Insert Sophomoric Genitalia Reference Here)*. Jerome, AZ: Puscifer Entertainment, no catalog number, 2009

Puscifer. *V Is for Vagina*. Jerome, AZ: Puscifer Entertainment, no catalog number, 2007

Tool. *Fear Inoculum*. New York: RCA Records, no catalog number, and Burbank, CA: Tool Dissectional LLC, 19075-95055-2, 2019

Tool. *10,000 Days*. Los Angeles: Volcano Entertainment II LLC and Zomba Label Group, 82876-81991-2 and 82876819912, and Burbank, CA: Tool Dissectional LLC, no catalog number, 2006

Tool. *Lateralus*. Los Angeles: Volcano Entertainment II LLC 61422-31160-2 CD, and Burbank, CA: Tool Dissectional LLC, no catalog number, 2001

Tool. *Ænima*. Los Angeles: Zoo Entertainment, 61422-31087-2, and Burbank, CA: Tool Dissectional LLC, no catalog number, 1996

Tool. *Undertow*. Los Angeles: Zoo Entertainment and New York: BMG, 72445-11052-2, 1993

Tool. *Opiate*. Los Angeles: Zoo Entertainment, 72445-11027-2, 1992

Notes

INTRODUCTION

1. https://loudwire.com/tool-itunes-top-10-albums-songs/ retrieved 6/17/20
2. *Ænima* at #2, *Lateralus* at #4, *10,000 Days* at #5, *Undertow* at #6, and *Opiate* at #8; *Salival* was not released to streaming
3. "Sober" at #2, "Schism" at #6, "Forty Six & 2" at #7, and "Stinkfist" at #8

2. GENERAL TAROT AND THOTH TAROT BASICS

1. Please note, some newer tarot decks include one or two "extra" cards that are special to that particular deck. This happens because card printings are done in multiples of 10. Some decks use the extra cards as title cards or advertisements, some decks use the extras as gifts of additional artwork, and some deck creators use the extra two cards as additional cards to be used during divination. Whether the tarot practitioner chooses to follow the creator's suggestion and use these additional cards in their practice is an individual decision (I personally do not), but regardless, the rest of the deck should conform to the standard structure outlined above if it is indeed a tarot deck.
2. *Understanding Aleister Crowley's Thoth Tarot*, p76

3. QABALAH BASICS

1. Namely the signs and planets, their meanings, and the concept of decans—all of which is readily available via thousands of websites and books.
2. In our graphic here, there is a dotted circle in this space.

4. SEPHIROTH AND ALBUMS

1. For those wagging their fingers at me that eMOTIVe is the obvious choice, yes! I agree; however, eMOTIVe is predominantly a cover album, and therefore ineligible for consideration here if I'm to adhere to my own "rules."

6. 0. THE FOOL: "GRAVITY," A PERFECT CIRCLE

1. *Book M: Liber Mundi,* p15
2. *Book of Thoth,* p53
3. p54

7. I. THE MAGUS: "LATERALUS," TOOL

1. *The Emerald Tablet: Alchemy for Personal Transformation,* p156-62
2. Ibid, p162

10. IV. THE EMPEROR: "INVINCIBLE," TOOL

1. *How to Operate Your Brain*

12. VI. THE LOVERS: "SCHISM," TOOL

1. *The Book of Thoth,* p80

15. IX. THE HERMIT: "FORTY-SIX & 2," TOOL

1. meaning hand; also the first letter in YHVH
2. *Book of Thoth,* p88
3. Ibid.
4. p88

16. X. FORTUNE: "DELICIOUS," A PERFECT CIRCLE

1. *The Book of Thoth,* p90
2. *The Book of Thoth,* p90

19. XIII. DEATH: "HORIZONS," PUSCIFER

1. p100
2. p43

20. XIV. ART: "AGOSTINA," PUSCIFER

1. p46

22. XVI. THE TOWER: "ÆNEMA," TOOL

1. Note the difference in spelling between the album and the track titles. The album title, Ænima, references the anima, the Jungian term for the feminine portion of the male psyche. The track title, Ænema, references an enema, a method of colon cleansing. It doesn't take much deciphering to see how the album and track have decidedly different themes.
2. Grey, *The Red Goddess*, p30

23. XVII. THE STAR: "GRAND CANYON," PUSCIFER

1. *The Book of Thoth*, p109
2. Chapter 1, verses 58, 61, and 63-65

24. XVIII. THE MOON: "CULLING VOICES," TOOL

1. *The Book of Thoth*, p112
2. *Understanding*, p146

25. XIX. THE SUN: "PNEUMA," TOOL

1. *Understanding Aleister Crowley's Thoth Tarot*, p148-49

26. XX. THE AEON: "GALILEO," PUSCIFER

1. insofar as humanity is concerned; the Sun is estimated to burn out in about 5 billion years.
2. And it is no small coincidence that wine making also coincided with massive changes in Keenan's art and apparent worldview, much like The Aeon archetype's general impact on us.

27. XXI. THE UNIVERSE: "THE GRUDGE," TOOL

1. p66
2. Sun, Moon, Mercury, Mars, Venus, Jupiter, and Saturn
3. which happens approximately every 28 years, so around the ages of 28, 56, and 84

30. KNIGHT OF WANDS: "EULOGY," TOOL

1. as well as a bit of Scorpio, because no one is purely the expression of any one sign
2. *The Book of Thoth*, p151

34. 2 OF WANDS: "THINKING OF YOU," A PERFECT CIRCLE

1. p189-190
2. as Keenan would infamously pantomime on stage during A Perfect Circle's early *Mer de Noms* shows

37. 5 OF WANDS: "PRISON SEX," TOOL

1. Incidentally, bones, teeth, and skin are all correspondences of Saturn.

39. 7 OF WANDS: "PASSIVE," A PERFECT CIRCLE

1. p182

40. 8 OF WANDS: "GREY AREA," PUSCIFER

1. *The Book of Thoth*, p193

48. 2 OF CUPS: "THE HUMBLING RIVER," PUSCIFER

1. Crowley described this card's title, Love: "Love, which recovers unity from dividuality by mutual annihilation" (*The Book of Thoth,* p195), which can describe both romantic and agape love, but most often indicates orgasm.

49. 3 OF CUPS: "INDIGO CHILDREN," PUSCIFER

1. *Sacred Places of the Goddess,* p144
2. p197

51. 5 OF CUPS: "MOMMA SED," PUSCIFER

1. Season 2, Episode 19, May 9, 2018
2. *Understanding Aleister Crowley's Thoth Tarot,* p229

54. 8 OF CUPS: "POTIONS," PUSCIFER

1. 8 of Cups' opposite card is 8 of Disks, Prudence, which is about digging in and staying for the long haul.

55. 9 OF CUPS: "DEAR BROTHER," PUSCIFER

1. p186

56. 10 OF CUPS: "SOBER," TOOL

1. See 7 of Cups

61. PRINCESS OF SWORDS: "COLD AND UGLY," TOOL

1. *Book M: Liber Mundi,* p213

63. 3 OF SWORDS: "FEATHERS," A PERFECT CIRCLE

1. *Understanding Aleister Crowley's Thoth Tarot,* p242

64. 4 OF SWORDS: "BREAD AND CIRCUS," PUSCIFER

1. p205
2. Ibid.
3. Ibid.
4. p180
5. Ibid.

66. 6 OF SWORDS: "POSTULOUS," PUSCIFER

1. *The Book of Thoth*, p206
2. Ibid.

67. 7 OF SWORDS: "7EMPEST," TOOL

1. *The Book of Thoth*, p207
2. *A Perfect Union of Contrary Things,* p189
3. Brown, Brian. *The Wisdom of the Egyptians*. New York: Brentano's Publishers, 1923. Accessed via Google Books on June 24, 2020. p265-70
4. *The Wisdom of the Egyptians*, p270
5. He was eventually banned from Twitter altogether, for posting inaccurate information and inciting dangerous violence.

68. 8 OF SWORDS: "ROSETTA STONED," TOOL

1. *The Book of Thoth*, p184
2. Ibid.
3. Ibid.

69. 9 OF SWORDS: "VICARIOUS," TOOL

1. *The Book of Thoth*, p186
2. Ibid, p208

72. KNIGHT OF DISKS: "SWEAT," TOOL

1. p164

76. 2 OF DISKS: "H.," TOOL

1. p160
2. *The Book of Thoth*, p212

78. 4 OF DISKS: "THE DOOMED," A PERFECT CIRCLE

1. *The Book of Thoth,* p213

79. 5 OF DISKS: "TICKS & LEECHES," TOOL

1. *The Book of Thoth,* p181
2. Ibid, p214
3. p261

80. 6 OF DISKS: "JAMBI," TOOL

1. p182
2. Ibid.
3. Ibid, p181
4. At 423 times, according to www.setlist.fm as of 9/16/22

81. 7 OF DISKS: "BOTTOM," TOOL

1. *The Book of Thoth,* p183
2. Ibid, p215
3. *Book M: Liber Mundi,* p170-1
4. *The Book of Thoth,* p215

82. 8 OF DISKS: "THE PATIENT," TOOL

1. *The Book of Thoth,* p185
2. Ibid, p216

83. 9 OF DISKS: "MONEYSHOT," PUSCIFER

1. *The Book of Thoth,* p216
2. Ibid, p187

84. 10 OF DISKS: "AUTUMN," PUSCIFER

1. *The Book of Thoth*, p188

85. FUN WITH MAYNARD TAROT

1. "Beyond As Above, So Below" playlist, @kyndyll.lackey
2. And that's just the beginning! The same can be done for all the rest of the planets in your astrological chart, if you're feeling fancy.

Acknowledgments

As I'm guessing is true for many books, the distance between the initial idea coming to me and the finished product coming to you spans years. In that time, I've been a grateful recipient of incredible support and love from friends, family, and colleagues.

First and foremost, I give thanks to my Master Thoth, Who inspired this wonderful ride, and all I have learned from it.

I also give thanks to Ascended Masters Aleister Crowley and Lady Frieda Harris for their works in this world that have inspired generations of occultists after them—myself certainly included—and surely more to come.

Likewise, I am grateful to Maynard James Keenan, M. M. Meleen, and the members of Tool, A Perfect Circle, Puscifer, Tapeworm, and Deftones for their artistic works that have collectively inspired, taught, mesmerized, and supported me for the past thirty years.

I am especially profoundly grateful to Ms. Meleen and Mr. Keenan for granting me permission to share pieces of their collected works here to aid me in this exegesis.

Thank you to my husband, Chris Lackey, for enduring countless hours of musings, geek-outs, and general endless chatter from me as I worked through this project; for reading and re-reading what must have felt like endless drafts; and for doling out encouragement, comfort, tough love, and brutal Virgo honesty on an as-needed basis.

Much love and deep bows of gratitude to Lon Milo DuQuette, T. Susan Chang, Gina Piccalo, Nikki Starcat Shields, Greg White, Roy Hamilton, Sara Holifield, Tabitha Jester, Lisa Presley, Kevin Webb, and M.M. Meleen for providing encouragement and instrumental guidance on publishing, bookcraft, marketing, and divine timing, and for providing critically important feedback on early drafts. And a deep bow to my attorney, Ramona DeSalvo, for help with appropriately and respectfully navigating the complex world of intellectual property.

And finally, to my family of origin and choice, my deepest love and gratitude. There aren't enough words in the universe to convey my fierce adoration of each of you: Chris, Alexis, Andy, Casey, Terry, John, Cheryl, Dustin, Amanda, and Dale, as well as beloved members of Fortune's Wheelhouse Academy and founding members of The Scarlet Temple.

To those reading these words, thank you for supporting my work! May you find every wonder and happiness in this practice, and may you keep reaching ever toward the Divine.

-MKL

www.ingramcontent.com/pod-product-compliance
Lightning Source LLC
Chambersburg PA
CBHW062356090426
42740CB00010B/1295